Charles H. Eden

Japan, historical and descriptive

Charles H. Eden

Japan, historical and descriptive

ISBN/EAN: 9783741169922

Manufactured in Europe, USA, Canada, Australia, Japa

Cover: Foto ©ninafisch / pixelio.de

Manufactured and distributed by brebook publishing software (www.brebook.com)

Charles H. Eden

Japan, historical and descriptive

A Barber's Shop. —p. 151.

Historical and Descriptive

REVISED AND ENLARGED

FROM "LES VOYAGES CÉLÈBRES"

BY

CHARLES H. EDEN

AUTHOR OF "INDIA, HISTORICAL AND DESCRIPTIVE," "RALPH SOMERVILLE,"
"THE TWIN BROTHERS OF ELFVEDALE," &c.

Numerous Illustrations and a Map

London:
MARCUS WARD & CO., 67 & 68, CHANDOS STREET
AND ROYAL ULSTER WORKS, BELFAST
1877

PREFACE

THE present work is a brief, but, we believe, complete and comprehensive account of Japanese life, character, and manners. It contains within a short compass what could otherwise only be discovered by an extensive perusal of large and expensive works, which contain a multitude of personal details and extraneous matters, uninteresting and unnecessary to the reader who seeks either for information or amusement. A history of Japan, as it has been and now is, forms, indeed, in itself a study as curious as anything to be found in the whole range of romance. A kingdom which for ages successfully resisted the intrusion of foreigners, and, surrounded on all sides by the dividing ocean, worked out within its own borders a complete and peculiar civilisation, is surely a remarkable phenomenon in human history. Leaving out of view the abortive attempts made in earlier times by the Portuguese and the Dutch to effect a settlement in the country, it may be stated that it is only within our own times that this spell of national privacy has been broken. The nations of the West, who had overrun the globe in search of "fresh woods and pastures new" for commerce, began to knock loudly at the doors of this antiquated prison, until the summons could no longer be disregarded. Japan was virtually thrown open to the trading communities of the world, and it need hardly be added that the British were the first pioneers who established and have since maintained a solid and influential position in the country.

Very singular must have been the experiences of our countrymen who first became acquainted with the social and political life of the people. They beheld many things which must have carried them back in memory to the early days of English history. A system of feudalism, more despotic than William the Conqueror ever contemplated, held in chains the entire country, and crushed out all notion of personal freedom. But no sooner did foreigners obtain a footing in the island than, as if by magic, this anomalous state of things began to vanish away. The people began to see that to real civilisation they were still strangers. From obstinate exclusivism they soon passed to extravagant admiration of everything foreign, and soon an *Anglo-mania* set in, which held that all things worthy of being worshipped and imitated had their home in Britain. The facility with which the Japanese have abandoned their old ideas, and taken to copying English ways and adopting English inventions, is at once ludicrous and extraordinary. So far has this been carried that artists are already beginning to lament the utter decay of everthing distinctively national and peculiar in their productions. Whether the Japanese will continue faithful to their new life remains to be seen. At present the British are being carefully copied in every particular, from ships of war down to neckties and tall hats. This is surely a stimulating flattery to our national pride, for the Japanese have also had the opportunity of becoming acquainted with Americans and Russians, French and Germans. In reforming their institutions it must be admitted, however, that they have shown much discrimination, having selected some distinguished German scholars, for example, to take charge of their Department of Public Instruction.

So long as "the proper study of mankind is man," books which tell us of the ways and doings of fellow-beings very dissimilar to ourselves must continue to be the most permanently interesting of all books. Especially is this true in the case of the Japanese, who form in so many ways a complete anomaly in civilisation. The reader of the following pages will find that they embrace a great variety of topics, from the life of the Mikado on his sacred throne to that of the peasant in his winter coat of straw. Popular tales and legends have been interwoven with the general account in order to render the book more attractive, and at the same time to exhibit the people in all phases of their character. We believe we present here, in the briefest space possible, the most complete account that has yet appeared of *Japan, Historical and Descriptive*.

CONTENTS.

	PAGE
PREFACE,	5

CHAPTER I.—Life and Manners—Anomalies—The Mikado and Tycoon—Earthquakes—The Theatre, etc., ... 7

CHAPTER II.—Early History—Idols—The Portuguese—The Dutch, . 25

CHAPTER III.—Relations opened with Japan—Ceremonials—Treaties—Embassy to Europe, ... 41

CHAPTER IV.—The Daimios—Opposition to Foreigners—They are Tolerated, ... 56

CHAPTER V.—Description of Japan—Origin of the Race—Legend of Sikono, ... 65

CHAPTER VI.—Worship of Kami—Curious Traditions—Buddhism—Reforms, ... 73

CHAPTER VII.—The Jesuits' Mission—Buddhism—Christians Persecuted, ... 86

CHAPTER VIII.—Japanese Religions—Their Gods—Mythology, . 92

CHAPTER IX.—Temples—The Bonzes—Matsouris—Fall and Re-establishment of the Mikado, ... 106

CHAPTER X.—Grades of Society—Rural Scenery—Literature—Legends, ... 123

CHAPTER XI.—Yedo—The Yakonins—City Life—The Lonins—Baths, 142

CHAPTER XII.—Tea-houses—Tea-house Girls, . . . 172

CHAPTER XIII.—Public Festivals—Jugglers—Mountebanks—Gymnasts, ... 184

CHAPTER XIV.—Wrestling—The Theatre—The Drama, . . 200

CHAPTER XV.—Popular Superstitions, ... 227

CHAPTER XVI.—Physical Appearance—Costumes—Surgery—Dwellings, ... 239

CHAPTER XVII.—Domestic Customs—Painting—Funeral Rites, . 252

CHAPTER XVIII.—Amusements—Festivals—New Year's Day—The Aïnos, ... 264

CHAPTER XIX.—Language and Literature—Division of Time—Shopkeeping, ... 282

CHAPTER XX.—Manufactures—Silkworms—Agriculture—Tea—Shipbuilding, ... 298

CHAPTER XXI.—Foreign Relations—Chief Towns—Probable Future, 319

Illustrations.

	PAGE		PAGE
Barber's Shop. *Frontispiece.*		Guitar Players,	179
Town and Bay of Simoda,	7	Japanese Family at Table,	185
Reception at the Court of a Mikado,	11	Gymnasts,	192
		Juggling Girls,	195
Buddhist Teacher or Priest,	30	Wrestling Match,	203
Nagasaki,	32	Samurai Child and Attendant,	213
Island of Desima,	36	Night Watchman,	225
Japanese War Vessel,	46	Spinning,	238
Ancient Japanese Warrior,	48	Types of Bourgeois Class,	240
Punishment for Stealing,	55	Porter,	241
A Daimio Reclining,	57	Peasant's Winter Dress,	243
Town and Harbour of Yokohama,	61	Japanese Court Dress,	244
Japanese Foot Soldier,	64	Interior of Japanese House,	248
Japanese Ladies on the Promenade,	67	Fac-simile of Japanese Drawing,	251
		Japanese Family Dining,	252
Japanese Women,	72	Tea Kettle,	253
Japanese God,	75	Japanese Painter,	254
Interior of Buddhist Temple,	81	Japanese Nurse,	260
Temple at Yokohama,	82	Burning the Dead,	262
Hermit of Kioto,	84	Female Dancers,	266
Execution by the Sword,	85	Marketing,	272
Japanese Young Women,	103	Fisherwomen,	281
Kami Temple,	107	Interior of Temple,	289
Religious Festival,	111	Fan-painting,	292
Japanese Cooper,	120	Fan-making,	293
Sailor, Soldier, and Courtier,	122	Curiosity Shop,	296
Ancient Japanese Warriors,	125	Japanese Workers in Metals,	297
Type of Lower Classes,	128	Japanese Weavers,	300
Japanese Hamlet,	131	Manuring the Tea Plant,	306
Sculptor or Statuary,	141	Women Gathering Seaweed,	308
Street in Yedo,	143	Transplanting the Rice Plants,	309
Mounted Yakonin,	146	Picking the Tea Leaves,	310
Yakonin on Foot,	147	Preparation of Tea—Sifting,	311
Japanese Salutation,	149	Rubbing the Tea Leaf,	312
Japanese Builder,	151	Fanning and Cooling the Tea Leaf,	313
Japanese Shoe Shop,	153		
Coolie,	156	Japanese Railway—Fac-simile of Native Water-colour Drawing,	318
Norimon,	161		
Japanese Postman,	163	British Consulate at Nagasaki,	321
Tea-house at Yedo,	173	Japanese Landscape,	326

JAPAN, HISTORICAL AND DESCRIPTIVE.

TOWN AND BAY OF SIMODA

CHAPTER I.

Japanese Life and Manners—Curious Anomalies among the Japanese—The Mikado and the Tycoon—Yedo—Earthquakes.—Japanese Theatre—Feudalism—Introduction of English Customs.

GREAT interest is felt at present throughout the civilised world in the insular empire of Japan. Universal history does not present such another instance of so singularly active and progressive a community shutting itself up in the strictest isolation from any point of contact with other nations, living for ages without either civil or foreign warfare, unknown to the great commercial communities of the West, and only desirous to remain so. Within the last few years this barrier of isolation has been broken down, and we are now comparatively familiar with what may be correctly termed the latest and greatest curiosity in the history of civilisation.

We shall anticipate in brief outline a few of the most striking peculiarities of the country and people of Japan, so as to present to the mind of the reader at a single view some notion of the more detailed information which will be contained in succeeding chapters.

First of all, a word of explanation as to the meaning of the term "Japan." This word is a singular instance of corruption, and as pronounced by us would never suggest to a native the name of his country. It arose thus. The largest of the Japan islands is called Nipon. It is compounded of two words written in the Chinese character, meaning the "place" or "rising of the sun." Originally the words were *Jih Pun*, which the Dutch spelt *Jeh-pun*. But the Dutch *j* is equivalent to our *y*, which would represent the native pronunciation. This, however, was overlooked by the English, who quickly transformed the word into *Japan*, in which form it continues in all our books and periodical literature.

We have said that the Japanese are an active and progressive community, but, being continually thrown back upon themselves by a rigidly paternal system of government, they have not advanced on all points with equal speed. In some things they equal, nay, surpass, the most skilled communities of Europe. In other respects they are so preposterously behind modern ideas as to suggest a state of society to be found only in the Middle or even the Dark Ages. In all the elements of material civilisation they leave other eastern nations at a vast distance. They make swords and cutlery to rival the best workmanship of Birmingham and Sheffield, silks and crapes that will compete with Macclesfield and Lyons. They launched a steamer without any assistance from foreign engineers, having actually constructed a working marine engine from some plans in a Dutch work. Yet in rapid locomotion, one of the greatest triumphs of modern science, so absurdly primitive are their ideas that they have no better mode of conveying Government despatches than by a courier, running at full speed, and stripped of all garments save his loin-cloth. This paradoxical character of the people shows itself in every relation of life.

/ The Japanese write from top to bottom, but from right to left, consequently their books begin where ours end. Their locks are made to shut by turning from left to right. Their old men fly kites, while the children look on at this solemn amusement of their grandfathers. Their carpenters draw the plane *to* them, and their tailors stitch *from* them. They mount their horses from the off side, while the horses themselves stand in the stable with their heads where we place their tails. So far from attempting to have white teeth, ladies vie with each other in imparting to them a brilliant black. The sexes mingle in the public bath-houses in a manner indescribable to western readers, being apparently no more ashamed of mutual exposure than our first parents before the Fall; yet if we are to place any reliance on the most authoritative testimony, the morality of Japan is superior to that of most eastern countries. They sleep without beds, and eat without tables.

As a people, they are perhaps the most peaceable, contented, good-humoured, and cheerful in the world, yet the country is without statute law or lawyers; but whether this last peculiarity should be classed under the head of paradoxes we will not undertake to say. They are at once one of the most sceptical and most religious people in the world. At times nothing can exceed the austerity of their devotions; but when this fit of enthusiasm passes away they relapse into a scepticism as complete as any Positivist could desire. This is particularly observable in their caricatures, a department of artistic work in which they particularly excel. The bonzes or priests are a favourite subject for Japanese sarcasm, and are pictured in every sort of ridiculous posture.

But if they can thus play fast and loose with religion, they have for ages obeyed a system of government such as no people ever paid allegiance to except themselves. They have had two emperors, two lords paramount. It is true that in rank and dignity the Mikado has always been the only emperor of Japan. His will alone has been law to all his subjects. All power has been derived from him, and has been considered on that account to have force and efficacy. But until within the last few years the Mikado

RECEPTION AT THE COURT OF A MIKADO.
JAPAN.—p. 11.

Shadow and Substance. 13

has been a mere phantom sovereign, shut up in a dismal prison of a palace, surrounded by innumerable body-guards, and positively *not allowed* to stir beyond the precincts of his palace prison. For many centuries until lately all real power has been in the hands of the Tycoon, the head of the Executive, the real and actual emperor of Japan. Yet the decrees of the Tycoon are supposed to derive all their efficacy from having the sanction of the Mikado superadded, the people all the while knowing such sanction to be no more than a mere mockery. How such a Government held together for so many centuries must certainly be reckoned as not the least of the curious anomalies that underlie the whole social fabric of Japan. The Mikado was the shadow, the Tycoon the substance; yet it would be hard to say which was the most real, for no decree of the Tycoon was necessarily binding upon the people unless it bore the mysterious *imprimatur* of the shadowy Mikado. This will account for the many insults and atrocities suffered by Europeans at their first entrance into the country, for which redress was asked in vain; the real fact being, as afterwards transpired, that the treaties by which Europeans held footing in Japan were signed by the Tycoon only, and Japanese *gentry* (everybody is a gentleman in Japan who can wear two swords) only obeyed them when it suited their purpose.

The Tycoon was, however, as much a prisoner in the walls of his palace as the Mikado himself. Such are the Japanese notions of court etiquette. Both their kings were prisoners. " Kneeling princes offer the Tycoon their lip-service, and flattering courtiers minister to his wants; but how often must he wish himself a common mortal! how wearily must he yearn for that bright world beyond his prison walls, for the pure air of those green mountains and the fresh breezes of the blue sea, so near, ever so near, and yet so hopelessly beyond his reach! How his courtiers must have chuckled when Lord Elgin, in the name of the Queen of England, presented him with a yacht! What would the cardinals say if the Sultan were to select the most lovely of his harem and send her to the Pope for a wife?"

Yedo, the great capital of the Tycoon, and the largest city in Japan, is also, as might be expected, a curious contrast to the other great capitals of the world. It is a city of orchards and gardens. No sooner do you turn off the main street, which is not less than eight or nine miles in length, than you enter the rural stillness of a lovely landscape. Instead of the bustle and din and smoke inseparable from our notion of a large town, you have green lanes, clumps of trees, and hedges of camellia, nectarine, peach, and jessamine. Owing to the bright sky and clear air of Japan, there is nearly always a gorgeous profusion of colour in these city landscapes. Such houses as are built of stone are without either mortar or cement. The Japanese are said to find this a necessity, for Yedo is a city of earthquakes, and the houses have to be constructed on the pattern of the willow rather than of the oak. They bend, but they do not break. The greater part of the town is, however, built of wood, and, as a consequence, fires are of daily and nightly occurrence. The Yedites are in this respect the most utterly careless people in the world. So accustomed are they to be waked up with the alarm of fire, that they look on conflagrations with the serene complacency of a Stoical fatalism, and seem to prefer spending their strength in trying to extinguish them to using a little ordinary vigilance in preventing their outbreak. As a consequence, it is computed that the whole of Yedo is burnt down and rebuilt once every five years. Yet, in spite of earthquakes and fires, the people are serenely happy. But, with fires both above and below the surface, it is of course vain to look in Yedo for architectural beauties.

Earthquakes in Yedo are seldom accompanied by any great loss of life. In spite of this, however, the heaving and vibrating of the ground have such a prostrating effect upon the nerves of Europeans that they never really get used to it, or manage to shake off the feeling of terror. The last great earthquake at Yedo was in 1783, and seems to have surpassed in intensity even the terrible earthquake of Lisbon. The accounts state that "at eight o'clock on the morning of the 27th of July in that year a great wind arose, accompanied by subterranean mutterings of thunder, which continued augmenting from day to day, in seeming menace of some frightful catastrophe, till August 1st. On that day an earthquake with loud thunders shook all the houses to their foundations, the intensity of the shocks each moment increasing until the summit of the mountain was rent open, and fire and flame appeared, followed by such an avalanche of sand and stones, tossed high into the air, and carried to incredible distances, that the darkness of night came on, the only light being the lurid glare of the burning lava and devastating flames. Vast chasms opened before the affrighted inhabitants in their flight, into which thousands, in the darkness and panic, urged on by the streams of fire and the showers of stone and ashes, are said to have been precipitated. The shocks did not entirely cease until the twelfth day, and were felt over a space of thirty leagues. Twenty-seven towns and villages were destroyed; the rivers boiling and overflowing inundated the whole country, to complete the work of destruction."

Unpleasant reminders of this frightful convulsion of nature have since occurred. As late as 1854 a severe shock was felt in the bay of Simoda, by which the town was reduced to ruins, large junks and boats were flung violently on the shores, a Russian frigate lying in the harbour was spun round and round like a top and nearly shaken to pieces, and the granite foundations of the harbour itself were flung into a chaotic mass of boulders. These earthquakes must be accepted by European residents as a slight offset to the beautiful climate, the balmy air, the blue skies, and the fragrant landscapes of Japan.

As a curious proof of the stationary character of Japan in certain respects, we may mention its Theatres and its system of Feudalism. The Japanese theatre reminds us in a very striking manner of the English stage at the close of the Middle Ages. It is not an evening's entertainment frequented by the upper classes who are in straits to know how to employ their wealth and leisure. It is a great national institution, supported by the middle and lower classes, who go to the play-house well furnished with refreshments, and sit it out from ten in the morning till six at night, eating their dinner during the intervals, sipping tea or the national intoxicating beverage called *saki*, smiling, chatting, now applauding some melodramatic deed of daring, now laughing with all the mischievous drollery of a British gallery at some "hitch" in the scenic arrangements, but all the while apparently determined to make the day as merry as possible, and to extract the very greatest possible quantity of enjoyment out of the brief span of life. With them the theatre is a whole day's amusement from morning to night, not a relaxation after the severe duties of the day. So it was in the old days of the Mysteries and Moralities of Western Europe, when the audience assembled at early morning to see the enactment of some Scripture story, which went tediously onward in all its changing phases from Monday at dawn till Saturday at sunset.

In one respect the Japanese theatre is far in advance of the early English drama. Its stage appliances, the whole arrangement of situation and scenery, are not surpassed, if they are equalled, by the best stage in London. In the Osaca theatres, which are the best in Japan, the brilliant costumes and the gorgeous dresses excel the most magnificent thing in spangles ever seen on the boards of Drury Lane. The plays themselves cannot be said to be of any great literary merit, and usually turn on some daring deeds of love and murder—the more heartrending the better for the audience. At the excruciatingly affecting passages the young girls may be seen weeping bitterly in a flood of sympathy. The childlike faith which some of these impressionable young ladies put in the reality of theatrical representations is excessively amusing. A Dutch resident at Osaka mentions that a friend of his one day met a young female, who was engaged in his establishment, apparently in the greatest mental anguish, sobbing as if her heart would break. On being asked what was the matter, she sobbed out in broken accents, "Oh, I am so miserable! They have killed him, they have killed him! that poor lover—the husband caught him and ran his sword through and through his body." "Who did it? where was it? and what have you to do with it?" he asked, believing it to be some domestic tragedy which had taken place in the neighbourhood—any lack of chastity in their wives being, according to Japanese law and custom, punishable with instant death. "Oh, oh! at the play." "Why, you little fool, it is all sham; he has not been killed at all, the fine gallant, and is most likely very busy eating his rice." "Oh, no! he is killed, indeed; I saw the sword go through his body as he fell!"

It must be confessed, to the detriment of our estimate of Japanese morality, that there are occasional scenes of a grossness that would be too bad for the worst theatre in Europe. Not a blush crosses the fairest cheek in the audience at these exhibitions of immorality, the female

Scenes of Grossness.

portion of the community on such occasions being apparently as little troubled by any qualms of shamefacedness as when they expose their persons perfectly nude in the public baths. This occasional grossness of the Japanese stage may in part be attributable to the absence of female actors, for in Japan the parts of women are taken by boys, a feature which the Japanese theatre shares with the early English. It is a peculiarity of Japan that a woman may enter a public bath with men; but that she should appear on the stage, decently clad, as an actress, is a pitch of impropriety not contemplated as possible by the Japanese mind.

The feudalism of Japan is its most extraordinary national feature. If the Mikado be but a phantom and the Tycoon a prisoner in his palace, who are the real governors of Japan? These are the Daimios, the great nobles or princes, the real owners of Japan, ruling their subjects with a power that knows little check save their own arbitrary will. Like our own early barons, these Daimios are followed by hosts of armed retainers, Japanese counterparts of the swash-bucklers of old England. These Daimios are worshipped by the populace as beings of a superior order, whom even to look upon is a stretch of daring never ventured on by a humble *bourgeois*. Does an ordinary man meet a Daimio travelling by street or road? Then, on peril of instantly losing his head (justice·is not slow in Japan), let him spring from his pony or leap out of his *norimon* (travelling-chair) and bow his face to the dust. The utter subjection of the middle classes to the Daimios is in Japan as complete as can be imagined. Such ridiculous western notions as those of the born equality of all human souls, or of the inalienable and indestructible rights of man, have not yet penetrated this versatile but unambitious race. Should any follower or dependant thwart the will of a Daimio, he is instantly commanded by his sovereign lord and possessor to perform the Hara Kiru. This is an operation unknown in any part of the world but Japan. It is neither more nor less than self-murder, and that too of the most horrible kind—disembowelment. This is the ancient and time-honoured mode of loyal self-immolation, but at present only a slight incision is made in the abdomen to satisfy the requirements of antiquity, and then a near relative or obliging friend, facetiously described as the "best man" on the occasion, draws his glittering sword and strikes off the head of the willing victim at a single blow. This practice is not confined to the retainers of the Daimios alone. It is a national custom, revered and honoured by the national mind, and practised by the Daimios themselves. One of the greatest of Japanese princes, on returning from the court of the Tycoon to his country residence, found that his wife's honour had been ruined by a friend who had fled. The indignant husband first killed his wife, and then committed the Hara Kiru on himself. Public opinion would expect the gay Lothario to do the same, but whether he so far obliged the *manes* of his injured friend is not recorded. It is from three families of these Daimios that the Tycoon is elected, and so powerful are princely notions in Japan that we find the Tycoon himself only ranks as fourth high officer in the Imperial hierarchy—a proof that the court guide-book is of no more consequence in Japan than in England.

Such is Japan as it has been for ages; but the last few years have seen a wonderful change pass over the whole social and political aspect of the country. The Tycoonate has vanished, and the Mikado has at length shown himself as the Sovereign *de facto* as well as *de jure*. Foreigners have now made good their footing, and have shown to the ever eager and quick-witted Japanese that in locomotion, in the rapid transmission of news, in ministering to bodily comforts, in all the arts of peace and war, western civilisation can show them a more excellent way than their own. After having so long struggled against foreign notions and failed, they now embrace them with a fervour corresponding to their former antipathy. A transformation without a parallel in history is gradually changing the habits and manners of all parts open to European commerce. Soon this change will make its way inland, for no people in the world imitate their betters more assiduously than the Japanese. It is well known that at present they are greatly enamoured of English ways and notions. An English gentleman on the Japanese legation speaks of the shock he experienced when meeting in the streets of Yokohama two Japanese " swells," dressed in full English costume, and making a circuit of the town on bicycles! Native merchants at Yokohama nearly all speak English, some of them with ease and fluency. Daimios refuse promotion among their followers to those who are not acquainted with the English or French language. One poor fellow, who had got into disgrace with his prince, instead of committing the Hara Kiru, was found not long ago by an English interpreter making desperate attempts to translate a French book on military tactics into Japanese, in order to ingratiate himself again with his offended master.

The upper classes are all sedulously imitating Paris and London fashions. The old wooden clog, on which Japanese ladies have hitherto hobbled about in rather ungainly fashion, is discarded for the high-heeled boot so prized among the belles of the West. Large numbers of young Japanese gentlemen have come over to Great Britain to have the benefit of an English education, and, with very fair intellectual powers, exhibit a patient plodding industry that in time conquers every obstacle. Thus, although Japanese music is as different from English as can possibly be imagined, English popular airs are now well known in Japan, and the *gamins* of Yedo or Yokohama may be heard whistling "John Brown's Body" or "Not for Joe" with perfect accuracy. Even the lower classes have taken to learn English with a systematic determination not usual with people of their position in life, and lately a vocabulary of English words has been published for their use, beginning with the names of familiar things, such as the sun, moon, and stars, and ending with some short familiar phrases, such as "Where are you going?" &c. The imitation of French manners that came into vogue in England in the reign of Charles the Second was confined to the court and metropolis, and never reached the real bulk of the nation. But in Japan the Anglo-mania is becoming universal, and as, owing to a recent revolution, the Constitution is still in a transition state, we need not be astonished if we hear shortly of the establishment of a Japanese House of Commons. Such extraordinary capacity for change marks a versatile but unreliable race; for we can hardly believe that a people who have parted with their ancestral notions with such a total absence of any pangs of sorrow will be likely to adhere with much steadfastness to their new-fangled acquirements. The following judgment confirmatory of this opinion is supplied to us by a gentleman who has been resident in Japan for nearly fifteen years, and who has had unrivalled opportunities of becoming acquainted with every phase of Japanese life and character:—

"Great quickness of imitation and judgment in discovering what is worth imitating seem to be the prominent characteristics of the Japanese. They want originality, and the independence of thought and character which accompanies it. The Japanese will not be slow in adopting the inventions of modern civilisation, and even in modifying them to suit their own convenience, but that they will ever add anything of importance to them seems doubtful. The same is true in a political point of view. The more enlightened of the Japanese are already beginning to discover the superiority of the European forms of Government, and where circumstances admit of it the Japanese

Constitution will sooner or later be reformed on the model of some European state; but their reforms, if accomplished, will be carried out under foreign guidance, and the Japanese Government seems destined for many years to become more and more dependent upon foreign powers. Japan can never be really independent so long as the mind of the nation is so entirely bent on imitating what is foreign. The nation it admires most and imitates most will always have a corresponding influence, which we may expect it will not be slow to exercise."

Of course as long as the Japanese continue to model after Great Britain we must believe them to be on the high road to perfection; and here we will for the present leave them, while we proceed in the following chapter to trace the history of the means by which the civilised nations of the West forced their way into commercial and political relations with the "Land of the Rising Sun."

CHAPTER II.

Early Notices of Japan—Idols Worshipped—Arrival of the Portuguese—Conversion of the Natives—Frightful Persecutions—Expulsion of the Portuguese—Imprisonment of the Dutch—Attempts of Russia and France to enter into friendly Relations.

THE existence of Japan seems to have been entirely unknown to the ancients. Ptolemy, the most thorough of all the ancient geographers, does not mention it; on the contrary, he says that unknown lands extend beyond the countries inhabited by the remote "Seres," which, from the indications he gives of them, are probably those we now designate as the inhabitants of China proper. This sufficiently proves that he had no conception of the islands since discovered beyond the frontiers of the Celestial Empire.

Marco Polo, the celebrated Venetian traveller, was the first who revealed to us the existence of Japan. In the account he gives us of this country he calls it Zipangu; but the Japanese have named it Nipon, a title which is applied by Europeans only to the largest of the group of islands. Polo admits that he never personally visited Zipangu, the Great Isle of the East, but he nevertheless gives us many particulars respecting it, the accuracy of which has been confirmed by the most recent accounts. He describes the state of the commerce then carried on between the inhabitants of Japan and Mangi, or Tonquin, as it is now known to us; the great fecundity of their seas and soil, which especially abound in pearls and gold; the form of government; the colour, stature, and religion of the natives; and the great number of smaller islands surrounding Zipangu. A stronger proof still of the veracity of Marco Polo's statement is found in his circumstantial recital of an important event, still celebrated in the minds of the two great peoples of the extreme East. This event is the disastrous expedition of the Tartar-Chinese fleet of the Emperor Kublaï against Japan, in the year 1284 of our era (as has since been certified by the annals of Japan); it must therefore have taken place during the residence of Marco Polo in the Chinese Empire, a period extending from the year 1261 to 1295.

His account of the Japanese idols is as follows:—" The idols worshipped in Zipangu and the adjoining islands resemble in form the Chinese gods. Some have the heads of oxen, swine, and other animals, others one head with four faces; sometimes they are to be seen with four, ten, and even one hundred hands, and with other members of the body equally multiplied; in fact, the more members these hideous forms possess, the greater is the devotion paid to them, and the higher the idea entertained of their power. The various ceremonies practised before these idols are so wicked and diabolical that it would be nothing less than impiety and an abomination to give an account of them in this our book."

Several navigators have disputed the honour of the discovery of Japan, and each has had his partisans. Historians are divided on the subject, and even disagree with regard to dates; some of them placing the discovery about the year 1535, others in 1543 and 1548, whilst a few bring it still nearer to our own time. To Mendez Pinto, a Portuguese, is, however, generally ascribed the honour of being the first European who stepped upon Japanese soil, and of bringing that country into communication with Europe. The following is an extract from his own narrative, and relates how, having set out from China, with several of his fellow-countrymen, to return to Malacca, they were overtaken by a storm, and their vessel stranded upon an unknown shore. "We were on the point," he says, "of springing on to the beach, when we saw two small *almédias*, each containing six men, push off from the land. After they had reached us, and the customary courtesies had been exchanged, they demanded from whence we had come. On our replying that we came from China with merchandise, and intended entering into trade with their country if they would grant us permission, they responded that the lord of the island of Tanixunaa, on whose coast we had struck, would willingly accede to this, provided that we discharged the customary dues exacted from foreigners on entering Nipon (Japan). 'For,' continued our interrogator,' such is the name of the great country you see before you.'"

Mendez Pinto and his companions remained at Japan for several months, and were treated by the different princes whom they visited with the greatest friendliness. Their muskets were the cause of the greatest astonishment to the Japanese, and there is no doubt it was they who first introduced fire-arms into the country.

Henceforward a few Portuguese ships were sent annually into Japanese waters for trading purposes; and as the Church considered any newly discovered lands its legitimate prey, missionaries also hastened thither.

In 1549 a Japanese of high rank, who had fled to Goa, under a sentence of capital punishment, was there baptised and received into the Christian Church. In return for benefits received, he disclosed to the merchants of this Portuguese-Indian capital the means whereby great riches could be made in his country. This prospect, added to the desire to promote the interests of their *protégés*, the Jesuit Fathers, induced the Portuguese to found an establishment in the Japanese Empire.

Admission into the country was at that period quite free. Every port was open, and the governor-princes of the different provinces—who were not so subject then to the Emperor as at the present day—showed themselves exceedingly hospitable towards foreigners; and each prince, in the interests of his subjects, strove to induce these new visitors to enter his port rather than that of his neighbour.

The Japanese, eager and acquisitive by nature, quarrelled for the European productions, and, not knowing their real value, paid any price that was demanded. One great advantage to the Portuguese was the possession of the Chinese town of Macao, which served as a depôt and warehouse, and thus enabled them to put their trading affairs on a surer footing; and they soon acquired immense riches by the exchange of their silk goods, fine stuffs, medicines, and curiosities both of art and nature. The missionaries also made a decided impression upon the natives by their modesty and the disinterested assistance they lent to both sick and poor; the splendour and solemnity of their religious services were also sources of the greatest delight to the natives. A certain similarity of character helped to cement the union; it is therefore not surprising that the Portuguese, under such favourable circumstances, should in a very short time have reached the height of prosperity. Such rapid success proved, however, the cause of their downfall.

Towards the end of the 16th century great discontent crept in amongst the natives, owing to the pride and avarice of these *nouveaux riches;* and the extortionate practices of many of their number soon brought discredit upon the whole nation; whilst the Jesuits also—forgetful of the example shown by Francis Xavier and their predecessors the first missionaries—began to display great pomp, and, not content with exacting the same outward respect as that paid to the highest dignitaries of the empire, gave way to even greater arrogance and presumption. At last one of them, whom a bull from Rome had suddenly raised from the rank of a poor priest to that of bishop of one of

Decline of Portuguese Power.

the Japanese towns, meeting a minister of state of equal rank to himself, refused to pay the courtesies always accorded to an official of his high standing. The latter was naturally greatly incensed at this insult, and so effectively portrayed to his sovereign the vanity and insolence of these foreigners, that the monarch's fears were

BUDDHIST TEACHER OR PRIEST.

aroused, and this incident proved the first step towards their disgrace.

The growing power of the Portuguese, added to the behaviour of the Jesuits, soon produced the greatest anxiety in the breast of a ruler who, not unreasonably, dreaded anything that would throw his country into trouble and confusion, or provoke any popular movements. The *bonzes*, or Buddhist priests, irritated by the hostile bearing of the young native Christians, who insulted them in their very temples, cunningly fanned these apprehensions, and soon the nobles became alarmed by the encroachment of the Europeans, and gave their aid. National feeling also was unfavourable to the foreigners, and when the sentiment, "Conversion is only one mode of conquest," had been heard from the mouth of a Portuguese, the storm of persecution broke forth. An imperial edict, issued in the year 1597, forbade any further teaching of the doctrines of the Jesuits, under the severest penalties, and the governors and rulers of the provinces received orders to compel all their subjects to abjure the new faith. Portuguese traders were forbidden to bring over any more ecclesiastics in their vessels, and all priests and members of religious establishments were recommended to leave the empire with as little delay as possible.

At the same time, the Japanese court did not intend that all foreigners should be included in this proscription. Trade and the propagation of religion were, to the Japanese mind, in no way connected with each other. The Portuguese were therefore allowed to withdraw to the little island of Desima, in the harbour of Nagasaki, and from thence to carry on their business affairs, but on condition they should never attempt to cross the boundary.

NAGASAKI.

In the year 1622 a frightful massacre of native Christians and some of their foreign teachers was perpetrated near that place. Mr. Steimnetz says—" The Jesuit father Spinola, a Dominican friar, and a Franciscan, were in the number of those who suffered, having been convicted of returning to the country after the Emperor had decreed their perpetual expulsion. Horrible tortures were employed, of which harrowing and revolting representations are given in the illustrations of the books of several of the old Dutch and Jesuit writers. Decapitation was the most merciful. The Christians were burnt to death; immersed in boiling water from the hot springs; beaten to death with clubs; suspended from the branch of a tree head downwards; crucified and speared; swung under a beam, feet and hands tied together over the back; their legs compressed between two blocks of wood, on which men trampled; hacked to pieces by bits at a blow; and, finding that the means as yet employed had little effect upon the missionaries and their native assistants, a new and more effectual, because more protracted, torture was invented—called the torment of the *Fosse*." Harrowing accounts of this fiendish torture have been given by Jesuit writers, with which, however, we should be sorry to lacerate the feelings of our readers. The Japanese persecutors appear to have rivalled, if they did not surpass, the worst phases of the Catholic Inquisition in Europe; and the *fosse*, in which the sufferer was hung head downwards until he should see fit either to die or make a signal of recantation, appears to have been the last stretch of their cruel ingenuity. Nevertheless, the constancy of the Japanese in many instances to the faith they had adopted is an undoubted historical fact, and seems to be admitted as such by writers of all denominations.

The relentless determination with which the Japanese rulers extinguished the last spark of Jesuitical teaching shows how keenly they appreciated the antagonism that must always exist between two powers, both of which make claims to absolute supremacy. Was the Tycoon to become a humble vassal of the Pope, as John of England had humbled himself to Innocent the Third? Taiko-sama, the man who first engaged in this terrible warfare which was to end in the extermination of all Catholic Christians, had just reasons for alarm when he found how the proudest nobles of Japan, who had embraced the Catholic faith, were vieing with each other in sending their humble submission to a distant power which claimed the right of electing and deposing princes. The Japanese nobles appear to have been by no means half-hearted in their adoration of his Holiness. The Prince of Omara, for example, thus expresses himself in a letter despatched to Rome—"With hands raised toward heaven, and sentiments of adoration, I adore the most holy Pope, who holds the place of God on earth." Thus, too, the King of Arima—"To the very great and holy Lord whom I adore, because he holds on earth the place of God Himself." And the Prince of Bungo—"To him who ought to be adored, and who holds the place of the King of Heaven, the great and very holy Pope." Taiko-sama was not so weak-minded as not to see that princes who thus gloried in their implicit obedience to a potentate beyond the oceans would be likely to yield a very qualified and half-hearted obedience to himself. He saw, in fact, that it was a fight for the mastery, and he flung himself into the contest with a determination to conquer ere it would be too late.

Matters stood thus until the year 1637, when a Portuguese vessel was seized, containing, it is alleged, certain treasonable letters, relating to an overthrow of the Government by the aid of ships and soldiers from Portugal. The Jesuits maintained that these were forgeries fabricated by the Dutch, who were not scrupulous in their efforts to eject their rivals; but an imperial proclamation was issued, decreeing that "the whole race of the Portuguese, with their mothers, nurses, and whatever belongs to them, shall be banished for ever," and laying down the stringent laws against intercourse with foreigners which have prevailed until the last generation, but from which the Dutch were exempted.

The Portuguese, on the first discovery of Japan, were shortly followed by the Spaniards and Dutch, both equally desirous of the privilege of trading with that country. The wide difference in their fortunes we learn from the very curious notes left by a Japanese historian.

The Spanish ambassador had a double mission to fulfil; first, to settle a slight difference which had suddenly arisen about the capture of a Spanish vessel; and secondly, to solicit, and exact, if need be, the expulsion of every European not a native of Spain. In case of refusal he was unhesitatingly to declare war. The reigning Emperor, highly incensed by this unreasonable demand, ordered the immediate destruction of the said Spanish vessel with all its crew—a precipitate action, the execution of which cost him the lives of some three thousand of his Japanese subjects, but destroyed any hopes the Spanish may have entertained of getting a settlement in the country. The Emperor's anger was at first extended to the Dutch, but they, with habitual placidity, calmly waited till the storm blew over, and allowed the Emperor to recognise for himself the difference between their mode of action and that of the Spaniards. He then gave them the small island of Firando, not far from the town of that name, and granted them the right of trading throughout the whole extent of Japan. Here they remained quietly established for several years, when they suddenly received the unexpected orders to demolish their offices and warehouses.

The director of the factory, letting his ambition get the better of his prudence, had built himself a magnificent edifice of hewn stone. The report of this, perhaps maliciously exaggerated to the Emperor, caused that sovereign to imagine that the Dutch were, in their turn, nourishing ideas of conquest; and that, under the pretext of trade, they had built themselves a strong castle. This was the sole reason for the pitiless decree issued against the Dutch manufacturers. They submitted to it without a murmur, knowing that, according to the laws of the country, any infringement, however involuntary, of the Emperor's commands, entailed the severest penalties.

The little colony then established itself in the island of Desima, situated in the port of Nagasaki, in front of the

ISLAND OF DESIMA.

town. This island had been constructed by the Portuguese shortly before their expulsion. The foundations were about twelve feet deep, and built of hewn stone. The level was raised about four feet above high-water mark, and the total length of the island was about 600 feet by 240 in breadth. It was formed in the shape of a fan, and within this miserable plot of artificial ground the Dutch remained for over two hundred years, during the whole of which time every movement was encumbered by the complete system of espionage under which they were placed.

In 1613 the English, under the guidance of William Adams, who had been second in command on board a Dutch ship, also established themselves at Firando. At first they lived in great harmony with their neighbours, but the spirit of rivalry soon produced enmity between the two nations, and each laboured to injure the other, instead of peacefully uniting to cultivate to the utmost the new field of riches opened before them. For several successive years the English endeavoured to place their trade both with Japan and China on a firmer footing, but without success. In 1673 they organised another expedition to Japan, but were repulsed on the pretext that Charles II., the reigning king, was allied to the kingdom of Portugal by his marriage with a princess of the house of Braganza.

More than a century afterwards, an English ship was not allowed to approach any part of the coast, and the expeditions of Captain Pellew in 1808, and Sir Stamford Raffles in 1813, were also unsuccessful, as was another attempt at reconciliation made in 1818 by Captain Gordon. One more trial was made in 1849 by Captain Matheson, but all pacific propositions offered by him were, as before, politely declined.

Russia also failed signally to break through the reserve of this exclusive nation. The first overture was made in 1792 by the Empress Catherine, who gladly seized the opportunity offered by the shipwreck of a Japanese merchant upon the Russian Kuriles to show her friendly disposition towards Japan. She instantly charged one of her officers, Adam Taxman, to convey the shipwrecked man safely back to Yedo. The Japanese Government, knowing the weakness of its northern possessions (Russia divided the Kurile group with Japan), expressed to Taxman a hope of making some commercial arrangements. But the subsequent propositions of the Russian ambassador, De Resanoff, were adroitly evaded; and he found himself treated with distrust and even uncourteousness by the court of Yedo. At length, contrary to the commands of his Government, he commenced hostilities. Later on, the Russian captain, Golowinn, was taken and detained a prisoner from the year 1811 till 1813.

The pacific disposition of Russia being at length comprehended by this extraordinarily cautious people, their apprehensions were for the time quieted; but they were ever watchful against any possible encroachments of so powerful a neighbour, who took every opportunity of adding to his already extensive territories. This feeling gained strength year by year, and they strove more than ever to avoid contact with foreigners, and prevent access to their country.

The French nation have only quite lately been admitted to any relationship with Japan, notwithstanding Colbert's endeavour to establish an embassy between the two countries. This great minister at once perceived that it was the religious question that had swayed the foreign policy of Japan, and in his instructions to his envoy we find the following curious passage noticed by Fraissinet:—

"Upon the matter of religion, you can say that France has two kinds, that held by the Spaniards and that believed by the Dutch; that His Majesty, having learnt that the Spanish religion is offensive to the Japanese, has commanded his subjects to embrace the creed of the Dutch. If the objection be raised that the King of France is as dependent on the Pope as is the King of Spain and others, you can reply that the King of France recognises no one greater than himself, and can illustrate the slight respect in which he holds the Pope's authority by an account of that which happened two years ago, after an insult offered to His Majesty's ambassador (the Duc de Créqui). The Holy Father not having immediately made the *amende honorable*, His Majesty had instantly sent an army into Italy—a measure which had caused such alarm to all the princes, together with the Head of the Church, that they at once despatched a legate, charged with the humblest apologies and supplications. His Majesty then mercifully ordered the withdrawal of all the troops encamped in the Roman States."

The sudden death of this envoy put a stop to these negotiations, and all efforts to obtain a footing in the islands were temporarily abandoned.

The next attempt made by the French was not till 1847, when a squadron under Rear-Admiral Cécille sailed for Japan, and anchored before Nagasaki. The fleet was immediately surrounded by boats filled with eager vendors of curiosities, merchandise of all kinds, vegetables, fowls, and edibles of every description. They were accompanied by a few more gaily-dressed boats containing some Government officials, who came on board to ask, in the name of their country, that no attempt should be made by these visitors to land. They were otherwise exceedingly polite, according to their custom, and exhibited the greatest curiosity, minutely examining the armaments, and putting many pertinent questions regarding the working of the ships. Admiral Cécille gladly showed them every attention, and they parted with mutual expressions of goodwill, though this pacific termination was followed by no immediate results.

CHAPTER III.

Efforts to open Relations with Japan—The Tycoon's Answer to the Dutch—American Address to the Tycoon—Imposing Ceremonial of the American Reception—Oriental Etiquette—Treaties with America, England, and France—Japanese Embassy to Europe.

SINCE the expulsion of the Portuguese more than two hundred years before, the Dutch continued, until nearly the middle of the present century, the only European nation in connection with Japan. But in the minds of the great maritime powers of Europe, the time had come when so important an empire could no longer be allowed to hold aloof in the great movement towards civilisation and modern commerce which, thanks to the immense progress in navigation caused by steam, had now extended to the farthest limits of the Western Hemisphere. Fresh attempts were therefore made by England, the United States, Russia, and France successively, to form some relationship with the Empire of Japan.

In 1844 the Dutch Government, taking advantage of the effect the opium war in China might be supposed to have upon Japan, conceived the idea of acting as a kind of mediator with the Government of Japan in the interests of European commerce. King William II. wrote to the Siogoun, or Tycoon, the temporal sovereign, begging him to open spontaneously certain ports to Europeans, in order to avert the danger of a similar attempt being made to that which had lately been the cause of the concessions extorted from China. "If you refuse any longer," said the King of Holland, "to take the rank among the commercial nations which you ought to hold, they will force your strongholds, and cause you to suffer the same humiliations as the Celestial Empire. Spare yourselves this shame, and by timely and generous measures gain for yourselves the esteem and sympathy of the European powers."

Two years elapsed before the Tycoon's answer was received. He then replied that he had observed attentively the events which had brought about a fundamental change in Chinese politics. These events, emphasised so strongly in the counsel of the King of Holland, were to him the clearest proof that a kingdom could only enjoy lasting peace by the total exclusion of foreigners. If China had never permitted the English to establish themselves on so vast a scale at Canton, the troubles which were the cause of the war would never have arisen, and a smaller colony would have felt themselves too weak to venture on such an unequal combat. "From the moment," added the Tycoon, "that one point is yielded, every other becomes more open to attack. This argument," he continued, "was that used by my great-great-grandfather upon a similar request of yours; and if it were not for the sincere tokens of friendship always shown by you towards our country, it is certain that you also would have been excluded, as were the other nations of the West. Now that you possess this privilege, I desire that you may continue to enjoy it, but I shall carefully watch against the advent of any other people, for it is easier to maintain a wall in a good state of preservation than to repair a breach when once it is made. I have given orders to my officials accordingly, and the future will prove to you that our policy exceeds in wisdom that of the Chinese Empire." Thus the efforts of the Dutch monarch to bring Japan into contact with Western civilisation proved abortive. We will now trace the consequences of the exclusive policy so rigidly maintained by the Tycoon.

The Americans were the first who ventured to subject Japan to the common law of nations. It was essentially necessary to the interests of their maritime commerce that, first of all, the ports should be opened to them, so as to form places for revictualling, coal depôts, and havens of refuge. It seemed also a necessity, in the interests of humanity, that some understanding should take place with a people who could, from year to year, calmly regard the destruction of many a fine vessel upon the reefs and unknown coasts of the islands they inhabited. Commodore Perry, in command of an American squadron, had the charge of the mission which was to accomplish these benevolent purposes.

The views of the Government of Washington are clearly set forth in the following letter, addressed to the Emperor of Japan by the President, Mr. Fillmore. After assuring the Emperor of the friendly feeling entertained towards his person and Government by the United States, the despatch proceeds as follows:—

"We know that the ancient laws of your Imperial Majesty's Government do not allow of foreign trade, except with the Chinese and the Dutch; but as the state of the world changes, and new Governments are formed, it seems to be wise, from time to time, to make new laws. There was a time when the ancient laws of your Imperial Majesty's Government were first made. . . .

"If your Imperial Majesty is not satisfied that it would be safe altogether to abrogate the ancient laws which forbid foreign trade, they might be suspended for five or ten years, so as to try the experiment. If it does not prove as beneficial as was hoped, the ancient laws can be restored.

"I have directed Commodore Perry to mention another thing to your Imperial Majesty. Many of our ships pass every year from California to China, and great numbers of our people pursue the whale-fishery near the shores of Japan. It sometimes happens, in stormy weather, that one of our ships is wrecked on your Imperial Majesty's shores. In all such cases we ask, and expect, that our unfortunate people should be treated with kindness, and that their property should be protected, till we can send a vessel to bring them away. We are very much in earnest in this.

"Commodore Perry is also directed by me to represent to your Imperial Majesty that we understand that there is

American Steamers in the Bay of Yedo. 45

a great abundance of coal and provisions in the empire of Japan. Our steamships, in crossing the great ocean, burn a great deal of coal, and it is not convenient to bring it all the way from America. We wish that our steamships and other vessels should be allowed to stop in Japan, and supply themselves with coal, provisions, and water. They will pay for them in money, or anything else your Imperial Majesty's subjects may prefer; and we request your Imperial Majesty to appoint a convenient port, in the southern part of the empire, where our vessels may stop for this purpose. We are very desirous of this.

"These are the only objects for which I have sent Commodore Perry, with a powerful squadron, to pay a visit to your Imperial Majesty's renowned city of Yedo—friendship, commerce, a supply of coal and provisions, and protection for our shipwrecked people."

The American squadron, composed of the steam frigates Susquehanna, Mississippi, and Powhattan, two sloops, the Plymouth and the Saratoga, and several smaller vessels, containing about 700 troops, left the United States, visiting several places of interest on their way, and anchored on July 8th, 1853, opposite the city of Uraga, situated on the western side of the bay of Yedo. The apparition of two steamers (unknown in this part of Japan), having in tow two brigs with furled sails, and going at the rate of several knots an hour dead against the wind, caused the greatest sensation amongst the Japanese, whose numberless trading barks carefully drew off to each side, leaving the squadron a free passage.

The moment the vessels anchored, two shots were fired from the battery, half-a-league distant, a sign of hostile intentions; and shortly afterwards the ships were surrounded with boat-loads of armed men, who presented the

JAPANESE WAR VESSEL.

usual address to strangers, enjoining them to retire. This request was refused; and the Vice-Governor of Uraga—the only Japanese received by Commodore Perry—was warned that, if any attempt was made to surround the squadron, such conduct would be attended with the gravest consequences. A few boats, however, still remained in the vicinity, till the sight of the warlike preparations on board the two steamers convinced them of the reality of the commodore's determination not to be trifled with, and they speedily dispersed. Whilst waiting for an answer from the court of Yedo to a letter demanding an interview, which had been despatched to that city, the Mississippi made a short excursion up the bay, and discovered beyond the promontory of Uraga a large fine creek, admirably formed for a safe and convenient harbour.

On the 12th of July the Emperor's answer arrived from Yedo, appointing a time and place for an interview between the commodore and one of his highest dignitaries. After some slight delay the little town of Gori-Hama, situated about a mile to the south of Uraga, was finally fixed upon as the place of meeting; and on the morning of the 14th the Susquehanna and Mississippi moved nearer inshore, so as to cover the village with their guns. The Governor and Vice-Governor of Uraga, and the commander of the forces, came on board to escort the commodore to the landing-place. Three houses had been constructed by the Japanese, one for the accommodation of the commodore and his suite, the others for the use of the two Japanese princes deputed to receive and deliver the American message to the Emperor.

The commodore's suite, consisting of as many officers, marines, and blue-jackets as could be spared from the vessels, numbered about three hundred; whilst the Japanese force was estimated at from five to seven thousand men. Their ranks were drawn out round the head of the creek for the space of a mile, their bright scarlet ensigns and flags of every shape and shade presenting quite an imposing appearance.

JAPANESE WARRIOR.

The commodore was escorted with much pomp, preceded by the Stars and Stripes of the United States, and by a band playing the national air, to the house of reception, the two envoys, Yoda, Prince of Idzu, and Ido, Prince of Iwami, rising and bowing as he entered, followed by the officers of his suite. The utmost formality prevailed. The President's message, together with the commodore's letters of credence, were then officially exchanged, a receipt for the same being duly signed by the two princes; and after more ceremonious bowing the interview terminated, the Japanese officials being powerless to negotiate further. The commodore had not provisions or water enough to enable him to remain on the coast more than a month longer, and also preferred waiting until the ensuing spring, when he would be able to concentrate his whole force, and be prepared with coal and store vessels, and all other conveniences for remaining an indefinite time, to secure whatever concessions the Japanese should be disposed to make. The squadron accordingly left on July 17th, after a visit of only eight days. Hardly were they clear of the bay when a Russian squadron appeared upon the coast, entrusted with a mission from the Russian Government to open communication with Japan. Several months later saw them still anchored before Nagasaki, patiently awaiting some reply.

On the 12th of February, 1854, the American squadron again anchored in the bay of Yedo. It was composed of the three steamships mentioned before, in addition to the sailing frigate Macedonian, the war sloops Vandalia, Saratoga, and Southampton, and the two transports, Supply and Lexington.

On the following day Commodore Perry received notice of the near approach of the grandee with whom he was to treat. At the same time the Japanese authorities endeavoured to persuade him to shift his quarters, which they considered too close to the capital of the empire. Twelve days were spent in discussion over this, and finally the American fleet anchored at Yokohama, about ten miles from Yedo. The 7th of March had arrived before the interview with the four emissaries employed by the Japanese Government took place.

The ceremonial which followed was, of course, of the usual pompous, formal character for which Japan is celebrated. Like all Oriental nations, the Japanese have extreme notions of dignity. When foreigners are to be received, seats and tables are arranged opposite each other on both sides of the reception hall. On the one side sit the Japanese officials, arranged according to rank. As the interview proceeds, lacquer trays are brought, on which are placed pipes, tobacco, lights, and spittoons; then follows a long service of native dainties: sweets of all kinds, fish, vegetables, seaweed, rice, tea — of course, usually voted "execrable" by Europeans who had travelled thousands of miles to the native home of the cheering cup. Then comes the *saki*, the Japanese spirit, strong enough, but by no means enticing in flavour. It does not seem to be very much relished by the natives themselves when they can get anything better, for they take to foreign wines with the utmost avidity. In the present instance the Americans had introduced judicious presents of sparkling champagne, a beverage in all respects suited to captivate the Japanese palate. It was passed about and drunk with an almost childish delight. When the visit is over, the guest is supposed to express his wish to retire. Both parties then rise, formal salutations are returned, and the entertainer conducts his visitor a longer or shorter way from the hall, according to his rank. These Japanese diplomatists are perfect masters of the art of "how not to do it." They can consume time to any extent in formalities and ceremonious twaddle, and only on the most pressing reminders can they be brought to deal with the real subject of the conference. They will inquire after your excellency's health with polite solicitude; they will tell you how honoured they are by your presence, hoping you like the country, admire the scenery, &c., &c., and look indescribably pained when, with western impatience, you insist on breaking through this crust of etiquette, and proceeding directly to business.

On this occasion the Americans especially remarked the profusion of crêpe and silken hangings; indeed the exceeding beauty and skill of all these productions of local industry were matters of profound astonishment to them. The elegance of the white straw mats carpeting the floors, the magnificence of the *braseros* of leather with which their halls were decorated, the brilliant colours and bright varnish of the furniture and walls, in fact everything, served to convince the American officers of the superiority of Japanese industry to Chinese—a superiority unhesitatingly acknowledged by the Chinese themselves.

Agreement with America.

In the excursions they made into the interior, by permission of the Japanese, it was evident that agriculture, and especially horticulture, had attained to a far higher degree of perfection in Japan than China; whilst the labouring classes appeared better off, better fed, better clothed, and cleaner in all their habits. In the matter of intellect, the Americans at once recognised that they had to deal with a most intelligent and cultivated people. Amongst the officials with whom they came in contact, they found several who could read, write, and speak both English and Dutch. They appeared thoroughly conversant with all that passed in other countries, and were not strangers to the discoveries and inventions of modern European science, for a telegraphic apparatus, and a miniature circular railway, that were worked in their presence, called forth most intelligent observations, and seemed to produce a great effect upon them. Meanwhile negotiations were progressing, and were finally brought to a conclusion at a general conference held March 31, 1854.

The agreement then signed was composed of twelve articles, and stipulated for the immediate opening of the port of Simoda to the ships of the United States, and, in a year's time, the port of Hakodadi. From these two places American ships could procure wood, water, provisions, coal, and every other necessary of which they were in need. Assistance was to be given to shipwrecked vessels by the Japanese authorities, who should also, if required, convoy them to one of the open ports. The United States Government was authorised to appoint a consul for Simoda eight months from the date of the treaty, and resident Americans in the two ports were granted full liberty to travel anywhere within a certain radius. Such were the principal clauses of the agreement signed at Yokohama.

England was the next power to negotiate with Japan; and on the 14th October, 1854, she also signed a treaty, by which the ports of Nagasaki and Hakodadi were opened unconditionally to British vessels, for purposes of revictualling, &c. The Russian admiral, Count Poutiatine, was about the same time rewarded for his long patience, and courteously welcomed by the court of Yedo.

Thus was the long-desired communication finally established between each of these three kingdoms and Japan, almost simultaneously, and upon equal terms; though, in consideration of its long connection with China and Holland, Japan still accorded these two countries a few especial advantages.

Four years later, in 1858, Lord Elgin, being engaged in the regulation of Chinese affairs, received instructions to proceed to Japan and commence more extensive negotiations. These he executed so successfully that a treaty was shortly signed at Yedo which placed commercial relations on the broadest foundations. A regular embassy was established at the court of Yedo, and consuls appointed to watch over the trade interests at Hakodadi, Kanagawa, and Nagasaki. Merchants could for the future enter into contracts with individuals without the interference of Government. Foreign moneys were rated at the same value as the Japanese coins of equal weight. The existing taxes on tonnage and transit were taken off, and a marked reduction made on the duties for exportation and importation. Having secured these advantages, Lord Elgin departed for China, previously presenting to the Tycoon, in the name of the Queen, a small steam yacht—a present which, for reasons explained in the first chapter, must have caused considerable astonishment, not to say amusement, among the Japanese courtiers.

France was now the only great remaining naval power not in connection with Japan. The pacific but fruitless attempt of Admiral Cécillé, in 1845, had been followed by no other until the month of September, 1858, when the French, encouraged by the success of the other nations, despatched a squadron, with Baron Gros as ambassador, to secure for France the good-will of Japan. No obstacles presented themselves, and in less than a month a treaty, containing similar clauses to that made with the English, was concluded; and thus Japan found itself suddenly placed in direct communication with Europe.

The spirited determination of the different European Governments to force upon Japan her rightful share in the commerce of the world being attended by such happy results, the most flattering hopes were entertained of the great commercial advantages to be gained from connection with this empire, hopes which were strengthened by the arrival of a Japanese embassy in Europe. The object of this embassy was to visit the principal courts, and to assure each individual Government of the friendly disposition of the Tycoon towards them. The ambassadors went in succession to London, Paris, the Hague, and Berlin, manifesting everywhere the same desire to see and know everything; asking the minutest questions about the institutions, customs, administrative proceedings, and industrial organisation; inspecting manufactories and foundries, collecting information, taking notes, buying samples, books, machinery, and yet never disclosing by word or sign their various impressions, only uttering the occasional exclamation of "Wonderful!"

Approaching events, however, soon showed that the Japanese were subject to the same laws of humanity as Europeans; and in this country, as elsewhere, the dawn of a more advanced civilisation was not ushered in without the futile opposition of a contracted patriotism, which stirred up much strife, and did not end without the shedding of blood.

PUNISHMENT FOR STEALING IN JAPAN.

CHAPTER IV.

Grievances of the Daimios—Hostility against Foreigners—Murders—The English inflict Chastisement—Europeans remove to Yokohama—The Daimios agree to tolerate Foreign Intercourse—Increased Acquaintance with Japan.

THE Government of the Tycoon had certainly agreed to open the four great Japanese ports to the ships of the nations with whom they had formally treated; but the original law excluding all strangers from the country—a law which was greatly favourable to the interests of the superior classes of Japanese society — had never been formally repealed. As will be seen during the course of this work, Japan was, in fact, governed by hereditary nobles called Daimios, who appear to have possessed the same rights as the owners of large fiefs in the times of the Feudal System in Europe; and it was this class who suffered most from the conditions of the recent treaties.

Certain natural productions, such as silk, tea, cotton, which till now had been exclusively consumed in the country, and were consequently very low in price, suddenly came into great demand in those towns where traffic with foreign countries had commenced. The result was an

A DAIMIO RECLINING.

instant rise in price, provoking a similar increase upon all other articles. If the system of free trade had been established throughout the empire, the Daimios—poor in purse, but rich in lands—would have immensely benefited by this new state of things; on the contrary, however, as all their goods passed into the hands of foreign merchants through agents of the Emperor, it was he alone who reaped the enormous profits. The inferior nobility also—who, not possessing an acre of their own, gained their livelihood by the profession of arms, or some public employment—were very soon involved in the greatest poverty, debt, and distress, as their salaries by no means kept pace with the advancing prices of all the necessaries of life.

An additional grievance to the nobility of all grades was to be found in the unavoidable wounds inflicted on their pride and prerogatives of caste by modern civilisation.

In a letter to the Tycoon they complain that these foreigners, far from gratefully accepting as a favour the privileges accorded to them after their reiterated humble demands, seemed now only to regard them as theirs by right in virtue of the treaties. "Such audacious pretensions are not to be tolerated; if these merchants will not subject themselves to our laws and rules of trade, let all their privileges, granted by us, be withdrawn. It is a universal law that he who abuses a favour loses all right to it. All good patriots sigh when they compare the glorious past with the present condition of the country. . . . We held one single nation in pawn as security for the good faith of the rest. This toleration has, however, proved a great error, as the advantages afforded to this nation have ended by exciting the cupidity of others. It is difficult for us to understand you when you say the world has changed, and that it is now impossible for one nation to remain isolated from others. Do you then think Japan is as other nations—as China, for example? You must understand that we speak of the modes of government amongst foreign nations. Is there any amongst them worthy to bear the name of government? Have they a Mikado, a grandson of the gods? Are not our principal families of celestial origin?" From these sublime notions of their divine origin, we can easily comprehend the almost insurmountable difficulties to be overcome before it was possible to establish any intimate relationship with the rulers of Japan.

These expressions of ill-will, however, took no definite form until August 25th, 1859, when, although the ink with which the Japanese officials had appended their signatures to the last pacific agreement was scarcely dry, a Russian officer and blue-jacket were foully murdered in the streets of Yokohama. A few months later the Chinese servant of the French consul, dressed in European clothes, was massacred; on the 30th January, 1860, the Japanese interpreter of the British legation was mortally wounded at the very gateway of the envoy's residence at Yedo; and a few days afterwards two Dutch captains were hewn in pieces in the principal street of Yokohama. And, most significant fact of all, these crimes remained unpunished.

Finally, after several other foreign officials had lost

their lives, amongst them four English residents, who were attacked and massacred whilst quietly riding one day in the environs of Yokohama, the forbearance of the British Government could stand no further trials, and they demanded instant satisfaction, with dire threats of vengeance if refused. No answer being returned to this menace, hostilities were commenced by the seizure of three steamboats richly laden with silk goods, &c., which were lying before the town of Kagosima, capital of the province of Satsuma. The forts immediately opened a formidable fire upon the English vessels, and a brisk action ensued for four hours, the advantage remaining with the English, who finally sailed out of the bay, after having fired the factories, foundries, and a portion of the town of Kagosima, and destroyed all batteries within reach.

Shortly before this an insult had also been offered to the French flag. Shots having been fired at some French vessels which were inoffensively sailing past the town of Simonasaki, two frigates, under the command of Admiral Jaures, were sent from Yokohama to demand an apology, but on their approach two forts opened fire upon them. The admiral, seeing that more vigorous measures were necessary, landed his men, who marched almost without molestation to the fort, which they found abandoned. Traces of blood were to be seen on some of the guns, and the French shot had slightly damaged the walls; but all dead bodies had evidently been carefully removed. The French spiked the guns, made a large fire of all the straw

TOWN AND HARBOUR OF YOKOHAMA.

JAPAN.—p. 61.

mattings and other inflammable materials they could find, and threw all the powder and ammunition into the sea.

These speedy and decisive measures at length led the Government of the Tycoon to perceive the gravity of their situation; they therefore deemed it prudent to manifest, at any rate for the present, a more conciliatory spirit, and strove to obliterate in the minds of the strangers the decree of expulsion, which it was impossible for them openly to retract. At the same time they sought by every means in their power to hinder a continuation of direct communication with Yedo, and finally, by their restrictions, succeeded in driving away all the Europeans, who settled themselves in Yokohama, then a poor village, but which in three years time became a large and flourishing town.

At length a general assembly of Daimios was convened, when the Tycoon and his ministers—who, from intercourse with the foreigners, were better able to judge of the state of affairs—at last succeeded (either by persuasion or the fear inspired by European reprisals, the horrors of which they graphically depicted) in bringing the Daimios to take a calmer view of their imaginary foes, and by sixty-five votes against forty-seven it was decided, after a long debate, that the time had not yet arrived to declare war against the strangers. The Government of the Tycoon has ever since preserved these pacific relations with Europe, the bond being further cemented by the return of their ambassadors from the West with a gratified recital of the warm and courteous receptions given them by the courts of England, France, Holland, and Prussia.

The fruits of this second victory gained by modern civilisation over the Japanese Government were soon visible. Expeditions were enabled to push into the interior of Japan, and, in spite of the hindrances opposed by the constant espionage of suspicious officials, the information gained, although still imperfect, gives us a true and just idea of a country and its inhabitants whose customs and costumes contrast so strangely with ours. The latest results of the most authentic information thus obtained will be detailed in the following chapters.

JAPANESE FOOT SOLDIER.

CHAPTER V.

Description of the Japanese Empire—Rich Vegetation of the Country—Conjectures as to the Origin of the Race—Story of Sikono and his Physician—Confirmation of the Legend—Singular Survival of Japanese Civilisation.

THE so-called empire of Japan is a collection of islands, of various dimensions, amounting to nearly four thousand, and situated to the east of the Asiatic Continent. The names of the principal ones are Nipon, or Niphon, Sitkoff, and Kiusiu. A sort of belt of defence is formed round these by a number of islets. The territorial area of the country is estimated at about thirteen thousand square leagues, and the population at about thirty-two millions.

Although we do not possess accurate information as to some of the more remote portions of the interior of Japan, the districts surrounding those towns accessible by strangers are most attractive to the eye. Vegetation of remarkable beauty and vigour begins almost from the seashore, covering so luxuriantly all the surrounding slopes that scarcely sufficient space seems left for the picturesque country houses, built by the richer Japanese, which lie dotted here and there, or for the numerous prettily situated temples. In no other part of the world is to be seen the strange medley of tropical plants and those belonging to temperate climes. Beneath the branches of the most beautiful of European trees grow a group of bamboos, or a cluster of enormous camellias, whilst the atmosphere is everywhere sweetened by the perfume of the camphor tree. The highest hills are clothed almost to their summits by richly cultivated lands, and cosy, cheerful little hamlets nestle amidst the bright green foliage of the valleys.

The people of such a pleasant country are, as we should imagine them to be, of a gentle and amiable disposition. All travellers unite in singing the praises of the Japanese, extolling their courtesy, refined sentiments, and love of the beautiful.

The conjectures concerning the origin of this strange race are numerous: some writers tell us that they are descended from the Chinese; others that Japan was first colonised by emigrants from Babylon, after the fall of that empire; others, again, make them of Tartar descent. The historian Fraissinet inclines to the first of these theories. He tells us that in the reign of On-Yé, the twenty-fifth emperor of the Xamo dynasty, the barbaric nations inhabiting the northern part of the Celestial Empire becoming too numerous, batches of them were drafted off to colonise the numerous islands situated in the Eastern Ocean. Now as On-Yé ascended the throne in the year 1196 B.C., this appears to tally correctly with other information derived from various sources.

LADIES ON THE PROMENADE.

JAPAN.—p. 67.

The Story of Sikono.

Five hundred years after the emigration described by Chinese historians, Zin-um-ten-woo—a name signifying "the Divine Conqueror"—chief of one of the still barbaric tribes, managed, by craft and force of arms combined, to gain authority over the entire colony. He was the founder of the dynasty of the Mikados, and the religion of the Kami, the worship of Ancestors. These events took place about the year 660 B.C. If the Japanese people had been indigenous, is it probable that they would have led a nomadic life up to the time of Zinmon, when China, so closely adjoining, had been already a powerful empire for fifteen centuries? It is much more rational to suppose that, taking refuge on the coasts of Japan, the expatriated Tartars remained there and multiplied, between the years 1196 and 660 B.C., by which time civilisation had so far advanced that they gladly welcomed a political and religious constitution.

Another Japanese tradition regarding their origin is told by some native authors, and is worth relating.

Sikono, Emperor of China, a great tyrant, and thoroughly detested by his people, was closely wedded to the pleasures of this life, but one day began to brood deeply and sadly upon the brevity of human existence. He said to himself it was very hard to be obliged to quit an empire, where he was surrounded by so much power and magnificence, in a space of time as short as that in which he had been born. This thought, having once taken possession of his mind, never left him by night or day. Insensibly it led him to consider if there did not exist somewhere some panacea against death. He therefore offered a magnificent reward to any one who should solve the problem, and for this end sent his most learned philosophers and wise men into all parts of the world. Sion-Fou, one of the first physicians of his court, had been for some time very uneasy under the rule of so despotic a master as Sikono. What else but an unquiet conscience was to be expected in a prince who, upon the slightest caprice or most trivial suspicions, cut off the heads of his most faithful servants? The physician felt that his own was by no means secure on his shoulders, and he therefore was constantly on the watch for a pretext to quit so dangerous a master. This new fancy of the Emperor's gave him, he thought, the long-desired opportunity, and, far from objecting to the foolish whim, he took the utmost pains to encourage it.

"Yes, resplendent Son of Heaven," he said to him, "it is certainly possible to constitute a universal remedy which can procure immortality to all here on earth. The ingredients of which it is composed are to be found in the islands situated beneath the rising sun; but they are so subtle and delicate in organisation, that they fade and lose all their virtue unless gathered by hands chaste and pure. Give me three hundred youths and as many maidens, all healthy in body and vigorous in mind. I offer myself as their leader, and we shall soon place in your hands this life-prolonging elixir."

Sikono fell into the snare. He equipped the whole band at his own expense, and forwarded them on their way. But instead of going to search for the immortal herb, in which he had only feigned belief to escape from the tyranny of Sikono, the cunning physician established himself and his companions at Japan, from whence they never returned; and thus out of the three hundred young men and the three hundred maidens sprang the thirty millions of people that now inhabit the "Land of the Origin of the Sun."

As to the truth of this legend, we find all that it relates of Sikono confirmed by Chinese accounts, which represent him as one of the three Neros, by whom they were governed at different periods. Popular tradition in Japan also clearly points to this chapter of their history. They still show the part of the coast where the Chinese physician landed, and point out the stones of the temple erected of old in his honour as a reward for his having introduced the first elements of civilisation, and of the arts and sciences.

But if the Japanese adopt this as a fact, still they do not regard the Chinese as the founders of their race and nation. Indeed, they place the arrival of these strangers at a date when the Japanese monarchy had already existed for 400 years. The most probable theory is, that this now rich and powerful nation was for many centuries only a poor secluded tribe, who had fled from the reach of their enemies to the far distant mountains of Japan, where they led a very simple life, maintaining themselves by their cattle, and living on fruits, roots, and plants. It was but very slowly that they made any progress in agriculture and the useful arts, probably not until the arrival of the Chinese as mentioned above. Whatever their origin may be, it is a very remarkable phenomenon that a nation, the contemporary of the great powers of antiquity—Egypt, Persia, Greece, and Rome—should have survived the downfall of those countries, and should still retain its ancient forms of civilisation, although brought face to face with that of modern Europe.

JAPANESE WOMEN.

CHAPTER VI.

Worship of the Kami, or Ancestors—Curious Account of Creation—Selection of Japan as a Divine Abode—The last Advice of Tzanaghi—Introduction of Buddhism — Superiority of Buddhism to former Systems—Feuds between the Old and the New Religions—Reforms of Fide-Yosi.

HISTORICAL research, confirming the data furnished by tradition, states that at the epoch when Japanese history commences—that is, about 600 years B.C.—the country already possessed a religion of its own. This is in existence at the present day, although in an altered form, and holding an inferior position to other sects of subsequent origin.

This religion, considered the national faith of Japan, rather on account of its antiquity than from any great number of its adherents, is the Sinsyn, or worship of the Kami, or Ancestors. But it is not ancestors in general, nor the particular ancestors of this or that family, who are thus venerated; they are fabulous personages of the Japanese cosmogony—that is, the protecting genii of Japan and its inhabitants.

In the beginning, says Japanese tradition, there was no

heaven and no earth. The elements of all things formed a turbid liquid mass, resembling the contents of an egg, the yolk and white of which have been mixed together. From the infinite space where chaos reigned there sprung forth a god, who called himself the Supreme Being, whose throne was in the midst of heaven. Afterwards arose the Supreme God, exalted far above creation; and then the Creating God, who is the Sublime Spirit. Each of these three primitive gods had his own separate existence, but nothing was revealed of them beyond their spiritual nature.

Chaos presently arranged itself into separate forms. Subtle atoms, rolling in diverse directions, united to shape the heavens. Coarser atoms attaching themselves, and adhering one to the other, produced the earth. The coarser atoms taking longer to solidify, this second creation was not consummated till a long period after that of the heavens.

When terrestrial matter was still floating like a fish on the surface of the water, or like the image of the moon trembling on a limpid wave, there appeared midway between earth and heaven a thorny branch, endowed with movement and susceptible of transformation. This changed into three gods, who are Kouni-toko-tatsi no Mikoto; Kouni-sats-outsi no Mikoto; and Toyo-Koumon-sou no Mikoto. All three were of the male sex, because their origin was solely attributable to the action of the Celestial Reason. After these gods were four couples of gods and goddesses, who lived without sexual relations, viz., Wou-

The Seven Celestial Gods.

hitsi-ni no Mikoto, and his companion; Oho-to-tsi no Mikoto, and his companion; Omotarou no Mikoto, and his companion; and lastly, Tzanaghi no Mikoto, and his companion Tzanami. The era of these seven celestial gods and their consorts comprises an immeasurable duration of many millions of years.

One day Tzanaghi resolved to call into existence an inferior world. When he had caused it to emerge from beneath the waters of the ocean, he felt a great attraction towards his new creation, and, addressing his divine companion Tzanami, proposed to her to descend to this earth. The goddess graciously accepted the pleasing invitation, and the celestial couple, casting their looks around for a

JAPANESE GOD.

desirable residence, were mutually charmed with the lovely appearance of the Sea of Japan. They therefore decided to direct their steps towards the beautiful Isle of Awadsi, lying like a basket of foliage and flowers upon the deep calm waters of the inland sea, which on one side laps the fertile coast of Nipon, and on the other breaks against the rocks of Sitkoff.

In this charming spot they lived for many ages, never wearying of the delights of their terrestrial abode, which was at length enlivened by the frolics of a group of merry children. As time went on, the gentle goddess Tzanami began to sadden at the thought that, whilst she and her spouse were immortal, they must some day behold the eyes of their earth-born children close in death. The anguish of this thought becoming daily more intolerable, her husband prevailed upon her to return with him to the celestial regions, before the spectacle of death should cloud their domestic happiness.

Before their departure, Tzanaghi called his children together, bidding them dry their tears, and lend an attentive ear to his last wishes. He commenced by depicting to them in images, for which the human language can find no expression, that state of immutable serenity which is the incorruptible inheritance of the inhabitants of the heavens. "Without," he added, "possessing here on earth the felicity reserved only for those of a superior world, there is no reason why you should not, by contemplation, partially participate in it, provided that you religiously follow my wishes."

After these words he desired them to sink on their knees before him, and raising in his right hand a disc of polished silver, which had so often reflected the image of his divine companion, in solemn tones addressed the following words to them:—

"I bequeath to you this precious souvenir, in order that it may recall to you the kindly features of your mother, at the same time that it causes you to contemplate your own countenance. This may perhaps often prove a humiliating comparison. Strive, however, to assimilate yourselves to this model of perfection, which henceforth can be only found in the heavens. Each morning place yourselves on your knees before this mirror, and you will at once see there reflected on your countenance the impress of any evil passions wilfully indulged. Obliterate all these traces of sin, and, when in a purer and more tranquil mood, address your prayers to your parents in all simplicity and sincerity; for be assured that the gods can read your inmost soul as easily as you can your countenance when you gaze into this mirror. If during the day you experience feelings of anger, impatience, envy, or covetousness, and find them difficult to subdue, hasten back to the sanctuary where you performed your morning devotions, and there renew your meditations and prayers. Finally, each evening, before seeking your rest, examine yourselves thoroughly, and let your last thought be fresh aspirations after the felicity of that superior world whither we have preceded you."

Here the legend ends, but tradition adds that the children of Tzanaghi ever after deemed sacred the spot whence they had received the adieux of their parents. They raised there an altar of cedar-wood, with no ornaments save the mirror of Tzanami, and two vases formed of fragments of bamboo, each filled with the flowers that she loved. A simple square shed, covered with rushes, protected this rustic altar, which, when bad weather rendered it necessary, they closed by means of folding doors. There morning and evening did the children of Tzanaghi conduct their worship as he had commanded them, and reigned, generation after generation, for a period of two to three millions of years, becoming in their turn the spirits of good, the immortal Kami.

The worship of their ancestors remained for a long time the only creed held in respect by the Japanese. It was not till 552 A.D. that a new doctrine was introduced into the country. This doctrine, which originated in India, and numbered hundreds of millions amongst its adherents, was Buddhism. Far from denying its foreign origin, the Japanese consider it a duty to recall the fact by various observances. Its introduction was due to the zeal of the king of Petsi, in Corea, who, anxious that a saying of Buddha, "My doctrine shall extend itself towards the East," should be fulfilled, presented to the reigning Mikado a statue of Buddha, together with a canopy, books, banners, and other objects necessary for the conducting of his worship. Its progress, however, was extremely slow, until a happy inspiration of one of its priests brought it into favour with the Mikado.

This man, when at the court one day, suddenly prostrated himself before the little son of the Mikado—a boy whose birth had been marked by extraordinary circumstances—and worshipped him, declaring he recognised him as the incarnation of a disciple of Buddha, the new patron of the empire, and the future propagator of religious light. The Mikado was persuaded to devote the child to the priesthood, and confide his education to the Buddhist bonze. The rest can be imagined. This boy became the initiator and first high priest of Buddhism in the empire of Japan, where his memory is now revered under the name of Sjo-Tok-Daisi, the holy and virtuous hereditary prince.

The great majority of the Japanese population were, without altogether abandoning the worship of their ancestors, soon won over to the new religion, whose rules, at once flexible, conciliatory, and insinuating, are easily rendered suitable to the consciences and habits of the most diversely constituted peoples.

Buddhism far surpasses, in many respects, the religions it has dethroned, owing this relative superiority to the truth and justice of its starting point, which is the confession of a need for deliverance, based upon the double fact of the existence of evil in man and the universal state of misery and suffering in the world. The grounds of doctrine of the Kami creed differ altogether from this, and relate entirely to the present life; its rules of purity were formed for the preservation of the faithful from the five great evils, viz., fire from heaven, sickness, poverty, exile, and an early death; and the magnificent festivals had no other aim than the glorification of their departed heroes.

But although patriotism be idealised even to the extent of its becoming a national creed, it is nevertheless a sentiment totally unable to comfort the soul or supply its needs. The human soul has perceptions of things higher than are to be found in this world, and therefore requires a religion which can assist it in their pursuit. Buddhism, in one sense, filled this void, experienced by so many minds, but never before recognised; and this sole reason explains the rapidity with which it was propagated in Japan—added, it must be confessed, to the judicious proceedings of the first Buddhist ministers, who soon managed to acquire the charge of all the shrines, and even the little chapels confided to their care. They were very anxious to join to their ceremonies symbols borrowed from the ancient national creed; and, in order to confound the two religions more utterly in the minds of the people, they introduced at the same time Kami, invested with the titles and attributes of Hindoo divinities, and Hindoo divinities transformed into Japanese Kami.

Regarding it superficially, Buddhism seemed to do no more than sanction all ancient national commemorations, and incorporate them with the new objects of veneration which would sustain the devotion of the masses; and thus it was that each of the thousand Buddhist divinities were so easily admitted into Japan. Temples, statues, and monastic brotherhoods were everywhere raised in their honour. Bonzes, monks, and nuns abounded throughout the land, especially towards the centre and south. Each convent vied with the neighbouring ones in matters of industry, and each strove to gain for itself the most thriving trade.

Little by little, however, this competition grew so unrestrained, that envy, hatred, and jealousy embittered all inter-

INTERIOR OF BUDDHIST TEMPLE—HIGH PRIEST AND SERVANT.

course between many of these powerful and ambitious orders. From virulent abuse to personal violence was but a step. The Japanese police at first interfered in the conflicts between these tonsured belligerents, but were wholly unable to stem the torrent of their fanatical rage. Bands of infuriated monks, in frock and cassock, armed with staves, pikes, and flails, rushed by night on the possessions of the offending brotherhoods. They robbed all who crossed their path, ill-treated, killed, or dispersed the conventuals, not returning till they had set fire to every corner of the priests' dwellings. Sooner or later, however, the aggressors were in their turn unexpectedly assailed, and made to suffer the same treatment. The outrages committed between these inimical brotherhoods occasioned immense disasters in neighbouring quarters, till at length, for the protection of their convents, the rich bonzes converted them into fortresses, the growing incapacity of the Government increasing their audacity.

Time, however, brought changes in the rulers of Japan, and at last a Tycoon—Fide-Yosi by name—endowed with a more enterprising spirit than some of his immediate predecessors, resolved to put a stop, once for all, to the quarrels of the monks. He surprised and occupied with his troops all the most turbulent monasteries, razed their defences, and transported to the farthest islands all the bonzes convicted of a breach of the public peace; placing the Japanese priests, without distinction, under the surveillance of a police force, active, severe, and inexorable. In addition to these prompt measures, he decreed that

TEMPLE AT YOKOHAMA.

henceforth the religious communities should be simply tenants, or temporary possessors, of the lands they held; the Government reserving to itself their proprietorship and all right of disposal. He also commanded all the dignitaries among the hierarchy to confine themselves and their subordinates strictly within the circle of their religious functions—an excellent law, which has ever since remained binding upon Japanese priests, and effectually prevented further disturbance.

Our readers will be struck with the curious parallelism which may here be traced between Eastern and Western history. In this isolated empire in the far East the same difficulties which threatened the very existence of early European States made their appearance, and had to be confronted. The subjection of all members of the priestly or clerical classes to the State, in so far as regards all the privileges and responsibilities of citizens, was found as necessary to the safety and well-being of Japan as of England or France, and the Tycoon, Fide-Yosi, may be regarded as an Oriental counterpart of our Henry the Second or the French Philip the Fair.

As will be abundantly evident from our account of the Japanese character, we need not look for many specimens of asceticism or monkish severity. Nevertheless there are to be found some who have chosen to retire from the world, and spend their time in vigils, and, perhaps, in prayer. In the neighbourhood of the large town of Kioto, where the proportion of priests to citizens is something quite remarkable, many of these sainted brethren are to

84   *The Hermit of Kioto.*

be found. Of these the most celebrated is the " Hermit of Kioto," who seems to have fairly earned this title *par excellence*, both on account of his extraordinary dwelling-

A Snug Retreat. 85

place and the mysterious awe with which he is popularly regarded. The habitation of this eccentric saint is in a nook or cleft of lofty rock, surrounded by the spreading branches of a tree. Between the rock and the highway is a pond, which secures him still further from molestation. But even hermits must eat, and to supply the necessities of nature the recluse has a pulley stretching over the pond and fastened to his den; and by this means he is kept in a constant supply of food by the bounty of the citizens, who send baskets of provisions up the pulley, and receive them back again when empty.

EXECUTION BY THE SWORD.

CHAPTER VII.

Establishment of Jesuit Mission in Kiusiu—Elasticity of Buddhism—Suspicions of Fide-Yosi—Designs of Iyeyas against the Jesuits—Completion of the Plot—Persecutions of the Jesuit Christians.

SHORTLY before Fide-Yosi had delivered the empire from these internal disturbances, important external events, of which we have already spoken, plunged the country into fresh troubles.

The Portuguese had just received authority to send yearly from Goa to Japan a cargo of merchandise. In one of their first voyages, the ship, returning to Goa, gave a secret passage to a Japanese gentleman named Hansiro, flying his country on a charge of homicide. The illustrious Jesuit, Francis Xavier, having lately arrived at Goa, undertook the religious instruction of this Japanese fugitive, and in course of time admitted him to the rite of baptism.

In 1549 the first Jesuit mission established itself in the island of Kiusiu, under the personal direction of Xavier, aided by Hansiro.

A feeling of surprise and holy fear at first seized the missionaries, when they discovered already established at Japan so many institutions, ceremonials, and objects of worship similar to those which they themselves had come to teach. Regardless of the antiquity of the Buddhist creed, they cried that this religion could only be a diabolical form of the true Church. But this resemblance they soon perceived could be moulded for the good of their own religion and its propagation. For the Buddhist creed is the broadest of Broad Church systems. With an elastic expansiveness unknown to sterner faiths, it receives within its borders any of the sons of men who, by their noble acts and devotion to the wants of their fellow-creatures, have earned the right of being regarded as divine. There was therefore nothing in the doctrine of Buddhism to oppose the admission of Jesus among the number of Buddhas who had appeared on earth during successive centuries, and by a similar argument the Virgin was without difficulty allowed pre-eminence over the many Queens of Heaven of the ancient Pantheon. In a word, every advantage was taken of the points of contact between the two creeds; and the sincerity of the faith of the many converts to Christianity made in all classes of Japanese society was afterwards indisputably proved by their steadfast constancy in the hour of persecution.

Some of the priests of Buddha, fearful that the old religion would sink in the estimation of the people, brought their most humble remonstrances to the foot of the throne.

"How many sects," demanded the Mikado, "are there existing in my empire?"

"Thirty-five," was the prompt response.

"Ah, well, then this will make the thirty-sixth," replied the jovial emperor.

But the Tycoon, Fide-Yosi, rendered suspicious by his recent experience of religious instructors, took a more serious view of the matter. The circumstance struck him that the foreign missionaries laboured not only to extend their doctrines amongst the people, but also to gain the favour of the great vassals of the empire, whose tendency to anarchy seemed to gather mysterious nourishment from the connection. Further inquiry revealed that the Jesuit priests had been brought up under a sovereign pontiff wearing a triple crown, and claiming at his will the power to dispossess the mightiest princes, distribute the kingdoms of Europe amongst his favourites, and even dispose of newly-discovered continents. He reflected that these emissaries from the great Ruler of the West had already created a party at the court of the Mikado, and had founded an establishment in his capital; that the former Tycoon, Nobounanga, had openly shown himself their friend and protector; and he also had reason to believe that in his own palace (his, as Tycoon in charge) dark plots were hatching amongst those persons surrounding his young son, heir presumptive to his power.

Fide-Yosi communicated these observations and fears to an experienced adviser, whom he had often entrusted with the most delicate missions. The profound and penetrating mind of this man, celebrated in Japanese annals by the name of Iyeyas, found an absolute pleasure in unravelling the coils of mystery, and he applied himself without delay

The Christians Persecuted. 89

to discover the extent of the danger. An embassy of the Japanese Christians had been, by order of P. Valignani, superior of the order of Jesuits, sent with a despatch to Rome. Iyeyas furnished proofs to his master that the Princes of Bungo, Omara, and Arima had taken the opportunity to write letters to the spiritual emperor of the Christians, Pope Gregory XIII. From these letters, specimens of which have already been given, it was perfectly clear, even to a less subtle and discerning mind than that of the minister Iyeyas, that, if things were allowed to go on without check, the time was not far distant when the Tycoon, and perhaps even the Mikado himself, would have to acknowledge the supreme authority of the Pope of Rome. The Tycoon restrained his indignation for the time, but only that his vengeance might fall the heavier. For nearly a year he and his favourite conferred together for the more complete organisation of the meditated blow. The first steps taken were in the month of June, 1557, by the distribution of bands of troops throughout the suspected provinces of Kiusiu and the southern coasts of Nipon, in sufficient numbers to repress all attempts at resistance. The preparations being completed, on a given day an edict was proclaimed from one extremity of the empire to the other, by order of the Tycoon, commanding, in the name of the Mikado, the suppression of Christianity within the space of six months. In order to effect this, all foreign missionaries were to be banished for life, on pain of death; their schools to be immediately closed, their churches razed to the ground, the crosses abounding in every direction to be thrown down, and all native converts compelled to abjure the new doctrines. At the same time, to prove the concord existing between the two powers, the Mikado paid a formal visit to his lieutenant; whilst the latter, to recompense the services of the faithful Iyeyas, elevated him to the rank of prime minister, and instituted him governor over eight provinces.

All the measures ordained by the edict were punctually executed, but did not meet with the success expected from them. To the profound embarrassment of the new prime minister, the native Christians of both sexes, of every class, and all ages, absolutely refused to abjure their faith. He then seized the goods of all those who possessed lands, and enriched his officers with the spoils. Others he cast into prison, or exiled to the convict islands. But no effect whatever was produced by these vigorous examples.

The recalcitrants were next threatened with capital punishment; but they offered their heads to the executioner with a resignation never before witnessed. Then tortures were employed, and the steadfast converts suffered both on the pile and on the cross.

In Japan the victim of crucifixion is attached to a cross with four limbs, the arms being extended on the two higher branches, the two legs on the lower. In this position he remains exposed from morning till evening; and at sunset two executioners, one standing on the right, the other on the left, each force a long spear from under the armpit out at the nape of the neck, and the corpse is then left suspended upon the cross for twenty-four hours.

The scenes of persecution which followed the imperial edict testified to the vitality of the faith, which, even in the uncongenial moral atmosphere of Japan, and overlaid as it was by many purely human inventions, could give rise to a race of martyrs such as other religions have never known. Dutch writers have paid an ample tribute to the heroism of the native Christians; and the ruthless persecution seemed, as not unfrequently happens, to have only excited, at least for a time, a more steadfast adherence to that religion in which they had learned to put their trust.

During three successive years did the fury of the Tycoon's officers exhaust itself in every refinement of barbarity and cruelty that their ingenuity could devise. Atrocities of a nature unutterably hideous were committed upon more than 20,000 victims, men and women, youths and maidens, old men and little children. Thanks to a war which broke out between Japan and China, the persecution suddenly abated, and the hope of the Christians revived, only to be again destroyed by fresh edicts launched against them. They finally all perished, though some of them certainly exist in small numbers, and in a surreptitious manner, to the present day.

CHAPTER VIII.

The Sinsyn or Kami Creed—Its Notions of Immortality—Buddhism; its History and Principal Tenets; its Reception by the Japanese—The Gods of Good Fortune; their Number and the Blessings they provide for Man—Effects of Japanese Mythology on National Character.

THE two great religions at the present time in force in Japan are the Sinsyn or Kami creed, whose votaries are denominated Sintoos, and Buddhism, the latter being peculiarly adapted to the habits of mind and customs of the Japanese. Sinsyn contains very few tenets; all are summed up in the belief that the gods who created Japan still continue to take an interest in their work, and that the heroes to whom the empire owes its power inhabit the abode of the gods, and intercede with them in favour of their country.

These heroes of the primitive ages were errant knights who, at a time when neither magistrates, laws, nor a regular army were in existence, caused justice to be respected by mere force of arms, and broke the power of the giants, dragons, and other monsters stained with the blood of human beings. Several towns derive their names from these noble deeds, and the victorious swords of the champions are religiously preserved in the temples. Respect for great men is so firmly rooted a sentiment in the heart of the nation, that all Japanese, of whatever creed, pay them public marks of veneration, to show their gratitude for the important services received from them. But that they may be deemed worthy to celebrate the festivals consecrated in their honour, or to visit the places rendered illustrious by their birth or exploits, it is necessary they should undergo a short ceremony of purification; and four rules of conduct are given to assist the faithful in discovering when he has arrived at the requisite condition of purity, or wherein he has failed to reach it. The only other religious duties required of him are to carefully cherish the two purifying elements fire and water, to testify by daily ablutions the pure state of his soul, and never to present any offerings to the temple but those of unquestionable fragrance and purity.

Pollution is the result of guilty connections, the death of relations, the touch of a corpse, the shedding of blood, or eating the flesh of domestic animals. To regain an unsullied state the penitent must submit to certain forms of expiation during a time, more or less prolonged according to the gravity of the offence. In extreme cases the men are obliged to grow their hair and beards to a great length, and to cover the head with a common hat of straw; and the women are ordered to envelop their heads in a piece of some white material; or both sexes are compelled to seclude themselves in their apartments, to undertake a pilgrimage, or to abstain from certain dishes and any gaieties. In no case, however, are the penances very severe.

The principal aim held in view by the Sintoos is the discovery of happiness in this world. They have only a very obscure and imperfect idea of the immortality of the soul, or of rewards and punishments beyond the grave; thus they never disturb themselves by vague theories of a life after death, but spend all their powers in trying to conciliate the gods who govern and direct the affairs of this life.

Buddhism is as full of complication as the Sinsyn faith is of simplicity. Although an immense number of documents exist upon the Buddhist religion, it is impossible to give its complete history, and perhaps this never can be done on account of its enormous extent and great antiquity; some fifteen to twenty nations, extending from Cashmere to China and Japan, embrace its doctrines, which have existed for a period of two thousand five hundred years.

The following brief synopsis of the principal tenets of the Buddhist faith will serve to convey to English readers some notion of the mystic and unintelligible jargon, with which Buddhist sages endeavour to keep the ignorant and unlearned from entering into the sacred mysteries of their creed :—

Buddha, or the Intelligent, the Sage, died at the age of eighty, in the year 543 B.C. Son of a king in the north of India, he was known by the name of Siddharta; he did not assume that of Buddha until he had, after long meditation, determined the basis of a new doctrine, formed for the instruction and salvation of the human race. This doctrine starts with the axiom that man has been condemned from eternity to perpetual renewals of existence, succeeding each other without end, and that the present life, exposed to sickness, old age, and death, is a fearful chain from which he struggles to be released at any price, so that he may never fall again into the abyss. In order, therefore, to procure the final liberation of the soul, the object of man is to strive to attain the state of *nirwâna*, or nothingness, which endures for ever. The mystic ladder by which this result is reached is contemplation, of which there are two flights, each divided into four stages.

To pass the first, the ascetic must detach himself from earthly desires. He may, however, still judge and reason, but he is sheltered from the seductions of evil; and the ecstatic feeling produced in him by the consciousness that he has progressed so far soon fits him for the second stage.

At this step the purity of the ascetic must still remain the same, but he casts aside judgment and reason, so that his mind, which fixes itself upon the one idea of apathetic tranquillity, feels only a sense of inward satisfaction, without the power to analyse or understand.

This feeling disappears at the third stage, the sage having reached that pitch of indifference when the experience of happiness is as nought to him. All the pleasure that remains to him is a vague sensation of physical well-being. He has not yet, however, lost his recollection of the various stages he has just passed, and he has still a confused consciousness of himself, in spite of the height of indifference to which he has attained.

Finally, the ascetic, at the fourth stage, no longer possesses even the feeling of physical well-being; all has become obscure; his memory has gone; more than this, he has even lost the feeling of indifference, and is now insensible to all causes of pleasure or sorrow, either within or without; his impassibility as nearly approaches to the state of non-existence as it is possible to attain to in this life.

And now he is admitted to the second stage of contemplation, or to the four regions presupposed in the world without form. He first enters the region of infinity of space. Thence he mounts a degree higher into the region of infinity of intellect. Thus the third region is attained, that wherein existence is lost. But as it is supposed that in this blank and gloom an idea of the nothingness into which he is absorbed may remain to him, one last supreme effort is made, and he reaches the fourth and final stage, where no ideas exist, and not even an idea of the absence of ideas.

Such were the mystic opinions promoted in Japan by Buddha Dharma. The first effect of the preaching of such a doctrine was to awaken the curiosity of the Japanese, who are of as inquiring a turn of mind as the Hindoos are taciturn and contemplative. Not evincing any special inclination to become nonentities, they occupied themselves in conjectures on the intermediate state between death and final extinction. Soon, by the assistance of the

Soul and Body.

bonzes, certain convenient ideas regarding death and the life to come were circulated throughout the towns and villages, without, it must be understood, in any way altering or harming those they had received from their forefathers touching the ancient gods and the venerated national Kami.

The soul of man, they said, resembles a floating vapour, elongated, indissoluble, of the form of a tadpole, with a thin streak of blood running from the top of the head to the extremity of the tail. If this were watched it would be seen to escape from its mortuary dwelling at the last sigh of the expiring man, and the cracking of the mortal frame can at any rate be heard. The attendant spirits of the great judge of hell are in waiting to receive the emancipated mysterious life, which they seize and carry before the tribunal, and the judge causes it to kneel before a mirror, which pitilessly reflects all the evils it has committed. The condemned souls are confined, according to the severity of the sentence, in one or other of the eighteen concentric circles that surround hell. Those under a vow of purification abide in purgatory, the cover of which is opened to allow them to pursue, without fear, the course of their pilgrimage.

Besides their two national religions, the Japanese have also a kind of private form of worship they pay to particular deities called gods of good fortune (or lucky gods); these are nothing more than the personification of human blessings. And thus, unsatisfied by the obscure and comfortless creed provided for them by their rulers, the people have materialised their inward yearnings by creating a mythology to satisfy them—a mythology as purely symbolic and human as that of the Greeks, with this great difference, however, that it is confined solely to types of terrestrial felicity, and is entirely free from any pretension to ideal beauty.

The gods of good fortune are seven in number, and their duty is to provide for men the following blessings:—longevity, wealth, daily food, contentment, talents, glory, and love. Their sanctuary is always to be found at the rear of the dwelling-house. The altar is composed of a slight scaffolding of cedar wood, generally of two small platforms entirely covered with red carpeting. The upper stage supports two idols made of hard wood, flanked by metal lamps, and the lower one three small round tables heaped with offerings of first-fruits. On the wall, which serves as a kind of super-altar, holy pictures are suspended; whilst at a short distance in front of the altar stand two high bronze chandeliers lighted by immense wax candles. It is here that the father of the family comes, sometimes alone, more frequently accompanied by his faithful partner, to kneel and invoke the tutelary divinities of his house. It rarely happens that a family places itself under the collective patronage of these gods. The principle of selection is perfectly admissible, and the man of the lower orders limits his invocation to the god of daily food, or associates therewith the deity of wealth. The merchant classes, in addition to these two, invoke the blessings of contentment and longevity. The four classed together are commonly called the gods of fortune and prosperity.

Shion-Rô.

The patron of longevity is naturally the most venerable of these seven types in the mythology of the Japanese people. They give him the name of Fkonrskon-Shion, or abbreviate it to Shion-Rô. During a life of incalculable duration he has observed, meditated, and reflected to such a degree, that his bald head has reached a development of prodigious height, and a long white beard covers his breast. When he walks slowly abroad, plunged in reverie, he holds in one hand a rustic crook, and with the other delicately strokes between two fingers the long hairs of his eyebrows. The chief emblems of this quaint deity are the tortoise and crane, but he is also represented accompanied by a stag, white with age, upon whose spreading antlers he suspends his roll or parchment wherever he desires to read or study. Shion-Rô has several young disciples, one of whom, by dint of continued application, has succeeded in endowing himself with a loftiness of brow which promises one day to rival that of his master. The latter never fails to attend the weddings of the *bourgeois* families. His portrait, usually delineated with large features upon nettle canvas, hangs on the wall immediately above the domestic altar. The artist often fancifully adds some accessories which give the picture an allegorical sense—such as the one most frequently met with, which represents Shion-Rô holding in his hand a large pearl, and descending from above seated on a crane; signifying that longevity is the most precious of all the heavenly gifts.

The god of daily food is personified as under the features of the patron of fishermen, Yebis, a disgraced brother of the Sun, who reduced himself to the condition of a fisherman and vendor of fish—an article of food which stands in the same relation to the Japanese as bread does to the inhabitants of other countries. No divinity is more popular amongst them than Yebis, who is represented as always at work, and smiling cheerfully, whether he has achieved the exceptional capture of the costly fish Tai, or, if less fortunate, he modestly carries to market a commoner description of goods, either on his own shoulders or in the panniers borne by his beast of burden.

His customary compeer and companion in domestic oratories is Daïkok-Fen, or Daïkokon, the god of wealth, who is as religiously invoked by every grade amongst the lower classes as Yebis. The native artists, however, do not seem to regard him with the same respect. They make him a wretched little figure, wearing a flat cap and large boots, planted on two balls of rice joined by a cluster of pearls. In his right hand is a pickaxe, whilst the left supports upon his shoulder a huge sack wherein to confine his treasures. They facetiously give him as a symbol the unclean rat, emblematic of the dirty paths so often traversed in the pursuit of wealth. The bonzes, remarking the assiduous worship paid to Daïkokon by the merchants, and also the more or less ironical favour accorded him by the poorer classes, painters especially, have devised a legend, according to which this divinity, the patron of subterranean wealth, volunteered to enter the service of Buddha in the capacity of a simple lay-brother; and thus it is that the grotesque image of the patron of wealth is placed in the vestibule of every Buddhist temple to serve as an encouragement and example to his adorers.

Hotei, a god always represented as carrying a sack of hemp, personifies contentment amidst indigence. He is the sage without hearth or home, and possesses no earthly goods; in short, he is the Diogenes of Japan. His only property is a ragged strip of canvas, a wallet, and a fan. When his wallet is empty, he only laughs and lends it to the children in the streets to play with. It serves him in turn as a mattress, pillow, and mosquito-net; and he uses it as a raft to ferry himself over rivers or arms of the sea. Hotei appears to lead rather a vagabond life, for occasionally he is seen careering about the country on a buffalo. He is the friend of all rustics, who show him the shadiest parts among the hills, where he lies down and enjoys soft slumber and the most peaceful dreams. Sometimes a group of children will stealthily approach and tease the happy sleeper, when he will smilingly awake, take the little scamps in his arms, and tell them stories, or talk to them of the heavens, the moon, the stars, and all the magnificence of nature's stores; incomparable delights which none knew better than he how to enjoy.

The god of talents, the noble old man Tossi-Tokon, shows the same kindness to little children. He inspires their games, and pleases himself, amongst other things, in teaching them all kinds of marvellous works in paper. Nothing disturbs the dignity of this grave personage. His emblems are the stole, mantle, cap, and slippers of a doctor, also a cross to which he sometimes suspends a roll of parchment and fan of palm leaves. A young deer accompanies him in all his wanderings.

Bisjamon, the god of glory, adorns himself in a casque and cuirass of gold, and holds in his right hand a lance decorated with streamers; but his only use is to fill a place amongst the seven Japanese blessings. He is never seen at the humble domestic altar; indeed, why should he be popular in a country where glory only awaits those fortunate beings belonging to the privileged caste.

Lastly, perhaps the most remarkable of all the seven household gods, and one that would be most interesting to free from all priestly touches and additions, is a feminine divinity, burdened with a double symbolism, both terrestrial and celestial.

Ben-zaï-tennjo, or simply Benten, is the personification of woman, family affection, harmony, and also of the sea, the fruitful foster-mother of Japan. She wears the sacred stole and an azure mantle, while her head is heightened by a diadem or resplendent image of Foô, the phœnix of the far East.

In the eyes of the women of the nation Benten is the type of maternity, or rather, more simply, the model mother; for she has fifteen sons, all, with one exception, highly educated, well conducted, very wise, and in good professions. The enumeration of the offices these young men fill is very interesting—one is a public functionary, one a writer of public petitions, another a master of foundries; while the others hold the professions of banker, agriculturist, merchant, baker, tailor, breeder of the silkworm, brewer, theologian, physician, breeder of domestic animals, and carrier by land and water. The fifteenth, with whom the legend ends, is a mystery to us, being the only one of the brotherhood not represented by an emblem.

JAPANESE YOUNG WOMEN.

Such are the principal elements of this mythology, the morality of which is perhaps, taking all things into consideration, the best in the world irrespective of Christianity.

Its extraordinary purity and humanity, its prosaic but acute good sense, have, more than any other cause, contributed to guard the Japanese people from the decadence of which they have found themselves in danger from the enormous pressure of Buddhism. To this cause also can be traced the source of the geniality, candour, and simplicity of character which are the distinctive traits of the labouring classes in Japan. That which redounds more to their credit than anything else, is the fact that their worship has only in the slightest degree been tainted with superstition. It hardly merits the name of idolatry. They recognise in the gods of fortune the children of their imagination, and therefore feel no scruple in drawing amusement from them whenever and wherever they like. They are the subject of innumerable caricatures. In one the god of longevity is delineated playing at backgammon with his exalted friend Benten. Four of their colleagues, squatting beside them, appear to be betting in favour of the goddess. The fifth god, Yebis, is holding a large fish in readiness to present to the conqueror. The seven divinities also seek for adventure in the capacity of itinerant actors. The god of glory is burdened with Yebis' fish, which he carries on the point of his lance. Benten, in an inn, displays her talents for needlework, by renewing the wardrobes of the troupe. During the representations she sings and plays the lute; while Daïkokou accompanies her by accurate blows of his stick upon a wooden drum. His emblems, the rats, are dressed to take the rôle of mountebanks. Clothed in a pretty fantastic costume, they climb to the top of Shion-

Decay of Old Beliefs.

Rô's long crook poised by the old tortoise. The god directs the performances, which he explains to the public whilst toying with his fan. In another corner the god of contentment is shampooed by Yebis, and the god of talents dexterously applies the blistering herb *moxas* to his own gouty legs.

It is unnecessary to multiply examples of this kind, all of which demonstrate in the same manner the extent to which the Japanese people trifle with the divinities of their own creation, while they lay aside the recognised creeds Sinsyn and Buddhism, which seem not to possess the least charm for them. They seem now to have put an end to all their ancient forms of idolatry; they no longer believe in the morality of their chiefs, and laugh at that of their priests; whilst their religious caricatures seem to protest by implication against the ancient objects of their worship, and to offer tacit homage to the unknown God.

CHAPTER IX.

Numerous Temples in Japan—Buddhist Monuments—The Daïbondhs—The Bonzes and their Duties—The Matsouris or Annual Festivals—A Moving Encylopædia—Procession of the Seven Beautiful Ladies—Faith of the Japanese in Greatness—History of the Fall of the Mikado—Greatness of the Tycoon—Arrival of Europeans and Re-establishment of the Authority of the Mikado.

RELIGIOUS scepticism has not, however, prevented the Japanese from raising immense numbers of temples, sanctuaries, and monuments throughout the land. According to official computation there are, at least, 150,000 religious monuments existing in the whole empire; of which about 25,000 are consecrated to the Kami faith, and 125,000 to the worship of Buddha.

The temples, more generally known as "Mias," are always placed in the pleasantest and most picturesque parts of the country, upon the best soil, and, whenever possible, close to a large town. They are approached by a spacious walk, bordered by lines of enormous cedar trees, which leads through an immense court, oftentimes containing several temples, and terminates at the principal edifice. In the entrance stands a clock, a basin filled with water for ablutions, and a large coffer in which the offerings of the faithful are deposited. The building itself is extremely simple, although the structure is very ingenious, consisting of beams curiously interlaced. The most celebrated of the

KAMI TEMPLE.

Kami temples is that one under the patronage of Hatchiman, in the town of Kamakoura. It is distinguished from all the others by the glorious trophies it contains.

The Buddhist monuments differ greatly in structure, in consequence of their being dedicated to one of the thousands of divinities, each having its own peculiar attribute. The most remarkable of these to which Europeans are allowed access is that dedicated to Daïbondhs, or the great Buddha. From the double point of view of art and religious sentiment, it may be regarded as the most finished specimen of Japanese genius known to us. The especial characteristic of this temple is its exceeding loneliness, although situated within a short distance of a populous town. Modest in dimensions, it is nevertheless peculiarly formed for a mysterious retreat, and well fitted to dispose the soul for the reception of supernatural revelations. The road leading to it is without any habitation; it first winds amongst high shrubberies, then rises straight into the midst of beds of flowers, and after making a detour in search, as it were, of some distant object, suddenly stops in front of a gigantic bronze divinity, in a squatting position, with the hands clasped, the head bent, and the attitude one of contemplative ecstasy. "The involuntary shock experienced at the first sight of this image," says Humbert, "soon gives place to admiration. There is an irresistible charm in the posture of this Daïbondhs, as also in the harmony of its proportions, the noble simplicity of the drapery, and the calm and purity of the features. All the surroundings harmonise perfectly with the feeling of tranquillity inspired by the sight. A thick hedge, encircled by beautiful groups of trees, forms the only protection to this sacred spot, whose silence and solitude nothing ever disturbs. Hardly observable, so hidden is it by the foliage, stands the modest cell of the officiating priest. The altar, whereon a little incense is always kept burning, is also of bronze, ornamented with two vases of the same metal, and of remarkable workmanship. The steps and space before the altar are covered with large flag-stones set in regular lines. The blue of the sky, the great shadow of the statue, the brilliancy of the flowers, the variegated hues of the groves and thickets, fill this retreat with the richest effects of light and colour." The idol of Daïbondhs, with the pedestal which supports it, is about fifty-five feet high, and in the foundations a peaceful little oratory exists. In essential points this statue exactly corresponds to the description of the great Hindu reformer which has been carefully preserved since his death.

In close proximity to temples of this severe style of architecture stand others so fantastic in form as almost to border on the grotesque. A traveller mentions having seen in one of the gardens "about three hundred divinities, of indescribably quaint construction, erected in rows like the pipes of an organ. The many coloured marbles of which they were made," he adds, "gave them a very gay aspect. There is also the temple to the thirty-three thousand three hundred and thirty-three divinities. Two amongst this multitude are held in great honour. One receives the petitions of young women that they may be blessed with a son rather than a daughter; they bring a cock as an offering; the priests eat the cock, and the god, say they, takes care of the rest. The other, represented by fifty most extraordinary pictures, is the god of toothache. The sufferers from this disorder first present their offerings, then after gravely masticating a small ball of paper until it is reduced to pulp, they spit it out at one of the pictures, and retire, under the conviction that a cure will speedily reward their pious act.

The Japanese who officiate at these numerous places of worship are called *bonzes*. Their life is passed entirely in repeating formularies of prayers, ringing the bells, beating the drums, and in begging food and drink, a part of their daily routine which they especially appreciate. As a rule—to which, of course, there are many creditable exceptions—the priests are an idle set of men, and although they belong to the middle class, between the nobility and *bourgeoisie*, they are held in no estimation. In earlier ages it was far otherwise. During the times of Buddhist revivalism in the seventh and eighth centuries, they did not exist in their religious capacity alone, but by their labour contributed to the prosperity of the country. The arts, especially sculpture and architecture, had no other representatives, but now their lives are almost completely unoccupied; their religious duties are so slight, that at most they need only preside at a few ceremonies, chief amongst which stand the anniversary festivals or matsouris.

As the Japanese Olympus includes a large number of gods and goddesses, the annual fêtes or matsouris abound in the calendar; but the lofty patriotism and noble

RELIGIOUS FESTIVAL.

JAPAN.—p. 111.

simplicity which formerly distinguished them in earlier ages have long been disregarded. Almost every temple has its yearly festival, which has now degenerated into a mere popular fair, with its various amusements of theatrical pomp and religious caricatures. The most magnificent of these fêtes is that annually given at Yedo, the capital of Japan, by the priests of the temple of Sannoô, consecrated to Zinmon, the founder of the Empire. The following account is given by Humbert, an eye-witness of the scene:—

"Tengon, the faithful porter and messenger of the gods, leads the procession. Attired in his finest celestial costume, he half unfolds a pair of large iris-coloured wings. His smiling air, roguish eyes, crimson complexion, and inordinately long nose, tickle the humour of the people, and inevitably secure for the *cortege* a most hearty welcome. The procession need be in no fear of any inconvenience from the spirits of evil, for when they see the image of Tengon at the door of the temples they hastily pass on.

"The municipal police keep wonderful order, preserving discipline among more than a million spectators admirably. In all the streets and places through which the procession passes, platforms are erected for the old men, women, and children. Places are reserved for all those who will pay the tariff demanded; and spaces are kept open for the common labourers; but all are bound to behave quietly, and remain stationary during the entire festival. Itinerant vendors of fruit, cake, tea, and saki only are allowed, in the prosecution of their calling, to enter the space roped off for the passage of the procession.

"The procession of Sannoô is a kind of moving national encyclopædia, where all sorts of historical memorials, mythological symbols, traditions, and popular customs are promiscuously crowded together. The scenic arrangements are as complete as possible. When art attains this democratic breadth, criticism can only bow to it. We will therefore pass on to the more picturesque details of the ceremony. Here is the patron of sacred dances. The image, attired in an old theatrical dress, is raised upon a high drum, supported by *figurantes* clad in gay costumes, and hats crowned with flowers. Next comes the procession of the white elephant. The pace of the pasteboard animal is regulated by that of his bearers, whose feet, though skilfully concealed, may still be seen moving under the colossal legs of the huge beast. He is preceded by a band of music; the sound of flutes and trumpets being accompanied by the noise of the great drum, cymbals, gongs, and tambourines. The men of this group wear beards, a pointed hat surmounted by an aigrette, boots, a long robe confined by a girdle, and some of them carry Chinese banners covered with dragons. Behind them a gigantic lobster, carried by a priest of the Kami worship, and surrounded by a troop of negroes, makes its way; a buffalo cart follows, drawn by a hundred labourers. The king of domestic animals is placed in the vehicle beneath the shade of a fir and a blossoming peach tree; he is accompanied by the demi-god who introduced him into Japan. Upon six other carts the instruments and products of the rice plantations are picturesquely arranged. Antique banners, some of which are ornamented with sketches of horses, precede a cavalcade of superior officers clad in the prevailing fashion of the court. Suddenly two terrible monsters appear. They have the face of a tiger, with the horns of a bull. Their enormous tails tower above the helmets of the armed men who surround them. They may perhaps be intended to recall to remembrance the tigers of the country of Corea, which caused so much annoyance to the soldiers of the heroic mother of Hatchinan. With this group is connected the exhibition of antique arms from the arsenal of Sannoô, lances and halberts, swords, long bows, arrows, banners and fans of war.

" Little by little, however, this exhibition loses its warlike character, and priests and bonzes file past under banners covered with hieroglyphic signs, and bearing reliquaries, sacred vases, and other appendages of their temples. Another troupe of bonzes balance paper lanterns on the end of long poles, whose transparency and varied colours are very effective.

" But the greatest attraction of the whole festival is the appearance in the procession of seven of the most beautiful ladies from the quarter of Sin-Yosiwara. Attired in robes of state, they advance majestically one after the other, each accompanied by her maid and a servant who carries a large high silk umbrella to protect her beauty from the fiery rays of the sun. Her hair is dressed to an enormous height in two or three stages, which require to be supported by large combs interlaced with crêpe, the entire edifice being crowned by a halo of tortoise-shell. The great brilliancy of her complexion is produced by the use of most scientifically prepared cosmetics. She wears five or six long robes, the collars of which are turned down on her shoulders. An ample cloak conceals them, which is prevented from sweeping on the ground by means of a broad sash of silk or velvet looping it up. High-heeled shoes complete the costume, and give additional height to the stature of the fair wearers. They are all seven well known to the people, and as their names are embroidered upon their rich dresses are easily recognisable.

"One is the lady of the Tan-of-War; it is spread out upon her velvet sash, upon which she has also added, as ornaments, four cocks of varied plumage; two are white, embroidered conspicuously upon the large sleeves of her mantle, and the silken feathers of their tails wave gracefully in the air as she moves. The second is the lady of the Golden Fish; one is worked upon each side of her dress, upon a ground of waves and foam in silver thread; the other embellishments represent little children playing with all kinds of coloured ribbons scattered everywhere over the mantle. Similarly appropriate attires are worn by the remaining ladies, whose emblems are death's heads, candelabra, cranes, and chrysanthemums. But volumes might be written if we attempted to describe fully the obsequious homage paid to this class of women by the priests and people of Yedo."

But the public appearance of courtesans is not restricted to the festival of Sannoô. Each year a fair is held in Sin-Yosiwara, under the patronage of the bonzes, in which the five thousand inhabitants of that immoral quarter have the privilege of taking part in a procession; the portraits of the queens of the fête being handed over to the priests, who suspend them on the walls of their sanctuaries. But one strange custom, that we cannot but admire for its appositeness, is the admittance into the procession of the statue of a monkey with a red face wearing a mitre, and carrying a holy water brush. As it is solemnly paraded about the streets, it cannot but open the minds of the spectators to the buffoonery of the religious parade they have just been assisting at.

All belief has, however, not entirely disappeared from the mind of the Japanese, as might naturally be supposed after witnessing one of their religious festivals, for they still have the most deeply rooted faith in, and respect for, the hierarchy, as well as for authority and human greatness. Their bigoted devotion to the Mikado is a striking proof of this. The tradition of the gods, demi-gods, the heroes and hereditary sovereigns who have reigned over Japan in a line of uninterrupted succession for 2500 years, is still carried on in the person of the Mikado, the little son of the Sun. He has absolute power over the people, although at one period this power was more fictitious than real, it having been absorbed in that of another sovereign, the Tycoon, by the force of circumstances, of which the following is an abridged account:—About two hundred and eighty years ago, a general, known in history by the name of Tycosama, was ordered by the Mikado to reduce to submission some rebellious vassals. Tycosama, instead of executing his sovereign's behests, profited by the power with which he was invested to put himself at the head of the Government. He shut up the Mikado in his seraglio, surrounded him with dignitaries to whom he gave pompous titles and small salaries, and succeeded in reducing the office of Mikado to the mere appearance of authority. The son of Tycosama was too young to gather with impunity the fruits of this audacious usurpation; he soon perished, assassinated by his tutor Iyeyas. The latter, leaving the Mikado in possession of his empty titles, went to establish himself at Yedo, which he made the second capital of the empire, and founded that dynasty of military chiefs who, under the name of Shio-goon, or Tycoon, have ever since reigned in Japan. The feudal organisation of the country proved, however, an obstacle to the immediate realisation of his plans, and a great number of princes refused to recognise his authority; he subdued some of the malcontents, and forced others to adhere to the laws made by Gongensama, a species of political compact which became the basis of the new constitution.

The new sovereign, supported by the princes whom he had created, seated himself upon the throne of Yedo; whilst the Mikado, still retaining his pretensions to absolute power, lived upon a pension granted him by the Tycoon. After this revolution, peace reigned again in Japan for some years.

The arrival of the Europeans, and the rivalries which resulted therefrom between the Tycoon and the princes of the empire, changed anew the face of things, and furnished an opportunity to the legitimate emperor to reassume his full authority, abase the wealth and power of the Government at Yedo, regain influence, and, in fact, cease playing the part of a phantom king. Of the two factions dividing the country at this epoch, the strongest and most popular was that one hostile to the reforms inaugurated by the Tycoon. The Mikado put himself at the head of the reactionary party to personify in himself the patriotic principle they were defending Secret agents of his throughout the country endeavoured to persuade the nobles that the public voice was opposed to the court of Yedo, and that the interests of the legitimate emperor were identical with their own. Pamphlets were circulated at the same time, advocating that matters should be pushed to the verge of war against the Tycoon. The princes, who for a long time had been regarding with jealousy or defiance the continually advancing power of the Tycoon, listened favourably to the words of the Mikado's agents. Several amongst them formed themselves into a league, and in the month of May, 1862, lodged a formal complaint against the Tycoon. The Mikado, who had been in daily expectation of this event, instantly despatched one of his officers with a letter to the court of Yedo, demanding the immediate presence of the Tycoon at Kioto, the residence of the Mikado, to answer to the charge brought against him. The Tycoon at first attempted to evade this command, but, seeing that the Mikado's party was each day gaining ground, found himself obliged to make some important concessions. But this was not sufficient. Old memories had been aroused; the great princes of the southern provinces conspired openly, bought guns, cannon, and steamers, and one day astonished Europe learned that the powerful Tycoon was in full flight, and that the Mikado had set up again the ancient banner of Zinmon, and had assumed direct executive power. Thus was the unity of Japan achieved by the re-establishment of the theocratic and legitimate emperor, under whose sway it now remains.

JAPANESE COOPER.

JAPANESE SAILOR, SOLDIER, AND COURTIER.
Japan.—p. 122.

CHAPTER X.

The Grades of Japanese Society—Changed Attitude of the Mikado—Disregard of Human Life—Beauties of Rural Scenery—Literature of the Lower Orders—Hero-Worship—Story of "The Fatal Star"—"The Old Woman and the Sparrows"—"The Physician in Spite of Himself"—Contentment with our Lot, or "The Stone-Cutter."

ALTHOUGH the different classes of Japanese society are not so rigorously separated one from the other as are the castes of India, they yet do not mix nearly as much as their European counterparts. There are three classes in Japan—the nobility, in which is included the royal house of the Mikado; the high dignitaries of the court; the Daimios, or peers of Japan; the Yakonins, or functionaries and soldiers of the houses of the princes; and the Lonins, or military retainers without employment. All the nobility, from the Mikado down to the Lonin, carry two swords. Next comes the literary class, in which the priests and physicians are included, who also have the right to wear two sabres. The third class includes agriculturists, farmers, artisans, merchants, fishermen, and sailors. Those belonging to neither class, and therefore excluded from society, are the mendicants, or Kotsedjikis, the Fettas, and the

Christians; these generally live outside the towns, and may only marry amongst themselves. The Kotsedjikis are divided into four classes, each of which recognises a chief; the Fettas are those people whose profession is to cure hides, and to shed the blood of animals; the Christians are the descendants of the ancient Christians, and are confined to certain districts, somewhat as the Jews were in towns of the middle ages.

But this division of Japanese society seems to be disappearing, in consequence of the transformation which the whole economy of the empire is undergoing. For several years, indeed, the Japanese Government has been animated with the sincere desire of equalising the different ranks. All men of power seem to work towards one object, namely, to denationalise Japan as soon as possible, and remodel it after the manner of European States. The army has already almost completely abandoned the helmet, the coat of mail, and the heavy sabres—in fact, all the military attire of the feudal times.

The system of administration has undergone equally sudden changes. The Daimiots, or possessions of the great feudal princes, have been transformed into imperial domains, the governors of which are nominated by the central power; and a great part of the country has been divided into prefectures of equal dimensions.

The Mikado himself, who formerly was invisible even to his own subjects, is now frequently seen either driving or on horseback, and he has issued a decree requesting the public to abstain henceforth from the manifestations of

ANCIENT JAPANESE WARRIORS.

JAPAN.—p. 125.

respect hitherto accorded him. It seems as if this sovereign, so lately surrounded by every form of reverence and veneration, has now no other aim than to divest himself of his divine attributes. Even the national court costumes, although not abolished, are frequently replaced by European vestments of various kinds, according to the fancy of the wearer. But as the tailors and milliners are utterly incapable of originating costumes in any way resembling ours in make, the most grotesque attires are frequently to be seen.

One reform, which is equally approved of by both foreigners and natives, is that which authorises the nobles, and even invites them, not to carry arms; a great advantage for the better preservation of the public peace. For the future also the nobles are forbidden to kill persons of inferior rank, as hitherto they were able to do with impunity, unless upon serious provocation; and the penal code has been remodelled upon a basis in every way much fairer for the common people. Notwithstanding this growth of a more humane sentiment, there still exists among the upper classes of the Japanese an extreme disregard of the value or importance of human life. Of this we mention one example, which occurred the day the Tycoon left Yedo. A coolie had so far forgotten the abasement of his position in life as to cross the road before an officer of the Imperial Guard. The officer, enraged at such a barefaced specimen of impudence and disrespect, ordered the coolie's head to be cut off on the spot. His sergeant, however, refused to carry out the barbarous order of the superior officer, upon which the officer immediately cut down his own man with a sword-cut across the head, and then, rioting in slaughter, killed the coolie also. Just then his own superior officer appeared upon the scene, and upon learning what had occurred, determined to punish an officer who had so far allowed his temper to get the better of his discretion. He therefore ordered his spearmen to run the delinquent through. With Japanese placidity this order was immediately complied with, and the officer's body was seen two days afterwards lying on the road-side by an *attaché* of the Dutch Legation who was coming from Yedo.

TYPE OF LOWER CLASSES.

As already stated, the Daimios or feudal nobles are the real governors of Japan. Public opinion, either as the origin of power or as a check upon the governing classes, can hardly be said to exist. A Japanese worships his superior with a depth of reverence utterly shocking to the western mind. To fight his way up through the different grades of the social scale is for him not only an impossibility, but the bare idea of entertaining so wild a project has never entered into his mind. Hence he is tortured with no feverish longings after a higher lot than the one in which he happens to have been born. The Japanese lower orders live in a state of happy contentment, amusing themselves in their own way, making the best of everything, and troubling themselves as little about the concerns of their superiors at home as about the interests of the mighty world that lies beyond the limits of their own island.

Every traveller praises the tranquillity and happiness of their rural life. They have cultivated the gifts of nature, so plentifully bestowed upon their soil, until their country has become a beautiful and well-ordered garden. Take the following description of a rural scene by Sir Rutherford Alcock, who certainly cannot be accused of exaggerating either the moral or physical attractions of Japan :—

"We now gain a shady lane, through which the sun's rays pierce only at intervals. On the banks above are to be found the pine, the evergreen oak (a noble tree, with leaves of a rich dark colour something like the laurel), the light bamboo, and all except the bamboo growing thirty or forty feet high, and of great value as timber. The beautiful maple, too, with its starlike leaves and ever graceful foliage, cannot be passed without a glance of admiration ; and Japan can boast of numerous varieties. At this season its leaves are of the brightest scarlet hue, but no pen can convey an adequate idea of the richness and variety of the autumnal tints. The brightest crimson and scarlet alternate with a golden yellow, and the deeper colours, brown and green, of the evergreens. The sere and yellow leaf has a beauty of its own here, which leaves little room for regret that the glowing hues of summer are wanting. The tall, well-kept hedges are thickly covered, cut and trimmed in the manner of Dutch gardening (a fashion which there is little doubt, I think, was introduced into Europe from Japan), and how admirably they are planted and trimmed! Nowhere out of England can such hedges be seen, and not in the British Isles can be found such a variety. Here is a low hedge, or border rather, made of the tea plant, two or three bushes deep, and growing about three feet high—not unlike the ordinary flowering camellia, of which it is a species. Now we have come to an enclosure fenced in with nectarines, and there is a hedge of pomegranate. Inside, a tall orange tree is laden with its golden fruit, and, stranger still, a cherry tree in full bloom this 25th day of November! O happy land and pleasant country!—that is, when no Daimios or officials intrude their presence. But I said I would not think of politics—let us return to the hedge-rows and their inexhaustible variety.

"Now it is a fine, tall, close-twisted fence of *cryptomeria*, while over that porch the *westeria* spreads with insatiable desire its far-reaching arms, to be covered in spring with glorious clusters of purple flowers. Little hamlets of farmers' homesteads are dotted about in a sort of picturesque confusion—generally nestled in the valleys and under the hill-sides amidst a clump of trees, where the *cryptomeria*, the bamboo, and the palm all tend to give an eastern character to dwellings otherwise claiming some resemblance to Swiss châlets. Their temples, gateways, and larger houses are eminently Chinese, only in better style, and infinitely better kept. The country can never look wintry here unless covered with snow, for its trees can never be wholly stripped of foliage, there is such a preponderance of evergreens." Such is the terrestrial paradise in which the fortunate Japanese pass a tranquil and easy existence.

JAPANESE HAMLET.

The lower classes have a very characteristic literature of their own, and a most amusing one it is. First of all, it is, as we have already said, full of the most ludicrous hero-worship. Here are a few specimens.

"Asahina-Sabro urges his steed in full career against a troop of enemies, lifting with his right hand and spinning into the air a warrior clad in both helmet and cuirass, while with his left hand he fells to the ground at one and the same blow two other warriors not less redoubtable." Or again: "Nitan-Nosiro, the mighty hunter, leaps astride upon the back of the gigantic wild boar, which has flung to the ground and mangled all the companions of the hero, and, clinging with his knees to the flanks of the furious monster, plunges, entirely at his ease, his cutlass into its neck." Or here is another to cap the classical story of the bow of Ulysses: "When the brave and heroic Tama-tomo made the conquest of the island of Fatsisio, wishing to avoid the spilling of blood, and anxious at the same time to convince the inhabitants that all resistance on their part would be futile, he called to him the two most powerful and vigorous men of the place, and sitting calmly on a boulder of stone, he presented to each of them in turn his bow, holding it by the wood and inviting them to bend the string. Each put forth all his force, but was utterly unable to bend the terrible weapon. Then they both united their efforts, but with the same result. The bow was beyond their powers. Finally, Tama-tomo arose, took hold of the string gently between his forefinger and thumb, soon to launch an arrow, which was lost in the clouds."

Such are some of the stories of the heroes of the olden time. The accounts of more modern historic anecdotes present a character totally different from the heroic tales and marvellous legends; they are marked by that air of cold reason which distinguishes the philosophical school of Confucius. In the writings of that sage it is stated, "If you turn not your heart from truth and right, the gods will take care of you, even if you do not invoke them. To be virtuous is to worship." A historic proof of the wisdom of this sage remark is to be found in the following story :—

"THE FATAL STAR."

In the reign of one of the ancient Mikados men beheld of a sudden in the heavens an unknown star. A celebrated Japanese astronomer, having attentively observed it, declared that it presaged a great calamity which must shortly fall upon one of the commanders-in-chief of the empire. Now at that time Naka-hira was commander-in-chief of the left, and Sana-gori of the right. Hearing the prediction of the astrologer, Sana-gori and his family rushed frantically through all the temples of Buddha that were to be found in the neighbourhood, praying and carrying costly presents, while Naka-hira and his family consulted neither priest nor oracle, but pursued the even tenor of their life. A priest, acting as spokesman of his order, repaired to the residence of Naka-hira, and told him how shocked and surprised was the religious world of Japan at his taking no part in the praying competition which was to avert destruction either from him or his colleague. "Sana-gori," said the priest, "visits all the holy places and pours forth his soul in prayer, with the hope of escaping the calamity which the unknown star presages, while you pass your time apparently in utter contempt of the prediction. My friend, have you lost belief in the gods?" Naka-kira, who had attentively listened to the priest, replied, "I have heard your remonstrance; now hear my justification. Since it was announced that this fatal star must bring misfortune upon one of the commanders-in-chief, I have, of course, seen that the predicted calamity must fall either upon

Sana-gori or myself. Now, on thinking the matter over, I see very plainly that I am well stricken in years, and that my military talents are failing me. Sana-gori, on the other hand, is in the very flower of his age, and at the height of his profession. Suppose, then, I were to offer vows and prayers, which might be heard so as to turn from my head the calamity which threatens it, this could only be done at the peril of Sana-gori, and therefore to the detriment of the empire. It is for this reason that I abstain from all intercessions on my own behalf, hoping thereby that the precious life of my colleague may be spared." On hearing these words, the priest could not restrain his emotion, and exclaimed, " Noble Naka-hira, such a generous self-sacrifice is the best act of worship that you could perform; and by all that is sacred, if there be gods and a Buddha, it is neither on you nor your family that this calamity will fall!"

There are large numbers of popular legends of the same class, belonging to what we might term "fairy lore," some of them of a highly imaginative and poetical character. Here is one which combines the quaint the comic, and the imaginative:—

"The Old Woman and the Sparrow."

Once on a time there lived together an old couple who had no children. One fine morning the husband brought home a sparrow in a cage; but the bird kept up such a perpetual chattering and squeaking that the old woman was nearly driven out of her wits, and she determined to get rid of the annoyance upon the first plausible pretext. One day, when she had gone out of the house, the sparrow, which was allowed occasionally to hop out of the cage, pounced upon a new dress which she had been sewing, and amused itself for a long time in undoing with its beak the stitches which the careful housewife had been all the morning engaged in putting in. So enraged was she upon returning, that she seized hold of the bird, clipped off its tongue, and flung it out of the window. Presently the husband came in, and, missing the accustomed twitter, inquired for the sparrow. His wife immediately confessed what she had done, and the husband began to bewail the loss of the bird, which, he said, he loved as if it had been his own child. So he went out, and began to search for the bird. As he was wandering over the hills in the quest, he beheld a charming girl approaching him, who thanked him for all the kindness he had shown her when in his house, and asked of him as a slight return to choose a present. "Here," said she, "are two baskets; one is heavy, the other light. Take whichever you prefer." "For a poor weak old man like me," he replied, "it is better to take the light one." So she handed him the basket which he had chosen, and, according to her directions, he did not open it till he had got home. It was found to be full of the most beautiful clothes. His wife, on seeing such wonderful luck, resolved that she, in her turn, would have a trial, so she started off at once to the hills in search of the sparrow. The same apparition of a beautiful girl also appeared to her, but, instead of thanking her for her kindness, violently upbraided her for her cruelty. At the same time, however, she presented her two baskets, and told her to make a choice. The old woman, whose thoughts were more avaricious than her husband's, instantly laid hold of the heavy basket and hurried home. "My husband will be astonished when he finds how much more I have brought with me than he did," she thought to herself. Arrived at her house, panting and blowing, she opened the basket, when, to her utter horror and disgust, out jumped two goblins! Japanese artists are very fond of representing the story at this crisis. You will see the picture of the old woman on her back, prostrated with alarm, her heels in the air, while the goblins rising out of the cage are dimly represented with faces full of fierce and ghoulish cruelty.

Another favourite legend of a somewhat similar nature is the following story of

"THE MAGICIAN IN SPITE OF HIMSELF."

There was once another old couple without children who had a favourite dog. Now a good spirit had taken up his abode in the body of this faithful animal. One day the dog conducted the old man into the wood, and showed him a place where a treasure was hidden. The wife began to talk about the occurrence, and a wicked neighbour was stirred with envy. He borrowed the dog from his master, and made the poor animal lead the way to a place in the wood, but on digging it up he found nothing but stones. Transported with fury, he killed the poor brute, and buried him on the spot. When the old man learned what had passed, he only asked in his sorrow where the body of his dumb companion rested. Being informed of this by the wicked neighbour, he went, and, cutting down the tree at the foot of which the dog was buried, he fashioned from its branches a little chapel in memory of the faithful animal, while from the trunk he formed a mortar to beat his rice. Hardly had he begun to use that utensil, when he found that it also gave forth gold. The old woman told this too, as a great secret, to a confidential crone, and the very next day, of course, the wicked neighbour came to borrow the mortar. With brotherly kindness, not to be found out of Japan, he lends the mortar, but the borrower can get no gold out of it, and in another fit of fury burns it. The old man begged for the ashes at any rate, and, having got them, he carried them carefully home. The same evening he beheld his dog appear to him in a dream, who told him the next day to repair to the border of the highway, and when he should see the train of a Daimio passing, not to kneel, but if summoned to do so to tell that he is a magician, having the power to cause trees that are withered or bare of leaves to burst into golden bloom. The next day he took his stand as directed, holding in his hands in a vase the ashes of the mortar, and soon saw the train of a Daimio approaching, and heard the terrible word, *Shitaniro!* "kneel down!" echoing along the road. Yet he had the courage to stand firm on his legs. The heralds of the prince renewed their challenge with their hands laid on the hilts of their sabres, but, learning from the reply of the old man that they had met a magician, they ran back to their master to see what they were to do. The prince replied that the stranger was to show proof of his pretended magic, upon which the old man flung a handful of ashes against a tree which spread its branches over the way. Instantly the tree was covered with glittering flowers. The prince gave orders that the man should be conducted to his palace, where he treated him sumptuously, and sent him away laden with costly presents. The noise of this wonder having spread through the country, the wicked neighbour again presents himself, and asks for the loan of some ashes, which, in keeping with his character, the good old man immediately gave him. He, too, armed with the magical ashes, presented himself at the road-side, faced the Daimio's swash-bucklers, and was asked for proof of his miraculous powers. Seizing a handful of ashes he flung them into the air, but, instead of covering the tree with golden flowers, the ashes were blown by the wind right into the face of the Daimio, who, enraged at such a terrible affront, drew his sword and cut the fellow down, while his attendants completed the job by hacking his head off. And so at last justice was done, and the wicked wretch got his deserts in a summary manner entirely characteristic of the country and people.

The great lesson that we should be contented with our lot appears in many forms in different lands, but there is surely no more romantic form that it has assumed than the following instructive tale:—

"THE STONE-CUTTER."

There was once in Japan a poor stone-cutter, who worked hard, made little, and was discontented with his lot. So bitterly did his hardships weigh upon him, that one day, in a moment of despair, he flung down his hammer and exclaimed, "Why was I not born to lie on soft mats, and to be clothed in robes of silk?" An angel heard him, and quickly answered, "Let it be to thee according to thy wishes." And, behold! he was forthwith rich, and reclined on a soft mat, and was clothed in a robe of silk. Now it so happened that the Emperor passed his way. He was preceded by couriers on horse and foot, followed by a brilliant escort of cavaliers, and surrounded by attendant courtiers, who held over his head a magnificent umbrella glittering with gold. "What is the good of my being rich," murmured the *quondam* stone-cutter, "so long as I have not the right of travelling with an escort, and of having my head protected by a golden umbrella? Why was not *I* Emperor?" "Thou shalt be so," said the angel. And immediately he was Emperor; he had an escort of cavaliers before and behind him, and courtiers who held above his head a magnificent umbrella glittering with gems and gold. The sun, however, with his burning rays, was parching the fields, and the dusty road, re-echoing the clank of his retinue, flung the dust into his eyes. "A fine thing to be Emperor, indeed," he exclaimed, "when the heat of the day overwhelms you, and the sun makes you his poor slave. Talk to me of being the sun, and then I would indeed be somebody!" "Behold! are you content?" said the angel. And lo! he had become the sun, and darted his rays up and down, right and left, and all around him. And he parched every green herb, and the faces of all princes who dwell on the earth. But a cloud interposed itself between the earth and him, catching the rays of the sun, and keeping them from striking the surface of the ground. "Look here," exclaimed the sun—" here is a cloud actually able to resist my power; better that I should be a cloud." "Let there be no hindrance," said the angel. And the transformation instantly took place; the new cloud placed itself so as to intercept the rays of the sun, and did its work so effectually that it saw the earth becoming green again under its shadow. Soon there fell from it great drops of rain upon the plains, and showers and waterspouts, so that the torrents foamed and the rivers overflowed their channels and devastated the lands. Nothing could resist the fierceness of the flood; a rock alone withstood it serene and immoveable. In vain did the boiling waters assail it with fury; the rock moved not; the foaming billows expired at its foot. "A rock then gives me law," said the cloud; "I choose to be in its place." "By all means," said the angel. And at once he was transformed into a rock, alike indifferent to the burning heat of the sun, to the torrents of rain, and to the shock of the tumultuous waves. It was not long till he beheld at his feet a man of poor appearance scantily clad, but armed with a pick and a hammer, who, with the help of his tools, knocked pieces off the rock, which he fashioned into shapely stones. "What!" cried the rock,

A Stone-Cutter again! 141

"shall a man have the power of ripping open my body, and making me into blocks of stone? Shall I be weaker than he? If so, let me become that man forthwith." "Thy will be done," said the angel, and he became, as in the time gone by, a poor stone-cutter, a simple workman in the quarries. His trade was rude, he worked hard and gained little, but—he was content with his lot!

SCULPTOR OR STATUARY.

CHAPTER XI.

Description of Yedo—The Yakonins—Lively Aspect of the Streets—Absence of Maritime Commerce from the Port—The Niphon Bass—Glimpses of City Life—The Billingsgate of Japan—Whale and Shark Merchants—City and Suburbs of Yedo—The Lonius : their influence on the National Character—The Great Road of Japan—Primitive Mode of Crossing Streams—Peculiarities of the Japanese Bath—Opposite Ideas regarding Modesty — A People's Parliament — Questionable Benefits of Hot Bathing.

YEDO, the capital of Japan, which has been thrown open to foreigners only during the last few years, is situated to the north of the gulf which bears its name, upon the east coast of the large island of Niphon. It extends over an undulating plain, to the south of which runs, parallel to the sea, a low ridge of hills, and to the north another range extends towards the west. Nearly in the centre of this plain rises a rounded eminence, on which stands a large castle, the old residence of the Tycoons, but occupied since 1868 by the Mikado. Clustered around this building is the town, which covers an area of twenty-eight miles, and is therefore, with regard to extent, the second largest city in the world. The river Ogava, or great stream, of imposing breadth towards its mouth, but elsewhere unimportant,

STREET IN YEDO.

flows through the city from north to south, and divides it into two unequal parts; the smallest to the east of the river bears the name of Hondjo, the other on the western bank is the town of Yedo proper. Only a very short time ago it was extremely dangerous to walk about Yedo, or through any of the Japanese territory beyond a certain limit called the treaty frontiers, which were traced round the five open ports of Yokohama, Hiogo, Nagasaki, Niegati, and Hakodadi. The chiefs of legation and consuls alone were, by virtue of the treaties, authorised to travel farther into the interior.

The class of men who rendered travelling in Japan so unsafe were not the peasantry, who are a gentle, amiable, kindly people, but the Daimios, or territorial princes, and the fierce Samurais, the nobles of the military class, who inspired even greater dread, for to encounter one was to run the risk of immediate death. The influence of European civilisation has, however, greatly modified this state of things; the Samurais have laid aside their weapons, and, in consequence, the dangers formerly attending locomotion have nearly entirely disappeared. It is still, however, wiser to bear in mind the proverb that " discretion is the better part of valour," and before venturing abroad in the streets of Yedo to be provided with an escort. This is usually composed of native guides, exceedingly clever horsemen, and called Yakonins, or policemen; their uniform is composed of a loose jacket, which is sometimes ornamented with emblematical figures; the pantaloons, where not covered by the flowing skirts of the jacket, are loose and wide, so that the general appearance is not unlike that of a female on horseback, riding after the primitive fashion. The absurdity of the figure to our ideas is increased by the appearance of the two swords which seem stuck through the body, and by the flat round hat, japanned and gilt,

MOUNTED YAKONIN.

which is poised on the head after the manner of a dessert plate. The Yakonins are skilful riders, but their horses are indifferent specimens of the equine race as far as size is concerned, being usually small and insignificant looking. Their

The Running Betto.

trappings, however, are handsome and even magnificent. The escort is completed by bettos, or running grooms, who, in order to give freer action to the limbs in their frequently

YAKONIN ON FOOT.

long and rapid journeys, divest themselves of all clothing except a straight scarf girded round the loins. This state of nakedness is, however, not so offensive as might be imagined, for they tattoo their whole bodies either with allegorical subjects or in shapes representing different articles of clothing. One of these bettos attached to the escort of a traveller had tattooed upon his figure the shape of a blue jacket with white buttons and red seams, and breeches—naturally of a very accurate fit—in black and white squares.

Yedo exhibits an air of gaiety and prosperity, which gives it a very cheerful aspect. If we picture to ourselves temples scattered everywhere; small houses, each a facsimile of the other—some isolated, others surrounded with one-storied outhouses; streets, appearing wider than they really are from the low elevation of the buildings, crowded with men and women of the lower classes (the ladies of quality show themselves very little), children, blind men in wonderful numbers, bonzes, files of palanquins filled with Japanese of both sexes, the exact image of those we see painted upon vases, fans, and leaves of rice paper, we can form some idea of the great capital of Niphon. This idea can naturally be but an imperfect one, as it is impossible to imagine the continual move and stir of the lively people of Yedo. The streets are always crowded with people smiling graciously, bowing profoundly one to the other, or prostrating themselves before some grand personage, but with such grace and dignity, that what might otherwise appear as an act of humiliation only seems one of common politeness and deference, though of course, to our notions, somewhat exaggerated.

Viewed from the side touching the sea, Yedo resembles an immense park to which access is forbidden. The richly-wooded hills are studded with cottages, and old temples with enormous roofs, beneath which lie long streets of wooden houses. The port of Yedo in no way corresponds to our ideas of what so large a town would be likely to possess for the convenience of its maritime trade; quays, docks, and wharves are nowhere to be seen, but in their stead stand walls, hoardings, and palisades. The absence of any maritime commerce explains this, for a few junks monopolise the whole of the coasting trade. Six polygonal forts, built upon piles within a few cables' length of the shore, debar entrance into the bay. To the south-west of these forts is the anchorage for European ships. Three or four large Japanese men-of-war and half-a-dozen junks

JAPANESE SALUTATION.

are also generally to be found there, too great draught of water preventing their entering what is commonly known as the junk harbour at the entrance of the river Ogava.

Hondjo, as we have already said, is situated to the east of the river. Five great canals, two running from north to south, and three from east to west, and crossing each other at right angles, divide Hondjo into eight parts, all of which are almost entirely covered with temples, the palaces of the Daimios, and the Government dockyards. But little animation prevails in this quarter. Four wooden bridges of solid yet simple construction unite Hondjo to Yedo, the longest of which is about 350 yards in length. Yedo is subdivided into three principal parts—Midsi, which is the town proper; Siro, or the imperial residence; and Soto-Siro, the district surrounding Siro. Midsi is a mixture of frequented and deserted streets—of gardens, rice plantations, parks, and temples—includes, in fact, all the town that is not either Siro or Soto-Siro, and of course is by far the largest quarter.

Siro stands in the centre, and being surrounded with high strong walls it forms a kind of large citadel. It is cut off from the rest of the town by means of two wide moats, over which eighteen bridges have been thrown at nearly equal distances, forming broad gravelled walks.

Around the citadel lies Soto-Siro, which contains the commercial buildings and shops, and is perhaps what we should call the *city* of Yedo. The streets are built with great regularity. Two navigable canals surround this quarter, spanned by fifteen bridges, one of which, the Niphon-Bass, or "Bridge of Japan," is made the geometrical centre of Japan, from which all the geographical distances in the empire are measured. The citizens' houses, as well as the Daimios' palaces, have an individual type of architecture. They are simply wooden buildings, with one story above the ground-floor, whilst to many of them a gallery is added, overlooking the street; the roofs are low, with slate-coloured tiles ornamented by mouldings in plaster at the extremities of the ridges. But though the houses are very uniform in their external appearance, the variety and originality of their picturesque interiors have an endless interest for the observer.

JAPANESE BUILDER.

Here, at the entrance of the street, is a barber's shop, where two or three of the townspeople in the simplest apparel have come to make their usual morning toilette. Seated upon a form, they gravely hold in their left hands a japanned plate, which receives the croppings of the razor or scissors. Artistic hairdressers, divested of all clothing that would in the least embarrass their movements, study carefully their patient customers from different points of view, using now the hand, now the instrument upon their heads, after the fashion that the sculptors of old modelled their cariatides. It is needless to say the illusion ceases when, taking between their teeth a silken cord, the operators twist it round and tie it in a bow at the ends of the curled locks of the gallant sons of Niphon.

A few steps further on is the bootmaker's shop. It bristles with wooden pegs, from which are suspended innumerable pairs of straw sandals. The merchant squats in one corner in the attitude of a Buddhist idol. Purchasers of both sexes stop in front of the stall, examine or try on the goods, exchange a few friendly words with the owner, and without disturbing him lay the price agreed upon literally at his feet.

The seed shops present also a very attractive appearance. The quantity and immense variety of the seeds exposed for sale, their diversity of form and colour, added to the art with which they are arranged upon the stalls, attract the attention at the first glimpse. Most effective too are the pretty little packets of different grains enclosed in paper, on which, in addition to the name, are coloured drawings of the plants themselves, frequently taken from some choice little album of Japanese flora. They are, however, generally the handiwork of one of the young workmen attached to the house, who may be seen lying at full length

JAPANESE SHOE SHOP.

JAPAN.—p. 153.

The Whale and Shark Merchants. 155

in his studio upon mats strewn with flowers and sheets of paper. Although in so singular an attitude, he skilfully contrives that not one stroke of his pencil should be ineffective.

The crowd increases towards the centre of the city, and the shops give way to the popular restaurants, confectioners of rice and millet, and retailers of hot tea and saki. A large fish-market adjoins.

The canal is covered with fishing barks. Fish of every kind are unloaded at the wharves, whilst the market-place is besieged with purveyors eager to lay in a cheap supply of provisions at the sales by auction. From the midst of the excited crowd vigorous arms can be seen emptying baskets full of fish into the hampers or japanned chests carried by coolies. From time to time the crowd opens to give passage to a couple of men carrying a porpoise, a dolphin, or a shark, suspended by a cord to a long strong bamboo, which they carry on their shoulders. The Japanese boil the flesh of these animals and preserve it in the fat of whales.

But one of the most remarkable sights of low life are the wholesale and retail whale and shark merchants near the Niphon-Bass. The stature, carriage, and gestures of these men, their extraordinarily fantastic attire, the size of the instrument that they plunge into the sides of the monsters of the sea, all betoken that to satisfy the consumption of this large city even such food as we should view with disgust must be utilised.

The town of Yedo is seen in its most picturesque aspect

from the high-arching bridge of Niphon-Bass. The banks of the canal are bordered with warehouses filled with silk, cotton, rice, and saki. Hundreds of boats, loaded with wood, coal, bamboo canes, straw mattings, covered hampers, chests, and small casks, may be seen, while enormous fish dart to and fro in every direction. The streets seem to be exclusively abandoned to the use of foot-passengers. Sometimes, however, amongst the crowd of pedestrians, a team of heavily-laden horses is seen making its way, or a two-wheeled cart containing five or six rows of bales, skilfully piled up and drawn by coolies. Otherwise no other sound of wheels can be heard. The echo of the wooden clogs upon the pavement, the bells of the horses, the monotonous cries of the coolies, and the confused clamour issuing from the canal, combine to form a strange combination of sounds without a parallel in any other town.

JAPANESE COOLIE.

The contrast is great in passing from the city to the suburbs of Yedo. They resemble a veritable English park, whose beauty is intensified by the singular vegetation of the country. The crowd is not so dense in these parts, and the people are always peaceable and quiet, and, although not actually taciturn, merriment seems to expend itself in laughter rather than words.

Sinagava is the most interesting quarter of the suburbs, and at the same time the worst-famed and the most dangerous. One part is occupied by fishermen, watermen, and labourers; the other by the same scum of society to be found in all our European towns, with the addition of a class of vagrants peculiar to Japan. These are the *Lonins*, or men of no occupation, belonging to the military caste, and possessing in consequence the right of carrying arms. Some of them are young men, who for their debaucheries have been banished from their homes, or by disgraceful conduct have lost their position in society; and others, again, were formerly members of a household, but their masters have been forced to reduce the number of their suite in consequence of hard times or misfortunes. The Lonin, deprived of his pay, and knowing only the profession of arms, has no other resource, whilst waiting for a new engagement, than to take refuge in these haunts of vice. A certain organisation and order amongst disorder is, however, maintained. Those constituted the chiefs hold whole bands of Lonins in abject dependence on them, and they are often employed by the Japanese nobility in the execution of bloody deeds to revenge private quarrels or political feuds. These miserable outlaws of society are so well aware of the loathing with which they are regarded, that whenever they leave their quarters they take the precaution to hide their faces beneath a large hat, the sides of which are fastened tightly down; or else they envelop their heads entirely in a piece of crêpe, only leaving the eyes uncovered.

Dangerous outlaws as these Lonins are, they often perform deeds of reckless daring which raise them to the rank of heroes, and embalm them in the popular memory. We may cite as an example one of the most popular legends in Japan.

The Story of the Forty-seven Lonins.

There was a small Daimio, who, having a feud in past time with one of the Tycoon's Council of State, determined to avenge himself by slaying his enemy when he met him in the palace. He made the attempt and failed, inflicting only a slight wound, some of the attendants having seized him from behind as he was aiming his blow. Foiled in his object, he returned to his house; and having collected his officers and retainers around him, and made his preparations for the solemn ceremony of disembowelling himself, he deliberately performed the operation in their presence, and then, handing the short sword covered with his blood to his secretary, he laid his dying injunctions upon him, as his liege lord, with that very weapon to take the life of his enemy. The latter, being freed from his antagonist, seized upon the house and property of the deceased Daimio, and turned out all his faithful servitors. These, to the number of forty-seven, became Lonins, under the command of the secretary, all bound together by an oath to accomplish the destruction of their master's enemy. Accordingly, choosing their time, they stormed his castle during the night, when they knew he was inside, and entered into a terrible conflict with all his retainers, amounting to some three hundred; and such was their desperate heroism that they finally vanquished them, and proceeded to search for their chief victim. He was concealed in a secret recess between two rooms, with one of his friends; but the Lonins had obtained information of the existence of such a hiding-place, and one of them thrust a spear through the partition. The blade wounded the Daimio, but not in a vital part; and as it was drawn out he took care to wipe it with his sleeve, so that on examining it, and seeing no mark of blood, the Lonins came to the conclusion that no one was there, and that he had escaped their vengeance. Nothing then remained but an act of self-immolation; and stripping off their armour and dress, they were in the act of performing the Hara Kiru, when a stifled cough reached their ear from the very hiding-place they had pierced in a vain search. Satisfied now that their enemy was still in their grasp, they sprang to their feet, tore down the walls, and dragged him and his friend out, when the secretary, with the very sword which he had received from his dying chief, struck off both their heads. Their vengeance thus satisfied, and not a living being remaining to be slain, they then performed the disembowelling with the greatest heroism and complacency. They were all buried in one cemetery in Yedo, and they live to this day in the hearts of all brave and loyal men in Japan as types of true heroism.

K

We can well imagine what must be the influence of such a popular literature and history upon the character, as well as the habits of thought and action, of a nation, when children listen to such fragments of their history, popular tales, and as they grow up hear their elders praise the valour and heroism of such servitors, and see them go at stated periods to pay honour to their graves centuries after the deed. Is it not plain that this general and unhesitating approval of what with us would be considered great crimes may have very subtle and curious bearings on the general character and moral training of the people? Is it any wonder that men, reared and nurtured under such a gospel, should be disposed to look on the massacre of foreign legations as simply the outburst of a noble patriotism?

A most picturesque and well-maintained high-road, called the Tocado, runs through Sinagava, from Nagasaki in the extreme south to Hakodadi in the far north, forming a great artery through the islands and cities of Kiusiu, Sitkoff, and Niphon. In the neighbourhood of Yedo especially the road has a most lively appearance, almost equalling the animation of a street. Travellers on foot, and in *norimons, kangos,* and *jinrikishas*—men, women, children, and bare-headed priests—follow each other almost without intermission. The old palanquin has been quite discarded for the *norimon*, resembling a covered box, and the *kango*, an open one. They are suspended from a strong pole resting upon the shoulders of coolie bearers. The *jinrikisha* is a modern invention. It is a highly-polished vehicle on two wheels, covered with a

NORIMON.

JAPAN.—p. 161.

The Running Postman. 163

white hood, and drawn, as its name signifies in Japanese, by one or more men. The coolie goes at a slow trot, and accomplishes from four to five miles an hour.

A messenger is now and then seen threading his way amongst the bustling crowd, his sole clothing consisting of a sash tied round the loins, and a large, round, perfectly flat hat, perched miraculously upon the top of his head. He carries over his shoulder a long thin bamboo, to one end of which is attached the small parcel containing his despatches,

JAPANESE POSTMAN

and to the other his own light luggage. He wears the customary straw sandals upon his feet, and runs with such marvellous grace and agility that he hardly seems to touch the ground. This is the running postman, or carrier of despatches, who can accomplish long distances with wonderful speed and facility. When great fleetness is not required, he usually dons something more in the shape of garments, as seen in our illustration.

The approach of some grand personage seems to cast a sudden spell upon the crowd; a silence falls over everything; employments are stopped, and many of the people hastily re-enter their houses and close them as a warning shout announces the approach of the great man. The *cortege* is preceded by two men—bareheaded, notwithstanding the burning sun—who are followed by soldiers armed, some with guns, others with lances, but all having swords buckled to their waist-belts; the heavy *norimon* comes next, borne upon the shoulders of a dozen powerful men; the rest of the suite follow in order.

The Tocado is crossed in several places by rapid rivers. Those over which the native engineers have been unable, in spite of their skill, to construct bridges, are crossed by flat boats upon the shoulders of a body of men who make it their profession. This peculiar calling is transmitted from father to son, and its members have formed a corporation amongst themselves to indemnify travellers in case of personal accident or damage to baggage. A handkerchief tied over the head and a sash round the loins is their whole costume. Tattooing supplies the place of

Mode of Crossing Rivers. 165

clothes on the other parts of their body, according to the prevailing custom of the coolies in large Japanese cities. Their choice of subjects is always in the heroic style, such as the combats of heroes with fantastical dragons, the tribunal of the great judges of hell, or the image of that incomparable hero who, at the same moment that his head was severed from his body, managed as it fell to tear out with his teeth a portion of his adversary's coat of mail. The charge for crossing the fords varies according to the number of bearers required; eight are necessary for the transport of a *norimon,* four for a *kango,* and two men to a hand-barrow, but single bearers are more frequently employed. When this is the case, the traveller seats himself astride the shoulders of his human steed, who seizes hold of him by the legs, and, bidding him keep his balance, advances with firm and measured steps slowly into the water. This mode of procedure is the same for natives of both sexes; the ladies preserve the same composure as the gentlemen, smoking their pipes and interchanging observations upon the height of the waters and the length of the journey.

A traveller alludes to this free-and-easy custom in the following terms:—" The women of the poorer classes are carried across on the men's shoulders, and as the men themselves are nearly immersed in water, it follows that the burden, below the waist at any rate, cannot be very dry; but in Japan such difficulties are easily met. The lady tucks up her clothes as she gets astride her steed, and he, on arriving at the other side, sets her gently down;

and before he is on his feet, or can turn round to receive his payment, the costume is all perfectly in order, and the lady escapes wet clothes for the rest of her journey, and probably a rheumatism for life. Really it is impossible to deny that a certain Spartan simplicity of costume and manners has its advantage in such a country as Japan at least." Now, however, that the rage for European dresses is extending to the lower classes, it is difficult to see how women are to be transported over rivers in the future. Parisian costumes might be seriously disarranged by such rude contact; and unless the Japanese build more bridges, there seems no course open for them but to adopt the latest thing in aerial locomotion, and carry their wives and daughters over their torrents in balloons.

It is impossible to fix the exact number of the population of Yedo, as the Japanese Government have been unable as yet to establish a regular census. According to one traveller, the population in 1862 was about 1,700,000, 600,000 of which were tradesmen and artisans, and 500,000 nobles and members of their households; but the fall of the Tycoon and subsequent departure of many of the princely families from the city seem to have considerably lessened this total, and at the same time to have deprived Yedo of the principal element of its opulence. In 1872 the English consul estimated the population at under 800,000, but it none the less remains still the most important town in the empire, and every phase of Japanese life can be seen in its streets.

Amongst the public establishments the most singular are

the baths and tea-houses. The former often occupy the whole side of a street. "Every one," says the Comte de Beauvoir, "goes there three or four times a day to perform their ablutions; men and women, young men and young girls—all in a state of nature—meet together in numbers of fifty or sixty to each bath-house. Crouching and springing upon an inclined plane, surrounded by pyramids of little tubs covered with leather, and filled with hot water, these human frogs sprinkle themselves from head to foot, till they gradually become as red as lobsters. They rub and scrub themselves unmercifully; then walk about, and gaily beg a cigarette from the foreigners looking on. The splendid tattooing of the men shines amidst the soft rose-colour of the sprightly nymphs who are soaped and dried by professional rubbers with the utmost *sang-froid*, as though it were the most natural thing in the world; and I verily believe we too should very soon join the party with the feeling that even social prejudice could scarcely call it shocking."

This custom of the Japanese, of taking their baths in common, has earned for them the reproach of a want of modesty. "It seems to me," remarks the traveller Lindau, "that it is a little hasty to judge them from our standard. There is a great difference between depravity and a want of reserve. The child knows no shame, but it is not therefore shameless. Modesty, Rousseau says with reason, is a social institution, which develops with civilisation; every age and every climate exercises an influence upon the different conceptions of this sense—a fact that every historian and traveller have been able to authenticate. Not only does French modesty differ from the modesty of a Mussulman, but our present ideas of modesty are in many points quite opposed to those held by our ancestors. Each race, according to its moral education and habits, has made for itself a criterion of what is decent or the reverse. We cannot with justice tax with immodesty the individual who, in his own country, wounds none of the social proprieties in the midst of which he has been brought up.

"The most refined and strict Japanese is not offended at the sight of a young girl taking her bath at the entrance of her house, in full sight of passers-by; and people of both sexes and every age have no thought of shame when they meet in the common hall for the purpose of performing their ablutions together. A highly-educated Japanese with whom I conversed on this subject was simply unable to comprehend the disgust and scruples expressed by Europeans at this custom. 'Well,' he said to me, 'when I see a woman in her bath, I see her entirely naked; what harm is there in that?' I could extract nothing else from him, till at length I perceived that we both started from such widely separate points of view that it would be impossible to arrive at the same conclusion."

We may here appropriately quote the following remarks of an acute observer :—" I cannot help feeling there is some danger of doing great injustice to the womanhood of Japan, if we judge them by *our* rules of decency and modesty. Where there is no *sense* of immodesty, no consciousness of wrong-doing, there is, or may be, a like absence of any sinful or depraving feeling. It is a custom of the country. Fathers, brothers, husbands, all sanction it, and from childhood the feeling must grow up, as effectually guarding them from self-reproach or shame, as their sisters in Europe in adopting low dresses in the ball-room, or any other generally adopted fashion of garments or amusements. There is much in the usual appearance and expression of Japanese women to lead to this conclusion. When the bath is taken, and the mysteries of the toilette are over, they will leave the bath-room a perfect picture of maidenly modesty and reserve—far more so, indeed, both in look and carriage, than a great many of those who frequent the streets and public places of resort in London or Paris."

Nor is the bath-house without its *political* significance. It is an important popular institution in Japan, being what the baths were to the Roman and the *café* to the Frenchman—the grand lounge. Towards the close of the day and in the early hours after sunset, as you pass along the streets of Yedo, at every hundred steps a bath-house is visible. You know their vicinity by the steam escaping through open doors and windows, and the hum of many voices, bass and tenor, in full chorus. And here all the gossip of the neighbourhood and town is no doubt ventilated. No one is so poor that he cannot secure a bath—no one so wretched that this luxury at least may not be his. Here, if they have any cares, the people seem to forget them all in the steamy atmosphere, and for half-an-hour out of the twenty-four they revel in the luxuries of a terrestrial paradise. But if this great institution of the bath be the source of public opinion—said by the ministers of Japan to exist, and invoked whenever it suits their purposes — it rises in dignity as the people's parliament or house of assembly (the only one, certainly, they are permitted), and we may overlook some of its deficiencies of costume, and other eccentricities, in the contemplation of its political and national uses. It certainly has a recommendation—wanting in all other parliaments—of acknowledging to the fullest extent the rights of both sexes and their equality. Not only are the women not excluded, as in the more pretentious parliaments of the West, but *their voice is unquestionably heard.* The gentler tenor often prevails over the deeper bass of the men; and the frequent laugh and shrill hilarity of the tone, heard from afar, ought to be a sufficient guarantee to the Government that no deep schemes of treason or sanguinary revolutions are ever discussed, at the same time that it affords a pleasant contrast in other respects to many debates in more solemn places. *The sex* is the State's protection, for, though one woman may plot a deed of vengeance, the history of the world does not furnish an instance of *a conspiracy of women*—or of any mixed assembly of men and women—for the enactment of scenes of violence and political convulsion. Long experience, or a deep insight into human nature, may have given the jealous rulers of Japan full assurance of the fact, and thus have supplied to the *vox populi* a free vent, as a sort of safety-valve, without any of its attendant dangers.

Assuredly they would allow no such gatherings of men alone. If so, they have made a discovery by which western states may hereafter profit, with such modifications of drapery and costume as our more refined habits would dictate.

The baths are considered of paramount importance in the hygienic practices of the Japanese. Independently of their morning ablutions, they each day, or nearly so, take a hot water bath at a very high temperature. They remain in it from twenty minutes to half-an-hour, either wholly or partially immersed, taking the greatest care never to wet the head. It not unfrequently happens that congestion of the brain, and even apoplexy, are the consequences of this irrational custom. All the houses belonging to the upper classes possess two private baths for domestic use, and even in the smallest household a little bath-room, furnished with the proper heating apparatus, is to be found. When the bath is ready, each member of the family and household makes use of it in turn. But these private baths are not generally used, as the expense of the necessary firing exceeds the amount of a family subscription to the public baths. Thus it is that the latter have become such a complete national institution, and are regarded, in a moral point of view, with the same indifference as we look upon the essential habits of sleeping, resting, eating, and drinking.

CHAPTER XII.

The Tea-houses—The Joro-jas or Night-houses—Unhappy Position of the Tea-house Girls—A Japanese Supper—Unconscious Demoralisation—The History of a Joro.

THE tea-houses scattered throughout Yedo, but more especially in certain of the suburbs, are of two kinds, the Tscha-jas and the Joro-jas. The former are considered the more respectable of the two, are frequented by the best society, and at the same time afford rest and refreshment to travellers. They are to be met with in the country as well as in the towns, and the sites upon which they are built show clearly the prevailing love of the Japanese for the beauties of nature. In all accessible places where the landscape attracts the eye, a tea-house invites the passer-by to rest awhile, and enjoy the prospect displayed before him. Upon frequented roads this establishment becomes a large hotel, but in more retired places it is simply a miniature house, built of wood and paper, and covered in by a thatched roof. A family, composed of a father, mother, and a nest of children, here manage in some mysterious manner to gain a livelihood. The traveller is oftentimes also pleasantly surprised, when

INTERIOR OF TEA-HOUSE AT YEDO.

JAPAN.—p. 173.

Description of the Night-houses. 175

he has wandered far into the interior, following the course of rivers, or penetrating thick groves, where no sign of any human habitation is apparent, to find himself close to one of these establishments, naturally a very humble specimen, and probably presided over by some old woman, who offers him, for the modest sum of a *zeni*—not quite the hundredth part of two pence—a cup of tea and small platter of rice. He is certain gladly to accept the welcome refreshment, and to smoke several pipes before quitting the lovely, though solitary spot. In all the tea-houses customers are waited on by young girls, called Nesans; they are exceedingly active and obliging in serving each one in turn, according to their respective wants, with eggs, rice, fish, saki—a kind of brandy made from rice—or tea, which the guests consume very slowly, sitting cross-legged upon soft, comfortable mats.

The Joro-jas are only to be found in certain districts, and differ from the Tscha-jas, inasmuch as they are only frequented by night. The following description of the latter is given by Lindau:—" After passing through a strong door guarded by soldiers, we found ourselves at the entrance of a street of a most singular aspect. Although very long and wide, it was intensely still, gloomy, and almost deserted. The houses on either side of it were unlike any I had seen elsewhere; they were larger than the merchants and artisans' dwellings, and yet they had not the great doorway usually seen at the entrance to all the noblemen's houses. Strong wooden gratings prevented ingress, but did not exclude from sight the view of the interior. Low massive doors were ranged round the side of the façade, and everything contributed to lend an air of mystery and strangeness to this isolated spot.

"The day had waned. Here and there paper lanterns were illumined. The foot-passengers hastened along, several of them having their heads enveloped in great handkerchiefs as if to avoid recognition. We had now reached the worst-famed portion of the town—the quarter of the Joro-jas, or night tea-houses.

"On drawing nearer to one of them we could discern a spacious hall, furnished with bamboo mats, and feebly lighted by four large paper lanterns. Beside us were a dozen or more Japanese, who, like ourselves, were minutely taking note of all that passed in the interior of the hall. There, in the customary squatting attitude, were eight young girls, magnificently dressed in long robes of the richest materials. Perfectly upright and motionless, they appeared to be gazing at the grating which separated them from us, but with that peculiar fixed look in their bright eyes which denotes a total absence of interest or observation. Their beautiful jet black hair was arranged with great art, and ornamented with yellow tortoise shells. They were very young; the eldest could hardly have reached her twentieth year, and the youngest looked little more than fourteen. Some were remarkable for their beauty, but all wore an expression of resignation and indifference most painful to see on such young faces.

"Exposed like animals in a menagerie, examined and criticised at leisure by every one, sold or hired to the first bidder, these unhappy creatures made the saddest impression on me. An old woman shortly appeared at the end of the hall and pronounced some words, upon which one of the young girls instantly rose and went out, but as mechanically and slowly as an automaton. We then passed through a door adjoining the grating, and crossed a straight gloomy passage which led into a large hall, raised some feet above the ground, and divided into two unequal parts. To the right we saw about thirty people, consisting of children, varying from eight to fourteen years, young girls, and women, whose age it was difficult to determine, as the Japanese, after reaching thirty, frequently look much older than they really are. This probably is the result of the hot baths they are in the constant habit of taking. Some of the children were already sound asleep, their heads resting upon a pillow of wood; the remainder, both women and young girls, very richly clothed in honour of the Matsowie, were seated round the *braseros*, eating, drinking, smoking, and chatting gaily.

"On our approach a neatly-dressed old woman came to meet us and inquire our wishes. The officer, our guide, answered that we wished to see the dancers and singers, and at the same time he ordered a good repast to be prepared in the finest part of the house. The old woman then conducted us through a garden planted with beautiful trees to a pavilion, where she lighted some paper lanterns and a dozen bad wax candles fixed in iron candelabra. The ground floor of the summer-house formed a single apartment; the first floor being, on the contrary, divided into a great number of rooms, or rather small cells, separated one from the other by paper partitions. The mats covering the floors were everywhere very clean, and of superior quality; the walls looked newly papered, and the top of the doors and side-posts were decorated with delicate carvings in wood.

"Our conductor, who was a sort of governess called *ô-bassan*, here left us after receiving our orders. She soon returned, accompanied by three little girls, each carrying a small wooden table varnished black, platters of the same materials but of various colours, china cups and bottles—in fact, all the necessary appendages of a repast. Very soon an exceedingly well-served Japanese supper was spread before us, consisting of hard eggs, lobster, uncooked and boiled fish, rice, fruits, sweetmeats; and for beverages the sweet Osaka wine, saki, and tea. The dishes were all excellent, and invitingly sent up, and our little attendants waited on us most cleverly and obligingly. These children are called Kabrousses or Kamerons, and are brought up by the Joros and the ô-bassans expressly to attend on them, or make themselves useful to the other members of the household.

"During supper several young girls entered our apartment; these were the Joros. They presented themselves one by one, each making a profound obeisance, kneeling and touching the ground with her forehead, and then retired into a corner of the hall. At our invitation they came and sat beside us, and modestly joined us in our meal; but they were very silent and reserved, and only

The Singing Ghekos.

responded to our queries by a few timid words. Their costumes were the same as those worn by the younger Japanese girls, only of more costly, bright-coloured materials. Some of them had tortoise-shell pins of the very finest quality stuck in their hair.

"Supper ended, the little girls cleared it away, and some other persons made their appearance. They were *ghekos*, or singers, four in number, beautifully dressed, and each

JAPANESE GUITAR-PLAYER.

carrying in her hand a sam-sin, the favourite instrument with the Japanese. After tuning them, they began to play, striking the strings with a piece of ivory shaped like an axe. Japanese music cannot be compared to ours, but some of the popular songs have very pretty agreeable airs. The Japanese are gifted with a very correct ear; they sing and play perfectly in unison, observing with great exactness the often very difficult rhythm of their melodies. In obedience to an order from the ô-bassan, the young girls rose to execute some dances. Their forced gestures and extraordinary contortions harmonised little with our ideas of grace, but their supple and precise movements were faithfully adapted to the character of the music, which, sometimes slow and sad, sometimes bright and lively, also served as an accompaniment to a poem recited by the ghekos.

"After the dance, which lasted for some time, there was a moment of repose and silence. We offered cake and saki to the ghekos, which they accepted with many thanks; the dancers also, encouraged by the ô-bassan, seemed now at ease, and talked a little, but in a very low voice. Some of them were remarkably pretty, but the excessive modesty which characterised them all struck me even more than their beauty. In one only did I notice a boldness of manner, which contrasted singularly with her pale handsome countenance. 'It is not to be wondered at,' said one of my friends, to whom I had imparted my observation; 'this young girl is considered a great beauty, and is very much sought after. Last year she was shy and retiring to a degree, but since then she has spent some months at Desima and Oora, where she associated a great deal with our countrymen, and in consequence has lost much of her former charming modesty. It must be admitted, as a general rule, that the natives degenerate morally from the moment they have any intercourse with us.'

"Space will not allow us here to inquire to what cause this effect may be attributed; but it is unhappily only too true that in Japan, as well as in China, the good, simple-minded people formerly to be met with in society have vanished wherever European influence predominates. The coolies, or porters, of Desima are incorrigible thieves; the tradesmen of Yokohama are becoming every day more unscrupulous; and every Japanese who holds any communication whatever with foreigners speedily loses that modesty which is as pleasing as it is rare.

"I cannot define the state of demoralisation in which the Joros live otherwise than by styling it one of perfect unconsciousness. The basis of every moral law is conscience; therefore where this is absent there can be no demoralisation in the ordinary meaning of the term. It is quite evident that there is nothing offensive to the Japanese mind in the life of a Joro. In one of the most venerated temples at Yedo, the temple of Akatza or Quanon Sama, the portraits of Joros celebrated for their beauty are suspended close to the altar, and are shown to the young girls sold to the tea-houses as models to be imitated. In the large town of Simonosaki there is a veritable monastery for Joros, founded by the wife of an ancient Emperor of Japan to assist in defraying the costs of a war undertaken against some rebellious subjects. A Joro can rarely be rescued from her unhappy condition by means of an honourable marriage, owing to the nature of the bonds which attach her almost indissolubly to her master. These unfortunate girls are generally the daughters of a poor family, either overburdened with children, or else, by the death of the breadwinner, deprived of their principal means of support. A livelihood, such as it is, is at any rate ensured for the girls by selling them to the tea-houses. Two forms of contract are drawn out on these occasions, according to their ages. If of a marriageable age, which is rarely the case, the young girl is hired to the tea-house for a certain number of years, for a sum varying from four to eight pounds, a considerable addition to the family revenue. If the child is young, she is sold once for all, and becomes the absolute property of her purchaser, who engages to clothe, feed, and educate her. Till about the age of fifteen or sixteen she is taught to read, write, dance, sing, and play the sam-sin; and, in fact, receives a very good education. She then becomes either a gheko or singer, an adoori or dancer, or else a Joro; she submits patiently to either of these conditions, without having either the power or the wish to complain. Before we pass judgment upon these unhappy creatures, we should take into consideration the fact that they exercise their shameless profession without will or profit. Towards the age of twenty-four or twenty-five the Joro ought, according to the tenor of the contract which bound her to the tea-house, to be released and allowed to regain her independence. But such is not the ordinary termination of the lives of these poor slaves. To be ugly or deformed is often their only chance of liberation; if, on the contrary, they possess any personal charms, the master takes advantage of their ignorance to retain possession of them. He teaches them to contract debts in procuring delicate food, buying nick-nacks or costly clothes, which he is not obliged to furnish; and as very few of them can resist these temptations, they soon become deeply involved, so that, at the expiration of their engagement, their only means of freeing themselves from debt is to sell themselves again for a new term of service.

"Thus, by a chain of overpowering circumstances, it usually happens that these poor creatures spend their entire lives in these houses to which as little children they were sold, and where, when their youth has faded, and they have become old and withered, they find a last asylum in the capacity either of servants, teachers in the school, or of dancing or singing mistresses. Here and there are isolated cases when one from her charms or good qualities has captivated some honest man, who ransoms her by paying her debts; but the greater part resign themselves to die in the state in which they have lived."

CHAPTER XIII.

Public Festivals—Animated Scenes—The *Champs Elysées* of Yedo—Various Jugglers—Mountebanks and Gymnasts—Wonderful Feats of Equilibrium—Juggling Extraordinary—Spinning Tops—The Butterfly Trick.

ALTHOUGH festivals are of frequent occurrence, the light-hearted people of Yedo have created for themselves a thousand other means of entertainment and recreation. They have evening as well as day amusements, the latter taking place in the public roads and in the temples or their courtyards, while the former have special buildings devoted to them—marquees, circuses, or theatres. The greater part of these places of amusement are within the reach of the humblest purse. The Sibaïa, which corresponds to our opera, is open to every class of people, and supports itself entirely, never soliciting or obtaining any assistance from the municipal or Government authorities.

The different quarters of Yedo have each their own separate recreations, more or less aristocratic, according to the tastes of the inhabitants of the district. The most interesting are those of Yomasta, where a permanent fair is held, and Osaka, which is both the Athenæum and the Pandemonium of Japan.

JAPANESE FAMILY AT TABLE.

JAPAN—p. 185.

The Cuisine of the Tea-houses. 187

The wooded hills of Yomasta, crossed and re-crossed by the great arteries of circulation, have very much the appearance of those verdant isles which are seen rising above the muddy waters of the great Chinese rivers, covered with thousands of junks. An immense temple with high galleries, surrounded by groves, forms the culminating point of the scene. All around are the tea-houses, towards which thousands of visitors are wending their way, either in search of refreshment, or simply for the sake of a sociable chat whilst they lazily sip a cup of tea.

Great animation prevails. The *nesans*, or servants, hurry hither and thither, carrying to each customer a little platter containing the customary Japanese dinner of fish soup, uncooked and boiled fish, rice, eggs, sweetmeats, fruits, etc. The cuisine of Japan is very varied, and quite that of a civilised people, but, like other countries, it has its own peculiarities. First of all, butchers' meat is not to be had, but poultry and fish take its place. The poor live entirely on rice and vegetables, but they manage to make this rather insipid food quite tasty, by seasoning it very strongly with horse-radish and capsicum. Fricasseed poultry and chicken soup are considered to form a very *récherché* repast, and are reserved for large entertainments or great gala days. But in the houses of the rich as well as in those of the poor rice forms the staple food, and takes the place both of bread and meat. Tea is the ordinary and universal beverage, although saki and the sweet Osaka wine, resembling Tokay in flavour, are also drunk.

The field where the fair is held at Yomasta is the

Champs Elysées of Yedo. Upon the wide pavements of the principal road, planted on both sides with maples, squat rows of small dealers, each on his own mattress, and all extravagantly puffing up while offering for sale the goods displayed at their feet. They have a sufficient variety of things to gratify the tastes of any and every one, and their wares are most picturesquely arranged amongst gay flags covered with coloured figures and large Chinese characters. The owner of one of these small shops deals in rat poison, and a heap of his victims lie beside him, to prove to the most sceptical the destructive properties of his drug; whilst his neighbour, muffled in a great pelisse, tries to tempt every one in turn with shells or paper packets containing bear's grease, which is much used in Japan for diseases of the skin. As a proof that the article he offers is genuine, he always carries about the head and claws of a bear, to which he is continually attracting attention. The skins of frogs are also sold at Yomasta, but it is difficult to conceive what use can be made of them. Bank lotteries and fortune-telling books, presided over by little horned demons, drive a thriving trade; and, proceeding further down the road, a knot of people will be seen taking turns in looking through a stereoscopic instrument, while another group watches a kind of bonze-juggler, whose specialty consists in playing harmlessly with fire. Vendors of water-melons, or tepid water slightly flavoured with tea, are also very popular, and the sale of pipes and tobacco is equally profitable. The dealer attracts customers by offering them the use of a lighted fusee which he

A Medley Crowd.   189

carries, and which they are glad to accept; for in Japan, though all the world smokes, the use of the flint and steel is unknown, whilst lucifer matches are generally useless from the effects of the damp weather. Travellers take advantage of any smoker they meet on their journeys to light their pipes from his, and the natives light fires, after the manner of savages, by the friction of two pieces of wood.

The crowd thickens greatly towards the large square of Yomasta, and the pavement is most inconveniently obstructed by stalls, some composed simply of straw mats, and others supported by bamboo poles. Here and there are some hardy fellows who follow their different professions all day in the open air; such are the popular astrologer, and the professional story and news-teller. The one explains to his circle of auditors the planetary system, allowing the public to make any observations they please, by means of his long telescope, upon the sun, moon, and stars. The other repeats mechanically the tragedy of the last capital punishment; and at the same time, in return for a small coin, he slowly distributes leaflets containing a printed account of the tragedy. The noise is incessant. To the confused clamour of the crowd is added the sound of cries, songs, and the tambourines of the mountebanks, players, and jugglers, all of whom make Yomasta their head-quarters, and offer every imaginable attraction for the amusement of the people of Yedo.

One of them dances a marionette, clothed like a jumping priest, upon the pavement. Another exhibits on a table the model of a temple; a white mouse climbs up the steps, rings the door bell, and makes his devotions before the altar. A third has trained some birds to shoot with bows and arrows, to pound rice, to draw water, and to drag a waggon loaded with bales of cotton. A street juggler balances himself upon two high upright poles, and whirls three or four bottles or china cups round his head; then breaks an egg, and extracts from it yards of string; or pounds a piece of paper in the palm of his hand, and a cloud of gnats rise from it a moment after. Further on, the discordant call of the fife, drum, and tambourine causes a general rush to view a representation given by the Lion of Corea. The player is muffled in a large striped or spotted cloak, surmounted by the enormous head of a fantastic lion, which causes great amusement and terror by its sudden bounds and loud roars. After a great deal of dancing and ridiculous caperings, the entertainment is ended by the monster suddenly casting off its disguise, and being transformed into an expert juggler, he seizes a drumstick and balances it upon the thumb of his left hand, then adds a second, and places a third crossways above the other two; finally he throws them in the air, catching them as they fall, and twists them round and round, faster and faster, adding to them without a pause one, two, and three bowls in succession, which have sprung no one knows from whence. This is the grand finale of the performance; the musicians carry round the plate—that is to say, the fan—and the juggler quietly lights his pipe from that of his nearest neighbour.

The Gymnasts. 191

At opposite corners of the square two troops of mountebanks have installed themselves. One company performs in the open air; amongst other exhibitions, they swallow swords and accomplish marvellous feats of jumping. One of them passes harmlessly through two hoops crossing each other and fixed at the top of a pole, on which is also balanced a jug at the point of intersection of the hoops. But their most masterly trick consists in darting through a cylinder made of bamboo trellis-work, about five feet in length, and resting on two supports. The mountebank lights and places at equal distances in the interior of the cylinder four large wax candles, above which he passes like a dart without extinguishing or disarranging them. His wife, who is seated on a chest close by, accompanies the different phases of the performance with appropriate airs upon her guitar, now and then, at especially critical moments, uttering shrill screams or sepulchral groans, in order to enhance the effect.

The troop on the other side of the square are gymnasts. They perform beneath a large shed, which contains all their stock-in-trade, such as poles and parallel bars, differing very little from those used in our gymnasiums. The company numbers a great many members, each of whom is a perfect master of his art. There is no professional clown, but all are buffoons in their own way, and from constant practice possess to perfection the art of jesting and repartee. The simplicity of their costume is very quaint to the eyes of a foreigner; a couple of pocket-handkerchiefs could contain their entire wardrobe. They wear on their heads a burlesque imitation of the caps worn by the nobles, which they never take off, not even when they perform the trick of seizing a straw hive between their toes, raising it from the ground and depositing it on their heads, maintaining their balance perfectly, with their arms crossed the whole time.

The Japanese acrobats are unrivalled in feats of equilibrium, which they perform by means of an inordinately

JAPANESE GYMNASTS.

long false nose or a bamboo pole, which in some mysterious way, known only to themselves, they affix to the middle of their faces. One of them, for example, will lie upon his back, whilst a child climbs to the end of his nose, upon which he balances himself on one foot, at the same time poising a parasol upon the end of his own nose; more than

Sleight-of-hand Jugglers. 193

this, the man, still keeping exactly in the same position, raises his leg in the air, and another child, pressing his nose upon the sole of the recumbent man's foot, gradually raises his legs till his whole body is perpendicular, and in this position he remains motionless for some moments. Other and even more incredible feats they perform with the aid of this long nose. The divine Teugon is the patron of these acrobats, who adorn themselves with his principal emblems, which, in addition to the long nose, are a large pair of wings and the costume of a herald.

Even more interesting than these are the sleight-of-hand jugglers. The best of them are generally to be seen at Yomasta, or in the courts of the large temple of Quannon, but they also make tours into the provinces.

"M. de Solsbrock," says Humbert, "invited one of these troops to exhibit before some notabilities who were then residing at Yokohama. My sitting-room adjoined the drawing-room, which we had converted into a theatre, and the two apartments opened on to the verandah, which the jugglers made use of as a green-room; thus I had the pleasure of assisting in all the preparations for their entertainment. They were six in number, besides the four musicians and several servants. Their furniture comprised, amongst other things, high three-legged stools, various stands, and elegant little tables varnished a beautiful red, besides large china vases, grotesque masks, and boxes of every size, some varnished black, others of white wood, and double-bottomed, with drawers or secret springs. These contained candlesticks, wax candles, a small magic lantern, china cups, answering to those used by our conjurers; marionettes, scarves, ribbons, turbans, string, paper pipes, swords, fans, and a regular assortment of tops, varying in size from a soup-plate to a nutshell.

"The orchestra was composed of a sam-sin, a pair of wooden castanets, a tambourine, and a drum. The music is not supposed to be an attractive accompaniment, but it is useful to deafen and distract the attention of the spectators at certain points, and also to announce the commencement of any new phase of the entertainment.

"Whilst I admit that the conjurers of Europe are equal in dexterity to those of the East, yet, taken altogether, the latter are certainly their superiors, and I can give no better impression of their performances than by describing them as charming mystifications. With the exception of the clever conjuring which the Yedo jugglers perform with astounding dexterity, their whole display seemed a mockery of the stupendous, worked by means of illusions of their own invention, admirable in their ingenuity and simplicity. Add to this the merits of a company, each member of which is perfect in the exercise of his art; a well appointed *mise en scène*; exquisite taste, or rather admirable tact in the arrangement of the costumes, decorations, draperies, machinery, and furniture, together with complete self-possession and grace; and it will easily be allowed that this especial class of juggler holds a distinct and honourable place amongst the numerous brotherhoods of that profession."

These men are especially clever in the almost impercept-

Juggling Girls. 195

ible manner in which they pass from simple tricks to the cleverest bits of jugglery, without the spectator perceiving or even suspecting the transition. For instance, one of them

JAPANESE JUGGLING GIRLS.

squatted before a high iron chandelier, and, fanning himself with one hand, seized with the other a lighted wax candle, threw it up in the air, and caught it again and again as if it were a ball, keeping time to a song he himself sang, accompanied by the orchestra. He finally restored the candle to its place, blew it out, and instantly there spurted forth from it a jet of water, which he received in a china bowl. Another of their number, kneeling before a low covered stool lighted on each side by great paper lanterns, exhibited two pretty marionettes, who performed a little comedy for four characters, intermixed with songs and dances. The changing of the different parts took place in full view of the spectators, and without the juggler moving for an instant from his place. The piece concluded, the marionettes were carefully packed away in their box by another person, whilst the juggler himself performed a kind of burlesque, which he brought abruptly to an end by flapping the wide sleeves of his jacket like the wings of a bird, and suddenly leaping upon a huge paper lantern, where he remained perfectly motionless for some seconds, supporting himself upon the points of his toes. A confederate again opened the box of marionettes and produced a complete breakfast-set. Seizing the teapot, he filled a cup to the brim and offered it to the lookers-on upon a waiter; but when they had received it into their hands, lo! it was empty. The juggler, in feigned astonishment, then put it to his own lips, but turned away with a gesture of disgust, for the cup now contained nothing but a swarm of flies. Another excellent trick is where the juggler makes an egg stand upright on his forehead, and then balances a saucer upon it.

Their varied and skilful manipulation of the fan is very wonderful. Each moment the interest grows more and more intense, until finally the senses become confused, and the tricks appear a complication of optical delusions and dissolving views. As the *chef d'œuvre* of the first series, the juggler produces for public inspection a large open fan; this he makes stand upright upon the back of his right hand, then hurling it in the air he catches it with his left, and sitting down on his heels, and fanning himself, he turns his head *en profil* and draws a deep breath, which issues from his mouth in the form of a horse galloping. Still fanning himself, he next shakes from the sleeve of his left hand an army of little fairies, who vanish dancing and saluting. The juggler then stoops down, closes the fan, and holds it between his two hands, while his head disappears from view, to reappear almost immediately enlarged to colossal proportions, only to be reduced again to its natural size, but multiplied several times. His manner of leaving the stage is also original. A kind of large bottle is placed before him, and he presently emerges full length from the narrow neck of this vessel, and vanishes in the clouds floating about the ceiling.

The next thing on the programme is the grand display of *tops*. A juggler produces two of the largest, and, taking them by the handle, rolls them for an instant between his hands. From that moment their rotatory movement never ceases. Another juggler seizes one and makes it spin on its side upon the tube of a pipe; then tossing it in the air he catches it in the bowl of the pipe, and finally sends it whirling off to a certain post on a highly polished table, where it obediently climbs over a viaduct crossed by an arched bridge. The other juggler now brings in a high stand, upon which he places a china bowl and fills it with water. On this he lays a lotus leaf, raises the second top from the ground and places it upon the leaf, where it continues to spin, and a beautiful little jet of water spouts out from the top of it.

Whilst the large tops are thus employed, the middle-sized ones and the smallest are unpacked. An almost imperceptible touch of the fore fingers suffices to put the whole set in motion; and while they are spinning, the manager displays to the audience a number of ordinary boxes and battledores, some perfectly smooth wire, and several swords, whose sharp edges he feels; then at a given signal three men appear on the scene, salute with the deepest reverence, and simultaneously commence the entertainment to the sound of the whole strength of the orchestra.

The first performs with a hoop and four or five tops; the second makes several more jump, one after the other, in regular file in and out of the boxes; the third makes a number run from end to end of a stretched wire, or on the edge of a sword, and moves and turns them at his will. In conclusion, a lively game with battledores is carried on, in which tops take the place of shuttlecocks. Incredible as it may sound, it is nevertheless a fact that not one of these tops ceases to spin, or falters for a single instant, during the whole time of the performance. It is useless to try to give an impression of the minor details of this spectacle. One little episode is that where the juggler carelessly cuts up a piece of paper into several little square bits, which he tosses into the air, and keeps them up by fanning them gently, till they change into a flock of birds and fly away.

An equally pretty sight is where another piece of paper seems to escape from his hands in the form of a butterfly, and, hovering round his head, eludes every effort made to seize it. At length it disappears in a bouquet of flowers, but emerges the next instant accompanied by another butterfly, and these two flutter hither and thither, always contriving to avoid the eager grasp of the juggler, till he at last imprisons them in a box and shuts down the lid. The moment he raises it, however, the captives escape, and the chase begins again with renewed spirit, till at last the juggler captures both at once and approaches triumphantly to exhibit them to the spectators, but on opening his hand nothing is seen but a slight shower of gold dust. This trick, as may be imagined, excites the enthusiasm of the audience to the highest pitch. The Japanese, however, never evince approbation by noisy demonstrations; holding their closed fan in their right hand, they strike more or less vigorously with it upon the palm of their left, at the same time accompanying the gesture with a slight cry of satisfaction.

The only sight which rouses them from their impassibility is a combat between man and man (prize-fighting). The public wrestling matches are also held in great favour in Yedo, but we reserve their description for another chapter.

CHAPTER XIV.

Antiquity of Wrestling in Japan—Ceremonies connected with it—Gigantic size of the Wrestlers—Description of a Wrestling Contest—Wrestlers strictly Professional—The National Theatre—Preparations—The Lady's Toilet—The Interior—Reception of the Favourite Actors—Females on the Stage—Scenic Arrangements—"The Shadow Cloaked from Head to Foot"—Stage Heroes—Out-Heroding Herod—The Green Room—Rehearsing—Love Songs and Dances—A long Drama—Night—Fire !

WRESTLING was one of the most ancient diversions of the Japanese people, and the tribe of wrestlers can trace the date of their foundation back to the seventh month of the third year of the reign of Zimmon, the first of the Mikados, that is, about the year 658 B.C.

Placed under imperial protection, this corporation, in concert with the Government, annually organises a fresh programme for the ensuing year, sending small detachments of performers to all the principal towns in Japan. They have no permanent house or place of entertainment, though the preparations made in their honour by the towns that they favour with a visit are sometimes very considerable; but no luxuries are ever permitted or offered.

The circuses in which these contests take place are constructed in tiers, which are placed in communication with the arena by means of simple ladders made of bamboo. No order is observed in seating people, men and women both hasten promiscuously to their places; and with the exception of a small number of boxes reserved for the authorities, the only difference in the seats is the two classes of tariff; the highest admits the payer to the upper tiers. The circus is well packed long before the hour for commencing, and much eager betting goes on amongst the spectators whilst awaiting the arrival of the performers. These gentry take an interminable time in their various preparations, arranging and re-arranging the long silken-fringed scarf again and again round their loins before their fastidious taste is satisfied, and adorning themselves with the velvet apron, upon which are embroidered their arms and the diplomas they have gained in their several victories.

At length the sound of a drum is heard from the summit of the tower, or rather the high wooden framework rising above the grand entrance to the circus. Stillness and expectation succeed the hitherto tumultuous impatience of the crowd, who from this moment watch the whole proceedings with unflagging interest. An exceedingly small personage enters the arena first. This is the manager, who is attired in the most elegant of costumes, and after a series of exaggerated bows and salutations to the public, proceeds to recite, in a clear and monotonous voice, the programme of the entertainment, together with the names and the distinguished titles of the two rival companies on the point of entering the lists together.

A second drum is the signal for the procession, and the

wrestlers file slowly in, their heads erect, their arms straight by their sides, and a low murmur of admiration follows them during the whole time of their triumphal march. They certainly are a splendid race of men, not to be surpassed in any part of the known world. After this parade the wrestlers divide and wheel off to opposite sides of the arena, take off their aprons, and squat down upon their heels, quietly waiting till they are summoned to the trials of strength.

The scene of action is a little circular eminence raised about eighteen inches above the floor of the amphitheatre. It is gravelled and surrounded by a double pile of straw sacks. The whole is covered over by an elegantly decorated roof, supported upon four wooden pillars. To one of these a holy-water brush is attached; to another, a paper packet containing salt; from the third is suspended a sword of honour; and outside the arena, at the foot of the fourth pillar, is a bucket of water with a ladle in it. There are four umpires; each one is posted at the foot of, or in proximity to, the pillars. The manager never leaves the arena. Provided with a fan of command, with long silk cords attached, he invites a representative from each of the rival companies to mount the raised ground in the centre, and then he proclaims, amidst the applause of the crowd, the titles of the two illustrious champions.

"I have never anywhere," says Lindau, "seen men so large and stout as these Japanese wrestlers. They are veritable giants, all over six feet in height, and the lightest of them weighing fourteen stone; whilst their chief, as

JAPANESE WRESTLERS.

JAPAN.—p. 203.

they will tell you with pride, is over twenty-four stone in weight. The object of the combat being to expel your adversary and remain master of the arena, explains the reason why choice is always made of men of such enormous size, as, naturally, weight is most effective in such contests.

"All those ready for action were almost naked, having nothing but a scarf of green silk tightly girded round their loins. Squatting in rows just outside the arena, they offered a curious but by no means a pleasant spectacle. One of the matches was just ended as we took our seats in the amphitheatre. An official advanced to the front and announced to the public who were the next two athletes to appear; and then he read from a paper a long list of proper names and figures; this was the state of the betting between the spectators on the chances of the next contest, and was thus read aloud in order to stimulate the spirits of the wrestlers. At the conclusion of this, two wrestlers stepped forward, and, after raising their arms above their heads as a salutation to the public, began their preparations for the struggle.

"These take a long time, but the audience, although they must be well accustomed to it, never lose patience, and are exceedingly entertained at the impatience exhibited by foreigners. The wrestlers first sprinkle some grains of rice and drops of water about the arena to propitiate the god of gladiators; they then slightly moisten their shoulders, arms, and legs, rub some sand violently between their hands, execute a few grotesque movements, probably to test the suppleness of their limbs, and finish by taking up their station opposite each other in the centre of the arena, in the attitude of men gathering all their powers for the ensuing tussle.

"Upon a given signal, the two men with a harsh cry rushed at each other, each striving to floor his adversary. The shock must have been terrible, for the sound of it echoed throughout the circus, and the combatants were instantly covered with blood. The blow had, however, been so skilfully calculated that the effect was in a degree neutralised, and the two men rebounded from each other as if they had been two inert masses of equal weight, which had been hurled the one against the other with corresponding velocity. They immediately returned to the charge, each trying to surpass the other in the strength of his blows, and both labouring their utmost to remain sole master of the arena.

"After several fruitless attempts they renounced this mode of conflict, and engaged in a regular hand-to-hand struggle, amidst immense applause from the audience, who watched every movement with feverish excitement. And indeed it was a stirring sight to see these two naked, colossal-like men grappled closely together in one mighty embrace, shoulder to shoulder, breast to breast, their arms intertwined, their legs planted well apart, and each sustaining without flinching the enormous weight resting upon him. Their limbs stiffened and their muscles swelled fearfully; but neither gave a sign of yielding, until suddenly one of them seized his adversary by the waist with one arm, held him suspended in the air, and then, with an immense effort, hurled him outside the arena, where he lay amidst the group of other wrestlers, who, like the audience, closely scrutinise the various vicissitudes of the combat. Breathless, staggering, and steaming with perspiration, the victor advanced to the middle of the arena, raised his arms in a salute, and retired amidst long-continued applause."

Even though the principal object of the Japanese wrestler be to push his adversary out of the arena, it seems contrary to all our notions of the fitness of things to choose for this purpose such enormous masses of human stoutness. It utterly upsets all our notions as regards muscular training in this country. In the days, not long past, when the Ring was a legitimate national pastime in England, it was abundantly proved that mere size had but little to do in deciding the issue of any hand-to-hand encounter. Wrestling is but a form of athletics, and in all athletic sports it is universally admitted, among those best able to judge, that well-trained muscles and an average build will come off the victor against the most ponderous specimen of human flesh and blood that can be brought forward. Indeed we are only repeating a truism when we say that, with us, great bulk is a positive drawback in physical contests. How comes it, then, that one rule holds with us and another in Japan? Is mere fat among Orientals capable of putting forth a power with which it is not endowed in these lands of the West? We cannot believe such an absurdity, and we are therefore brought to the conclusion that the national tastes and feelings of the Japanese serve to account for this singular discrepancy. They are a vain-glorious and boastful people, taking an extravagant delight in their fancied superiority over all other peoples on the face of the earth. With a trace of primitive barbarism which their civilisation has not been able to eradicate, they unconsciously associate mere size with power. Nothing can give them greater pleasure than to believe that the Japanese are a race of giants. A small, spare man, however muscular and vigorous, would therefore fail to "take" in the same way as a gigantic, overgrown monster. And the men being all of this latter type, the mode of wrestling is modified by common consent to suit the motions of such organisms. Such seems the only rational reconciliation of the typical Japanese wrestler with our conception of physical culture.

The Japanese athletes, or *Soumos*, as they are called, form a peculiar class, and enjoy a certain consideration. The middle classes are very proud to be seen in their company, and invite them to their houses; even the nobles do not disdain their acquaintance. There are different orders of these wrestlers. The champion of each is also the head, and, like the heroes of our own prize ring, wears a belt, which he fastens round his waist. It is usually the gift of the lord of his native province, and he takes every opportunity of wearing it, rarely appearing without it, except when actually engaged in conflict.

Wrestling, as a profession, is not practised indiscrimately. Every professional must be incorporated with some society, and is obliged to be content with whatever salary is accorded him. The chief helps himself liberally from the profits of their entertainments. He, nevertheless, is not absolute master of the company, but is, in his turn, under the authority of the king of the wrestlers, who presides over the principal society at Yedo or Rioto, and to whom he pays an annual tribute. The chiefs of these societies hold the rank of officers, and wear two swords, the sign of nobility. They travel continually through the various provinces, sojourning in the principal towns during a period fixed by the Emperor. They amass immense sums, for the Japanese are enthusiastic lovers of their art.

The open-air theatres and the puppets, or lay-figures, are other favourite pastimes. At the former, pieces answering to our farces and light comedies are played. "I have seen at the Palais Royale," says Baron de Hübner, "farces less witty and more indelicate, with this difference, that with us everything is uttered, whereas with the Japanese everything is acted. The audience is composed principally of women and young girls, who laugh out loud. They are for the most part very respectable people, I was told, but all belonged to the lower classes."

The puppets, or lay-figures, are of life-size, made of bamboo or *papier-mâché*, dressed in silk clothes. They are kept in small houses, and miraculous scenes, the various apparitions of gods, combats and legendary deeds, are represented by them. Each group is separate and placed in a niche, which is arranged to suit the character of the place where the event represented has taken place. The intention of the lay-figures is to depict reality, natural sentiments, and the different passions of the human heart, such as anger, fear, impatience, and love. Here, again, the Japanese tendency to caricature is evident. The first intention is to impress the spectator, not to amuse him. But, involuntarily or ignorantly, the *artiste* blends comedy and tragedy, as if to hint that the truth of these historical masquerades should be received *cum grano salis*.

These little theatres form the principal amusement of the lower classes at Yedo, but the more educated attend the larger houses, where dramas are performed by a full and permanent company of actors. The large theatre in the suburb of Osaka is the most celebrated, and therefore most fashionably attended.

The Sibaïa, as it is called, affords one of the most interesting and curious sights in the world. If the literary merit of the pieces or the perfection of the acting does not equal that of the Chinese theatres, yet the one has a poetry about it which the other lacks. The character of its pieces is more ingenuous, impassioned, and tender. In China, the audience looks on at the play, and criticises the actors; in Japan, the audience assists the actors by its sympathy, which seems to produce an interchange of sentiment between them. These representations begin very early in the day, sometimes at six o'clock in the morning, and terminate about eight or nine o'clock in the evening. Some idea can be entertained of the endurance both of the dramatists and spectators by the fact that three days are not always sufficient for the performance of certain plays.

The sun has scarcely risen, when, at the sound of a

drum, a numerous and motley crowd hasten towards the doors of the theatre. Amongst them are tradesmen who have closed their shops for the day, and sunburnt peasants giving themselves a treat in consequence of some successful bargain made the previous evening; clerks or employés, who, under the common pretext of illness, have obtained a days' leave; artisans taking a holiday; and a few of the very lowest of the people, such as porters, watermen, and others, who have come to spend their earnings of the day before, leaving the future to take care of itself. Etiquette forbids the great dignitaries of any class to show themselves at a theatre; their wives sometimes venture to go alone and incognito; but the great majority of the audience is composed of heads of families, their children and servants, all arrayed in their smartest apparel. The men do not think it necessary to make any great additions to their working-day garb; but the ladies make up for the sombreness of their husbands' or fathers' toilet by a most elaborate one of their own. The evening before, the skill of the hairdresser is called into requisition, and such a splendid tower is built up on the cranium of the fair lady that she is obliged to sleep with her head resting on a block of wood. The following morning she rises at daybreak, and, after her usual ablutions, washes her neck, shoulders, and arms with milk-starch, which produces a very faint suspicion of a white skin—so great a matter of envy to the Japanese ladies; she next darkens her eyebrows with a black pencil, and puts a thin coat of gold on her lips, which in a few hours turns to a vermilion hue. She finally dons several layers of robes, all sloped out towards the throat, and confined by the obis, or silk sash, which she twists round her hips and loops up behind in the shape of a gigantic bow. Similar care is bestowed upon the children's attire. They all partake of a slight repast, provide themselves with some little dainty for refreshment, draw on their inconvenient shoes, and then very politely beg " the gentlemen-bearers of the norimon, or palanquin, to conduct them to the doors of the theatre, if it is not giving them too much trouble."

Arrived there, they take their tickets, hire cushions, buy an illustrated programme at an adjoining tea-house, answering to our ticket offices, and finally install themselves in their places without a trace of fatigue being visible on their countenances. On the contrary, merry looks and bright faces are seen all around; for these people, in their simple delight in pleasure, are determined to be amused, and possess the secret of enjoyment as much as if they were children.

A few steps lead up to the door of the hall, which is a large room on the ground floor with galleries running round it. It is quadrilateral in shape, and lighted by high windows; whilst the stage, concealed by a curtain, takes up an entire side. The whole floor is divided into uniform little squares, resembling a chessboard, and are what we should call boxes. The roomiest and most luxuriously appointed are on the upper tier, and an amphitheatre above that is consigned to the minor aristocracy. In the centre is a small platform, from which the whole hall can

SAMURAI CHILD, FOLLOWED BY HIS SISTER CARRYING THE SWORD OF A YOUNG GENTLEMAN.

be seen at a glance, and where a sort of overlooker watches to keep order. In front of the stage, to the left, is the choir and the orchestra, composed of drums, flutes, and three-stringed guitars. The musicians, clothed in priestly garments in remembrance of the first ballets dedicated to the gods, hardly cease playing for an instant, either for the enlivenment of the audience between the acts, or for the accompaniment of the recitatives during the performance. The imperturbability of the Japanese character is more than ever evident, when fifteen hundred persons can listen for twelve hours at a stretch to this horrible squeaking with apparent satisfaction.

Two long boarded platforms, joining the stage on each side, and on a level with the boxes, stretch the whole length of the hall. The actors make frequent use of them in their entrances and exits, although under the very noses of the spectators. The boxes are only divided by a wooden partition, upon which a ledge is placed to form a path for the waiters, who are most assiduous in supplying the wants of the audience. They hand cushions about, attend to the braziers, or offer refreshments and various dainties between the acts, which they cry in the nasal tone of voice peculiar to the profession in all countries. Each box holds four persons, who face each other and look sideways at the stage. In the middle is a little brazier, at which they constantly light their small copper pipes, at the same time partaking of some slight refreshment. But in spite of these distractions, they bestow great attention upon the play.

Popular Applause. 215

On the entrance of a favourite actor the crowd is electrified. Cries that no combination of consonants could accurately render are heard, here and there unequally prolonged, like the sound of a shower of stones. Sometimes it is a general and momentary explosion; but during the performance itself Japanese audiences are very apathetic, and the only thing that will rouse them is the exaggerated acting of some popular player. In pathetic scenes they never applaud, but merely give quiet signs of approbation.

Although belonging to the lowest ranks of society, these actors are the objects of intense admiration, and are very often entirely supported by some of their ardent admirers. Instances have been known of an actor at his death being mourned by the whole population, and magnificently interred by public subscription. The fixed salary of the greatest actor rarely exceeds two hundred pounds per annum; but it is usual for them to participate in the profits made by their performances. A few play gratis, being sufficiently satisfied with the honour of becoming known to the public.

The only women allowed upon the stage are those belonging to that class whence the singers, dancers, and joros are taken. It is considered profanation to bring any of the privacy of family life before the public. The legitimate wife, mother, or daughter has full liberty to occupy herself as she pleases in her amusements or duties; but any exhibition of feeling, either at home or abroad, or the smallest expression of the sentiment of love, is regarded as quite abhorrent by even the least refined

N

minds. The female parts are generally, therefore, undertaken by men, who, by the aid of ample robes and extensive head-dresses, manage very successfully to conceal their harsher features and forms. It is their voices which betray them; instead of the soft tones of a woman, the ear is jarred by a strained and nasal utterance, which vilifies without disguising the masculine organ.

The scenic arrangements of Japanese theatres are superior to those of China, and are far in advance of those of the Shaksperean period. In the painting of the scenes, the perspective, as in all Japanese drawings, is peculiar, but the accessories, at any rate, are exact, and, it may be said, are even very true to nature. The shifting of the scenes is worked by means of a turn-table, such as those seen at our railway stations. The scene represented is in the form of a semi-circle, which revolves upon a pivot, and at a given signal turns slowly round, bearing with it all the actors, who continue their action till out of sight. The reverse side shows a fresh set of people already engaged in conversation or variously occupied. But by far the most unique arrangement on the Japanese stage is the presence of an individual whom we can only denominate the Shadow. He is clothed entirely in black, wears a black cowl, and stands close behind the actor, whom he never takes his eye off for an instant, and whose every movement he follows as though he were his reflection. He hands him all the little accessories he is in need of, and places a small stool at the right moment for him to sit upon and prevent the inconvenient posture of squatting.

Exaggerated Acting.

The eye cannot at first accustom itself to this black form stalking so silently about the boards; but in a theatre all is so conventional that the quaint impression soon wears away, and, once admitted, this shadow certainly fills a most useful part. Amongst other services, when the day wanes, he holds a lighted candle at the end of a stick under the nose of the actor, to render his gestures and features distinguishable.

A traveller records that he once put the following question to a celebrated actor—" Why do you thunder so with your voice, and use such exaggerated action in your tragic parts; surely it is not thus a daimio or soldier would speak or act?" "No," he answered; "but if we comported ourselves upon the stage like the world in general, who could recognise that we were heroes?" This response embodies the secret of dramatic and scenic art in Japan. They feel instinctively that, above the common level of human passions, others far nobler and higher exist, which, therefore, must belong to the domain of the drama; and these it is they seek and strive to represent. In a word, they are searching after an ideal; but it is in the pursuit of it that they go astray. The simple beauty of the Greek drama has never been recognised in the far East, where the conception of a superior world can only be interpreted by the irrational magnifying of the real. Beyond the trivialities of daily life, they can only imagine the monstrous; thus they think to find beauty in enormity, and to excite admiration by causing stupor and astonishment. The actors out-do the authors in this matter. It is not sufficient to expend their lamentations or their fury in interminable monologues, but they emphasise and deliver them with the most insupportable exaggeration. Their action is equally forced and unnatural. To represent rage, the actor foams at the mouth, roars, throws himself about, falls exhausted to the ground, to rise again with renewed expressions of fury; he shows his teeth, rolls his eyes, plucks out whole handfuls of hair from his head, writhes in frightful convulsions, then taking a moment's breath he abandons himself again to fresh paroxysms of rage, till at length the curtain falls to interrupt a pantomime seemingly without end, which has worn out the actor before the public even begins to weary.

Sometimes, on the contrary, the entrance of a new arrival causes the enthusiast suddenly to restrain himself, and the next moment beholds him resuming the conversation in a perfectly calm tone, quietly squatting on his heels, chatting and smoking in the most natural manner in the world. The same spirit which makes them so faithfully represent all the minor details of familiar scenes in their tragedies, produces situations of indescribable horror. The head of the murdered adversary is infallibly seen to roll upon the ground; every agony is prolonged, simply in order that the cries and groans of a suffering purely physical may be heard by the attentive audience.

As a matter of course, it would be impossible that this excessive mimicry could be sustained without a break for the whole day; the acts are, therefore, interspersed with little episodes of genuine comedy, rather prosaic, perhaps, in conception, but sparkling with humour, and acted throughout with a comic faithfulness that convulses an audience perfectly callous to the most heart-stirring scenes of tragedy. They certainly have the advantage of being written in the popular dialect, and are therefore comprehensible to the educated and uneducated alike; whereas tragedies are only written in the loftiest and most stilted style, which is intelligible to comparatively few.

Although the exaggerated and realistic character of Japanese art has caused tragedy thus to degenerate into melodrama, it has not had the effect of transforming comedy into mere farce; on the contrary, this inferior branch of the drama has here reached a very high stage of perfection, and has many striking qualities. The European who attends one of these little plays, perhaps out of curiosity only, is astonished at the hearty enjoyment it has given him. The subjects are all borrowed from family life; the characters are finely drawn and well rendered; and the action, which is not impeded by a straining after historical fidelity as in the drama, proceeds with greater force and unity. The accuracy of the characters is even strengthened by the substitution of every-day mortals and their ordinary passions for the legendary types and grand conventional sentiments of tragedy. In fact, these playwrights of Yedo possess an instinctive talent for the definition of the niceties of character so striking in its precise truthfulness, that it places them quite on a par with our best comedians. They possess the comic vein also in a very high degree, and have the gift of seizing upon the ridiculous, and of bringing into prominence the grotesque side of humanity.

To show that their women are sometimes credited with nobler feelings than they are usually supposed to possess, a French traveller, M. Bousquet, describes at length a Japanese comedy in which a woman plays the principal part. O'Haré, as she is called, is passionately attached to and loved by a married man, Djiye by name; but at the piteous entreaty of her rival, the legitimate wife, O'Haré heroically sacrifices her own inclinations and feelings to restore peace to the heart and hearth of the neglected spouse. She feigns inconstancy with such art that her lover, indignant at her apparent fickleness, throws her over and returns home, where it is presumed happiness will reign for ever after; and several essentially comic scenes are skilfully managed by the absurd jealousy of a rejected admirer of O'Haré's. The misery of the latter, heart-broken at the loss of her lover, excites no commiseration in the breast of the audience, for she is only a woman and a gheko, and must, therefore, play the same subservient *rôle* upon the stage as in real life.

The Japanese theatres have, like ours, their green-room, side-scenes, and refreshment room; and, to the foreigner, the life which is here seen affords far more interest than the crowded hall or the pieces acted. In general, men only frequent the green-room, but sometimes female servants are seen bringing refreshments to some actor or female *artiste* employed as a dresser. Although the whole room is crammed, the Japanese habit of extreme courteousness is never forgotten, and every one does his best to maintain order. Various groups are scattered about; here are a lot of musicians refreshing themselves till the manager summons them to their post again; there are a couple of comedians rehearsing the different *poses* and gestures which in a few moments are to excite the admiration of the public; whilst another, squatting before a mirror, puts the finishing touches of paint to his face, and adjusts more exactly his feminine head-gear. In the wings, carpenters are hurrying backwards and forwards with different portions of framework for use in the shifting of the scenes, or the artificer arranges his apparatus for the fireworks and clouds of flame which will shortly astonish the audience; and the play still drags slowly on to the noise of drums, and amidst the conversation of the audience and the desultory chatter of unoccupied actors. In the refreshment room the confusion seems inextricable. There, all except the servants are squatting in groups upon mats, each more or less clothed according to his individual taste. It must be explained that, though the large sash is indispensable, the other garments are merely considered as accessories, to be donned or laid aside at pleasure, dependent on the different degrees of temperature. Some are eating and drinking, and, indeed, a good basin of fish-soup and a bowl of rice are by no means to be despised after three or four hours of continued acting; others content themselves with a few cups of tea, and in smoking, playing draughts, backgammon, or dice. During the interval, a man furnished with a beautifully polished box makes his appearance. This box is divided into four compartments, containing red, blue, black, and white sand. These he casts separately or together upon the floor, as a sower sows his seed, producing coloured designs of flowers and birds, and in conclusion, amidst the noisy laughter of the assembly, amorous subjects worthy of the secret chamber of Pompeii. The accuracy of the drawing and the harmony of colour in these sand-pictures, executed in so strange a fashion and in so short a time, is most remarkable.

It is not a rare thing to see the restaurant itself transformed for the nonce into a theatre. The singers come and install themselves there regardless of the noise, and give some of their most popular songs and melodies. The listeners chat and laugh with them, but they never exceed the strictest bounds of propriety, unless, indeed, they have been persuaded to imbibe too freely of the spirituous liquor saki; then, sometimes, their excitement momentarily leads them astray. Dances, or rather pantomimes, succeed the songs, the subjects of which are generally on the sentiment of love. These women are very often young and pretty; their attitudes are full of grace, though perhaps sometimes a little extravagant. They wear a silk robe, confined by a sash of various colours, and when acting they change their apparel several times. The conversation carried on by the frequenters of these restaurants appears to be inexhaustible. They argue, criticise, talk scandal, and gossip about every great or little topic of the day; and traces of a movement which marks the spirit of the times may be discovered in songs of the following description, which are frequently to be heard—" Ah! .that I could travel by telegraph, for the jinrikisha is so slow; it drags along so wearily; it bruises one's limbs, and crushes one when it is overturned." These are the echoes of young Japan's progress,—imitation of all things European, and contempt of all things native.

Suddenly the gong sounds; it is the signal for a grand performance by the mountebanks during one of the interludes. Now the restaurant completely changes its aspect. Its present occupants hasten back to their seats in the theatre, and are succeeded by dramatists, *literati*, patrons, and *dilettantes* of the Sibaïa, who, with their wives, meet together to refill the deserted rooms. The conversation now takes quite another character; nothing is talked of but literature and art. The restaurant is transformed into an academy. These meetings serve as invaluable training schools for young writers; for it is here that authors of established repute go through the salutary ordeal of public discussion upon their works, and that doctrines and received traditions undergo a revision which operates gently but irresistibly in the domain of letters, and even in the sphere of religious institutions.

Night has arrived before the play is concluded. The streets, all fantastically illuminated, assume a most extraordinary aspect. Every one is provided with a paper lantern, upon which is engraved, in large characters, the name of the proprietor, or, painted in Indian ink, his armorial bearings. The tea-houses are closed. Little by little the noise ceases ; the number of lanterns diminish ; the streets become almost deserted, and a profound silence reigns, broken only from time to time by the night watchmen, who perambulate the different districts of the town provided with a club and paper lantern.

The slumber of the inhabitants of Yedo, however, is very frequently disturbed by the ominous knell of the tocsin. It is sounded by a watchman from one of the thousand towers which overlook the temples or principal residences ; he has perceived a fire, and rings for aid. The signal of alarm is repeated in every direction ; the houses are opened, and the inmates hurry out, ask excited questions of passers-by, rush towards the threatened quarter, or climb upon the roof to discover the direction of the danger they are in search of. The fire is still some way off, but, fed by the highly inflammable materials used in the construction of Japanese houses, it advances rapidly. It is no longer a house that is burning ; it is a street, and soon an entire district is in flames. The precautions for the safety of life and property are conducted with great activity and intelligence ; but they are powerless in the presence of such an enemy as they are struggling to subdue, and the only thing finally effectual in arresting the progress of the conflagration is to make a large empty space by the destruction of several buildings.

NIGHT WATCHMAN.

JAPAN. p. 225.

CHAPTER XV.

Popular Superstitions in Japan—The Demon Cat—A Baffled Guard—The Courageous Volunteer—The Enchantress Foiled—A Tragic End—A Rat-hunt—Commemoration—Story of the Fox-cub—A Marvellous Cure—The Fox-god.

BEFORE entering into the subject of the domestic life of the Japanese, we may here give some account of the many curious superstitions which exist in the popular mind. Of course Japan has its complement of ghosts and goblins, good fairies and malicious ghouls. What nation has yet existed without developing in the course of its history a goodly literature of the elfin land of fairy romance? It is a curious circumstance that, among nearly all nations, the same animals are associated with the power of assuming the uncanny shapes of men and women. The cat and the fox may be taken as typical specimens, and in Japan there is an abundance of alarming stories told of the various devilish deeds done by these same animals. The badger, which exists in considerable numbers in Japan, also comes in for its share of popular superstition; and many are the tales told around the country firesides of the strange spells which these animals have put forth to lure too confident man to his own destruction. The cat is very often associated with legends of faithfulness and devotion to man. It follows faithfully the steps of its mistress, or devours some venomous rat which was about to bite her with its poisoned fang. Often, however, it is connected with darker deeds, with acts of bloody sorcery; and one such story is preserved in the traditions of the family of the Prince of Hizen, one of the principal Daimios of Japan. This legend may be correctly termed

"The Story of the Demon Cat."

The Prince of Hizen had broad lands and great possessions, and all things smiled upon him, so that he was very happy. As is usual in Japan, he had more wives than one; but as is the custom, not only in Japan but all the world over, he loved one in particular. Once he was walking in his garden with this favourite wife, who was both young and beautiful. It was the spring of the year; the birds sang on the boughs, the blossoms gave out their sweet scent, the air was fresh and balmy, and the minds of the prince and his dear wife were filled with indescribable happiness. After a while they walked back to the castle. They did not look behind them as they went, but if they had, they might have seen a monstrous black cat with two tails, marking thereby its infernal origin, skulking after them through the trees and shrubs. The cat entered the palace unobserved, found its way into the wife's bedroom, and, to make a long story short, waited for its opportunity, seized the poor woman in its murderous fangs when it found her alone, and quickly devoured her. Having swallowed her, it instantly assumed her personal appearance—became *her*, in fact, so that the prince himself had not the slightest idea of the foul wrong that had been done to him. And he talked and slept with her, and knew her not from his beautiful wife. But a wonderful change began to be seen in the appearance of the poor prince. His eye grew dim, the colour fled from his cheeks, his gait grew feeble and tottering, the flesh was fast disappearing from his bones. All his council viewed the change with terror and dismay. It was daily becoming evident that some deadly sorcery was acting against his health and his life. But none could so much as guess at the real cause. The bonzes were consulted, but the high priest was of no more use in staying the sorcerer's hand than the conclave of court physicians. Clearly the case was desperate.

Now it had been observed that the prince was always much worse in the mornings, and it was resolved that a watch should be held all night in his sleeping chamber. So a number of their lord's retainers, men of rank and position, were chosen and appointed to the solemn duty of keeping watch over their master during the night vigils. They did so, and with what effect? Every night, exactly at ten o'clock, the foul enchantress, in the form of his wife, stole gently into his bedroom, and instilled a poison into his bones by her caresses. Yet the guard did not perceive this, for the enchantress had power over them also, and cast a deep sleep on them, so that they were all unaware of her presence. Thus the prince grew worse and worse; and the high priest, as well he might, began to tremble for his reputation.

One night he was sitting wrapt in deep thought, looking out of his study, when he saw a young soldier bathing in the clear light of the moon. After having performed his ablutions, he engaged in prayer in audible tones for the recovery of the prince his master. The high priest was touched at such devotion, and spoke to him. The soldier expressed great anxiety to be allowed to form one of the body of watchers who kept nightly vigil over the prince. Could it be allowed? Apparently not; for the man was but a common soldier, and not of rank high enough to allow him to enter the princely presence. But as the poor lord was getting rapidly worse, all considerations of etiquette were waived, and the faithful soldier was duly installed as one of the watch.

His first night came, and with beating heart he took his place. Ten o'clock approached, and the guard, one by one, began to drop over into the region of dreams. Even he felt the drowsiness of enchantment taking silent possession of his faculties. And now let the reader mark the personal devotion to superiors which has been so distinguishing a feature of Japan in its past history. What did the good soldier do to keep himself awake? He drew his dagger and stuck it in his thigh, and then laid below him a piece of oiled paper, for fear his blood might soil the floor of the apartment! The pain kept him awake for a time, but as the effect was beginning to wear off, he took hold of the dagger and moved it in the wound, thus causing him the most excruciating pain. This had its effect; he had earned distinction, and was now wide awake. And sure enough the door opened gently, and in walked the enchantress, richly clad, and filling the room with her dazzling beauty. She stole forward and bent over the prince. "How does my lord?" she murmured. The prince raised his languid eyes and answered with a feeble smile. But she suddenly turned round, for she felt there was some one awake, and her eyes fell full on the young soldier sitting in the corner with the dagger stuck in his thigh. "Ha! how comes it that you are awake?" she said. The soldier glared at her, and pointed at the dagger. The enchantress was foiled; she could do nothing with a waking man in the room, and so she glided out as noiselessly as she had entered.

Morning came; the guard awoke, and lo! the young soldier had been awake all the night, and had seen the enchantress; but as yet none knew that she was not the prince's wife. Next night came, and he still kept himself awake by self-inflicted agonies. The enchantress came, and, finding herself still watched, she departed. And the joy was great, for the prince was growing better, daily and visibly improving. All properly attributed the change to the young soldier, and his fame began to spread over the whole country.

When the prince was almost completely better, a council was held under the presidency of the high priest, and it was resolved that to the young soldier should be committed the task of slaying the princess, as an enchantress who had conspired the prince's death. He found the royal lady in her chamber, and she turned fiercely on him, and ordered him out of her presence as a base scullion and a low-born wretch. But the hero was not so to be turned aside from his purpose. He drew his sword and made a plunge at her; whereupon, seeing that he was determined to make an end of her, she suddenly changed into the monstrous cat that she really was, and made a bound at the window. In spite of the quickness of her pursuer, she escaped and made good her way to the hills. Here she did great hurt by devouring, in her rage, both man and beast. But the prince instituted a grand hunt, at which the cat was killed and captured. Such was the tragic end of the Bloody Cat!

The popular idea seems to be that the cat has the power of assuming the personality of any human being it chooses, and of so deceiving friends and relatives. Thus another common story tells how a certain young lady was always followed about by a tame cat. So persistently did the animal keep on all occasions close by its mistress that her parents grew alarmed. They began to suspect that the cat had assumed the personality of some wicked enchanter who had fallen in love with their daughter, and that it was about to cast a spell upon her. They accordingly proceeded to drive the animal from about their place, when, by a miraculous interposition of the gods, the cat was suddenly endowed with the power of speech. It turned upon its pursuers, and informed them that a monstrous rat, which had its home in a neighbouring barn, had taken a violent fancy for the young lady, and would have long since exerted its baneful powers upon her had it not been for the ceaseless vigilance of the speaker—the faithful and devoted cat. The parents were thunderstruck at thus hearing the cat address them in their native tongue, and began to devise plans by which the rat might be destroyed. "Your plans will all be in vain," said the cat; "the rat will not come forth so long as you are in the vicinity. It has the craft of its kind, and knows how to elude human beings; but there is a cat belonging to your neighbour" (mentioning a farmer who lived near), "and I believe, if he were to join me, we would be able to kill the rat."

The terrified couple agreed at once, and the following night the two cats joined and held a watch. The neighbours gathered from all sides at the news of this extraordinary rat-hunt, and the greater part of the night was spent in keeping a solemn vigil at a proper distance. At length a low growling was heard, then the noise of a scuffle, which grew louder and louder, the shrill screams of the cats, and the unearthly sounds uttered by the demon rat, forming a compound which made the teeth of the listeners chatter with terror and their blood curdle in their veins. At length the tumult began to abate, and it being impossible to tell which side had been victorious, the excitement of the crowd broke through the bounds of reserve; they rushed in to the scene of the conflict, and there beheld a gory spectacle. The rat was lying, but not dead, the blood still oozing from its swollen veins. The two cats were on their haunches, gazing at their enemy in a state of great exhaustion. The people cut the throat of the rat, which turned out to be of supernatural dimensions, and brought away both cats. Yet though they bore no mark of wound or scar upon their persons, they both began to sink rapidly. No restoratives had the slightest effect upon them; the spell of the rat had begun to do its work, and in a short time they were both numbered with the ghosts of departed cats. But the people were not unmindful of the great services that these faithful creatures had rendered them at the cost of their own lives. Every year a great feast is held in the district to commemorate the self-sacrifice of the faithful cats, and toasts are drunk in honour of the animals that destroyed the monster who plotted the ruin of a peaceful household.

We have mentioned the fox as another of the animals which has the power of assuming the external appearance of a human body. That this power may be exercised for the purpose of benefiting humanity, the following story, which we may entitle "The Marvellous Cure," will serve to exemplify.

It happened, one bright day in early spring, that two Japanese friends of the *bourgeois* class were out on the mountain to spend a holiday. As they were wandering about among the fragrant shrubs enjoying the fresh air of the country, they suddenly spied, a short distance away, two old foxes playing with their young one in the bright sunshine. The innocent gambols of the unconscious animals were so pleasing that the two friends stood struck with admiration. Presently they observed a number of young urchins, who had also observed the foxes at play, and were now stealing up to intercept them in their retreat to their den. These naughty boys carried sticks, with which they beat off the old foxes, and then they proceeded to tie the limbs of the young one together, and to carry it off in triumph. At this juncture the two citizens interposed, and demanded to know where the boys were taking the fox to. They answered that they were taking it to a man who had asked them to catch him one, and had offered them a sum of money for it. One of the friends, being naturally of a kind heart, was grieved to see the poor little cub so cruelly tied and treated, so he offered the boys twice the money which they expected to get on their return. The bargain was concluded, and the cub handed over to its purchaser. The kindly man, who had thus interposed to save the life of a dumb brute, showed his kindness still more by the manner in which he treated the fox when it had become his property. He gave it to eat of the provisions which he had brought to regale himself and his friend; he stroked it on the back; he took it in his arms and cherished it. After a time he began to observe that the old foxes were looking at him from the other side of a bunch of ferns, and he thought he could perceive in their silent countenances their sense of grati-

tude for the kindness with which he had treated their
offspring. Antagonistic feelings began to hold a warfare
in his breast. Would he take the fox home with him, and
make it a household pet, to be the delight of his family
and the envy of his neighbours? Would he keep it as a
perpetual safeguard against the possible enmity of the
whole generation of foxes? or would he restore it to the
parents who were now looking at him with such beseeching
eyes? Pity and natural affection prevailed. He released
the cub, which darted off like the wind, and, at a bound,
was once more fawning upon its father and mother.

Now it so happened that this good man had a son who
was very ill. The physicians could do nothing for him;
they tried all their drugs and potent philters, but in vain.
At last his parents were told that nothing but a live fox's
liver could cure the malady. A fox was searched for, but
in vain; the cunning animals had all hidden themselves
in their dens, and were nowhere to be found. Meanwhile
the poor boy continued to sink rapidly, when one evening,
just as his friends were giving up all hope, the man whom
they had commissioned to get the fox's liver for them
called and handed in the prescribed cure. The parents were
overjoyed, and pressed the man to accept their hospitality.
He thanked them, but was sorry he could not; a friend
was expecting him. So he departed. The liver was ad-
ministered, and, sure enough, the boy began to mend.
When he was convalescent, the same man who had brought
the liver called again to say how sorry he was that he had
been unable to get one for them. The poor people began

to thank him for the liver he *had* brought. But he denied all knowledge of it, asserting most positively that he had hunted far and wide, but had never been able to capture a fox. Both parties were, as might naturally be expected, much astonished; the presumed benefactor going away wondering what good angel had taken his place, and the overjoyed parents abashed at having thanked a man who protested that he had done nothing for them. The same night, as the good man lay in bed, a woman appeared to him in a dream, and spoke to him after the following manner:—" I am the mother of the young fox which you saved from cruel boys. The foxes do not forget a kindness, and they know how to return a benefit. It was rumoured abroad among our tribe that a fox's liver was the only remedy for your son's disease; and I am now come to tell you that my partner and myself killed our own offspring in order that you might be recompensed for your good deed. My husband called at your house disguised as a fox-hunter, and I have thus come to unravel to you the mystery." So astonished was the honest burgher that he sprang up in his bed, and in doing so he awoke. The woman had fled, but he now knew the meaning of the mystery. In his excitement he had awaked his wife, to whom he explained the purport of his vision. They were both smitten with admiration and gratitude to the gods for having thus put it into the minds of the foxes to save the life of their son. They rose from their bed, and spent the night worshipping before the family shrine; and when the morning dawned, they told their dear boy how the goodness of the gods and the gratitude of the foxes had rescued him from the jaws of death. And the boy grew up healthy and strong, and became a tall man; nor did he forget what he owed to the foxes, for he reared a costly temple to the fox-god, Juari-Sama, and there he might often be seen bending reverently before the altar, and thanking Heaven for the goodness of the dumb creation.

SPINNING.

CHAPTER XVI.

Physical Appearance of the Japanese—Married Customs—Female Costumes—Unhealthiness—Extraordinary Cures—Acupuncture and Cauterisation—The *Yashkis*, or Palaces—Palace of the Tycoons—Cheerful Dwellings—The "Lily" Tradition—Park-like Grounds.

THE Japanese are much of the same type as the Spaniards and the inhabitants of the south of France. They are of middle stature; the men about five feet six inches in height, while the women rarely exceed five feet; the difference in height between the sexes being greater than in Europe. When dressed, the Japanese look strong, well-proportioned men; but when in the exceedingly slight costumes which they very often are pleased to adopt, it is then apparent that though their bodies are robust, their legs are short and slight. Their heads are very much out of proportion to their bodies, being generally large, and sunk a little between the shoulders; but they have small feet, and pretty, delicate hands. The resemblance the Japanese bear to the Chinese is much less marked than is usually supposed; the faces of the former are longer, and on the whole more regular, their noses are more prominent, and their eyes less sloped. The men are naturally very hirsute, but they never wear beards; their hair is glossy, thick, and always black; their eyes are equally dark, their teeth white and slightly prominent. The shade of their skin is totally unlike the yellow complexions of the Chinese; in some cases it is very swarthy or copper-coloured, but the most general tint is an olive brown. Children and young people have usually quite pink complexions.

The women follow the Chinese type much more distinctly. The eyes are narrower and sloped upwards, and the head is small. Like the men, their hair is glossy and very black, but it never reaches the length of European women's hair. They have clear, sometimes even perfectly white skins, especially among the aristocracy; oval faces, and slender, graceful forms. Their manners are peculiarly artless, and often remarkably elegant. But the harmony of the whole is spoiled by an ugly depression of the chest, which is observable in the handsomest and best-formed amongst them.

Custom obliges the married women to shave off their eyebrows and blacken their teeth—a sacrifice they submit to more heroically than would be supposed, for they are well aware that the power to charm does not entirely depend upon the possession of white teeth and finely-arched eyebrows. As a compensation, perhaps, they make a most immoderate use of paint. Their brow, cheeks, and neck are covered with thick coats of rouge and white; the "fast" ones even go so far as to gild their lips, which is certainly no embellishment, but the more modest are content to colour them with carmine.

The *kirimon*, a kind of long open dressing-gown, is

TYPES OF BOURGEOIS CLASS.

JAPAN.—p. 240.

Peculiar Costumes.

worn by every one, men and women alike. It is a little longer and of better quality for the women, who cross it in front, and confine it by a long wide piece of silk or material tied in a quaint fashion at the back. The men keep theirs in its place by tying a long straight scarf round them. The Japanese use no linen, the women alone wearing a chemise of silk crêpe; but it must be borne in mind that they have a daily bath, and that simplicity is affected by all. The middle classes, however, wear, in addition to the kirimon, a doublet and pantaloons, which are easily laid aside when desirable; these are also worn in winter by men of the lower orders, the pantaloons fitting tightly and made of checked cotton. The peasants and porters usually wear a loose overall in summer, made of

JAPANESE PORTER.

some light paper material, and in winter not unfrequently consisting of coarse straw, as shown in the illustration opposite. The women also envelop themselves in one or several thickly-wadded mantles. Linen gloves, with one division for the thumb, are very generally worn. Sandals are made of plaited straw, and in bad weather are discarded for wooden clogs, raised from the ground by means of two little bits of wood under the foot and heel. As might naturally be expected, locomotion under such circumstances is performed with difficulty, and the hobbling gait which these props necessitate has often been commented on. This peculiarity is most noticeable among the fair sex in Japan, whose naturally easy gait is almost as much diverted from its normal movement by these small stilts as that of their sisters in the West by high-heeled shoes. The costume of the country is exactly alike for both the lower and the higher classes, with the difference that the latter always wear silk materials; this custom has, however, become much less general since the arrival of Europeans, which has occasioned a far greater demand for the product, and consequent rise in the price.

The women dress tastefully and even coquettishly. The Comte de Beauvoir thus describes them:—" They are charming; they arrange their jet-black hair in three large divisions, fastened together by ornamental pins; they are laughing, bright, lively, and rosy, a little like painted tallow, especially when they take it into their heads to daub themselves with purple or to gild their lips. They trot along upon their little wooden sandals, enveloped in a

PEASANT'S WINTER DRESS OF STRAW.

loose wrapper, which they fasten or not as they like. A thick green or scarlet sash tied in an enormous bow about a foot square at the back, and resembling a cartridge-box in shape, gives them a pretty quaint look, which is very fascinating."

The costumes worn by officials and those of the Mikado's suite are distinguished by the amplitude of the folds and the richness of the texture. Wide floating pantaloons are often substituted for the kirimon, which trail on the ground, completely concealing the feet, and give the wearer the appearance of walking on his knees—such, in fact, is the delusion it is intended to produce. A kind of overcoat, with wide sleeves reaching to the hips, completes the costume.

The excessive cleanliness of the Japanese, the simplicity of their apparel, which allows their bodies to be so much exposed to the open air, added to the salubrity of their country, might reasonably lead one to imagine that they enjoy excellent health. Such, however, is not the case; several travellers tell us that diseases of the skin, and chronic and incurable complaints, are very prevalent. The hot baths are the great remedies for everything; but in certain cases the aid of the physicians is always called in. These form a society, which has existed from a very early date, and enjoys certain privileges. They are divided into three classes: the court physicians, who are not permitted to practice elsewhere; the army physicians, who occasionally give their services to civilians; and, lastly, the common physicians or doctors not employed by Govern-

JAPANESE COURT DRESS.

ment, and who attend all classes of the community. As no formalities are required for the practice of medicine, each member enters on the career at his pleasure, and practices according to his own theories on the subject. It is a profession often handed down from father to son, but it is not a lucrative one, and is looked upon as an office of little importance or consideration.

Medical men nevertheless abound in Japan; and in addition to recognised practitioners, there is a class of quacks exactly answering to those of our own country. Their science principally partakes of the nature of sorcery, and their remedies necessitate the accomplishment of various preliminary ceremonies more or less peculiar. When hot baths fail to produce the desired effect, they have recourse to acupuncture and a kind of cauterisation. Acupuncture consists in pricking with a needle the part affected—a mode of healing which has been practised from time immemorial in the East. Any kind of needle is used, provided it is very fine, polished, and exceedingly sharp-pointed. Those employed by the Japanese are rarely of gold or silver, as they pretend to maintain; they are more often of steel manufacture, and imported from Holland. After the skin has been stretched sufficiently tight, the needle is thrust in perpendicularly, either by rolling it between the fingers, by a direct gentle pressure, or else by striking it lightly with a small hammer made for the purpose.

Cauterisation is performed with little cones called *moxas*, formed of dried wormwood leaves, and prepared in such a manner as to consume slowly. One or more of these is applied to the diseased part and set alight. This mode of cauterising wounds has frequently the effect of strongly exciting the nervous system, while it only changes the seat of irritation, and produces eruptions of the skin.

As an aid to medical knowledge, they have little anatomical models in cardboard, painted a flesh-colour, upon which the spinal column and other salient points of the human frame are distinctly marked with characters or numbers attached to them, corresponding with similar numbers in a book which contains a full and detailed account of every disease that especial part is addicted to, and instructions how to prick or cauterise it, and how often. Nearly every Japanese family possesses this species of medical manual, and such is the reputation of the remedies therein recommended, that many people make use of them at fixed periods and as preventatives.

The simplicity the Japanese affect in their dress is also carried out in the arrangements of the houses. Those of the middle class are much the same in construction as the nobles, but they differ in the internal disposition. They are rarely more than thirty feet high, and are mostly composed of one story only, occasionally two, but then the ground floor, which is very low, serves only as a larder for provisions. The frequent earthquakes in Japan are the reason why they build in this manner; but although their edifices do not equal ours in solidity or elevation, they are by no means inferior in cleanliness and accommodation. Almost all of them are built of wood; the ground floor is

The Royal Palace.

raised about four feet above the ground; the walls are made of planks, covered with coarse mats, joined together with great art; the roof, which is also boarded in, is supported by four pillars. In a two-storied house, the second story is generally built much more solidly than the first; experience having shown that the edifice can thus better resist the shock of an earthquake. Sometimes the walls are plastered with a coating of soft clay or varnish, and are decorated with gildings and paintings. Instead of these, at the back and front of many of the houses, simple panels, covered with paper and moving in grooves, are substituted.

The *yashkis*, or palaces in which the people of rank reside, are no more than ordinary houses grouped together, and surrounded by whitewashed outhouses with latticed windows of black wood. These outhouses serve a twofold purpose, viz., as habitations for the domestics, and as a wall of enclosure. Always low, and, if the ground allows, rectangular, they look very much like warehouses or barracks.

The palace of the sovereign is merely a yashki of larger dimensions; it has, however, a certain character of its own, resembling the style of architecture in which the Kami temples are built. It is a perfect labyrinth of courts and streets formed by the many separate houses, pavilions, and corridors, or simple wooden partitions. The roofs—which are the exact counterpart of those of the temples—are supported by horizontal beams, varnished white or gilded at the extremities, and decorated with small pieces of sculpture, many of which are very beautiful works of art. The corridors uniting the houses are either of stone or wood, and roofed over with cement. The partitions are the same as those in the smaller dwellings; they are moveable, and have little bits of white paper pasted over them by way of ornament. Sometimes they are protected by a wooden grating. The shutters, originally of the natural colour of the wood, become of a clear grey or pale mahogany, according to age or species. The effect of the imperial palace as a whole is indescribable. The sombre, soft harmony of the colours; the beauty of the details; the finish of the decorations, which must be closely studied to be appreciated as they deserve; the exquisite taste, elegance, and noble simplicity dominant in these mysterious regions, make one utterly forget the barbarous character of the architecture.

The ancient palace of the Tycoons is, on the contrary, remarkable for boldness and richness of outline. The apartments, larger and finer, but otherwise a repetition of those in the Daimios' palaces, are especially noticeable for their elevation. Everything breathes the spirit of the times when the power and prosperity of the Tycoonate was at its height. Upon the ceilings of dead gold, sculptured beams cross each other in squares, the angles where they meet being marked by a plate of gilt bronze of very elegant design. The moveable partitions and the walls are decorated with bold and simple sketches of trees upon a foundation of gold.

A peculiar feature in the physiognomy of Japanese towns

INTERIOR OF JAPANESE HOUSE.

Interior of Dwellings.

is the fireproof storehouse, in which property of value is hastily placed by the owners in cases of fire or the typhoon, whilst they seek their own safety in flight. It is a sort of low wooden tower, cased with cement and plastered with black stucco. The windows are small, and closed by means of massive iron shutters.

All Japanese dwellings have a cheerful, well-cared-for appearance, which in a great measure is the result of two causes: first, that every one is bound constantly to renew the paper coverings of the outside panels; and secondly, that the frequent fires, which each time make immense ravages, often render it necessary to reconstruct an entire district. In the interior, the houses are generally divided into two suites of apartments; the one side being· apportioned to the women, who rarely show themselves, at least in the upper classes; the other side being used for the reception-rooms. These apartments are all separated the one from the other by partitions made of slight wooden frames, upon which little square bits of white paper are pasted; or else a kind of screen is used, which can be moved at pleasure, and the room enlarged or contracted according as the occasion requires. Towards nightfall these screens are usually folded up, so as to allow a free passage of air throughout the house.

But the greatest novelty in the eyes of foreigners are the gardens attached to every house. The smallest tradesman has his own little plot of ground, where he may enjoy the delights of solitude, take his siesta, or devote himself to copious potations of tea and saki. These gardens are often of exceedingly small proportions, and give the effect of a fairy park seen from a distance through the large end of a telescope. They consist of a quaint collection of dwarf shrubs, of a purple or dull green hue, extending their little distorted branches over miniature lakes full of gold-fish; liliputian walks in the middle of diminutive flower-beds; tiny streams, over which little green arches to imitate bridges are grown, just high enough for a rat to pass under; and, lastly, arbours or bowers beneath which a rabbit might just find room to nestle. Sometimes the roofs of the houses are covered with a thick crown of flowers, amongst which the favourite blue lilies abound in profusion.

"It is a charming sight," says the Comte de Beauvoir, "and the history of these gardens, suspended like a halo of loveliest azure on the tops of the slight pavilions, greatly surprised and interested me. It appears that from these blue lilies the Japanese distil the pale pink oil with which their women perfume their long black hair. There is a very quaint tradition extant regarding the cultivation of these lilies; it is supposed to have been an ancient decree of the Mikados, and is as follows:—

"'The goddess of the sun has given us the earth to cultivate in order that it may produce useful plants for the use of women, who are the ornaments of the hearth, and for the warriors who fight in the name of glory; you should therefore not cultivate any but useful plants! As to the lilies, which are emblems of women's luxury, the goddess forbids them to be reared upon the sacred soil,

Rustic Scenery.   251

but they may be sown upon the roofs of your houses, a place useless for other purposes; and at the same time that they beautify the hair of your women, they will be a living covering to your paternal roof.'"

In the suburbs, many of the houses stand in the midst of park-like grounds, in which are condensed all the charms of a diversified landscape—rocks, valleys, grottoes, fountains, and ponds being arranged, distributed, and combined in the most ingenious way. If these habitations are not sufficiently isolated by nature from the public gaze, the new enclosures are carefully surrounded by hedges, palisades, or by bamboo fences covered with creeping plants. If the garden opens into the street, a rustic bridge is thrown over the canal which is opposite the entrance gate, and this they conceal by clusters of trees or thick shrubs, so that on passing through the gate one might imagine oneself upon the borders of a virgin forest, and far from any human habitation.

FAC-SIMILE OF JAPANESE DRAWING.

CHAPTER XVII.

The Japanese Mat—Night-dress—Japanese Ideas of Cosiness—Clever Painting—Marriage Ceremonies—Curious Symbolism—Concubinage—Baptism—The Selection of a Name—Funeral Rites—Cremation and Sepulture—Carefully kept Cemeteries—Incapacity for Sorrow.

THE interior of a Japanese establishment is extremely simple, its scrupulous cleanliness forming its chief ornament. The rooms are usually low, and all are furnished with thick mats made of rice straw, plaited with the greatest neatness and regularity. They are about three inches thick, and soft to the touch; all are of the same size—six feet by three nearly. The inhabitants never soil them with their boots, but always walk bare-footed about the house. The mat in Japan answers the purpose of all ordinary furniture, and takes the place of our chairs, tables, and beds. For writing purposes only they use a low round table about a foot high, which is kept in a cupboard, and only brought out when a letter has to be written. This they do kneeling before the table, which they carefully put away again when the letter is finished. The meals are laid upon square tables of very slender dimensions, round which the whole family gather

JAPANESE FAMILY DINING.

sitting on their heels. At bed-time, thick coverlets of silk or cotton are spread upon the mats, and ample dressing-gowns of more or less costly materials.

When a Japanese has taken off his day-garments, he envelops himself in a warm, large night-dress, rests his head upon a wooden pillow, which is stuffed at the top, and in shape and dimensions resembles a flat iron, and so composes himself to sleep. Everything is put away in the morning in a sort of black cabinet, all the partitions opened to give air, the mats carefully swept, and the now completely empty chamber is transformed during the day into an office, sitting-room, or dining-room, to become again the sleeping apartment the following night.

There are, however, two pieces of furniture which are to be found in the houses of every class: these are the brazier and the pipe-box, for the Japanese is a great tea-drinker and a constant smoker. Every hour in the day his hot water must be ready for him, and the brazier is kept burning day and night both in summer and winter; it serves in addition to light his pipe, which he will fill and empty five or six times in as many minutes. To sit round the brazier and gossip and smoke with a select circle of friends is the only idea of cosiness this otherwise easy-going people seem to possess. The Japanese lounges through life; he only works to live, and only lives to enjoy existence. Oblivious of the bygone day, careless of the morrow, he regards life merely as the season for material enjoyments, and as a succession of hours, days, and years. Hence the absence of all domestic comforts which are the result of forethought. Another reason may be that the Japanese never make their house their home; it is nothing more to them than a resting-place, a temporary shelter, where they take refuge when external occupations are over.

The principal meal takes place about the middle of the day, and after it the family indulge themselves with several hours' sleep, so that at this time the streets are almost deserted. In the evening they have another meal, and then devote the rest of the time till bed-time to all kinds of amusements. In the highest Japanese circles, the dinner-hour is sometimes enlivened by music from an orchestra stationed in an adjoining room. Songs are now and then given; but they are most uninteresting and monotonous, being little beyond a constant repetition of the same theme.

When the table is cleared, pencils, large pieces of paper, brushes, and moist colours are produced, and every one sets to work to draw or paint. The Japanese have a

JAPANESE PAINTER.

marvellous faculty of doing anything with their hands both correctly and rapidly : a drawing is made in a few minutes. This is no doubt partly the result of constant practice; the artist has learned by heart a number of subjects, which he reproduces so often that it becomes at length almost mechanical, and one of these forms the foundation in the composition of every drawing he attempts. His various and separate treatments of them are, however, original. He tries to puzzle the lookers-on by the oddest combinations, to baffle them and leave them as long as possible in doubt as to the form his picture will take, until a last touch makes the whole thing clear. For example, he will commence by drawing a horse's head, then a man's, then other heads, then some hocks, feet, hands, legs, etc., all jumbled together in such a manner as to render it most difficult to discover the subject of the drawing. At the end, when every one has guessed in vain, the artist, with a few strokes of the pencil, joins all these heterogeneous members, and a group of horsemen is evolved out of the puzzle.

Other games succeed these *jeux d'esprit*, some of which are positively infantine for the Japanese have a regular passion for playthings, and a traveller relates having seen three generations, grandfather, father, and son, all intently occupied in flying a kite. One very fashionable game is played with fans. A small, light wooden box is placed upon a mat, and upon it an imitation butterfly, made of reed and covered with silk, is set. The players, sitting on their heels a short distance off, take aim at the insect by turns with their fans, the handles of which are to raise the butterfly without upsetting the box. The hits and misses are calculated according to a list which indicates the different methods of striking the butterfly.

This frivolity of character does not, however, distinguish the Japanese in the serious branches of life. All their domestic solemnities, marriage especially, are made subjects of deep and careful meditation. In the upper classes, a marriage is arranged between two young people when the bridegroom has reached his twentieth and the bride her sixteenth year. The wedding is preceded by the betrothal, a ceremony which offers an occasion for the several members of both families to meet together ; and it not unfrequently happens that the future couple then learn for the first time the wishes of their parents respecting their union. If, perchance, the bridegroom elect is not satisfied with his choice, the young lady returns home again. This inconvenient custom has little by little fallen into disuse. Now-a-days, if a young man wishes to marry into a family of good position, or one which it would be advantageous to his prospects to enter, he endeavours first to see the young lady, and then, if she pleases him, he sends a mediator, chosen usually from amongst his married friends, and the betrothal is arranged without any further obstacle.

Titsingh relates a curious custom which for some time was prevalent in certain Japanese provinces. Whoever entertained a preference for a young girl wrote his name upon a bit of wood, which he concealed somewhere in her house beneath the mats. By this means the fair damsel knew the number of her admirers, and the owner of the label she chose became the happy possessor of her hand.

The will of the parents is now almost without exception the dominating power in matrimonial arrangements, which are simply carried out as matters of business. Thus, when a Japanese, whose family consists of daughters only, is fortunate enough to marry one of them, her husband becomes his adopted son, assumes his name, and succeeds him in his business or in the administration of his affairs. The betrothal and wedding are usually solemnised on the same day, and without the assistance of any minister of worship. The customary ceremonies are all of a homely nature, but at the same time are extremely complicated and numerous.

Upon the day fixed, the trousseau of the young bride and all the presents she has received are brought to the house of her *fiancé*, where the ceremony is to be performed, and arranged in the apartments set apart for the ceremonial. The bride arrives soon afterwards in a norimon, dressed in white and escorted by her parents. The bridegroom, arrayed in gala costume, receives her at the entrance of the house, and conducts her into the hall where the betrothal takes place. Here grand preparations have been made. The altar of the domestic gods has been decorated with images of the patron saints of the family, and with different plants, each having its symbolical signification. When all have taken their places according to the recognised form of precedence, the ceremony is

begun by two young girls, who hand round unlimited
quantities of saki to the guests. These two damsels are
surnamed the male and female butterfly, the emblems of
conjugal felicity, because, according to popular notions,
butterflies always fly about in couples. The decisive
ceremony is tinged with a symbolism which has quite a
touch of poetry in it. The two butterflies, holding between
them a two-necked bottle, approach and offer it to the
engaged couple, who drink together from the two mouths
of the bottle till it is emptied. This signifies that husband
and wife must drain together the cup of life, whether it
contain ambrosia or gall; they must share equally the
troubles and sorrows of existence.

The Japanese is the husband of one wife only, but he
is at liberty to introduce several concubines under the
conjugal roof. This is done in all classes of society,
especially amongst the Daimios. They assure us that in
many of the noble families the legitimate wife not only
evinces no jealousy, but has even a certain pleasure in
seeing the number of her household augmented by this
mode, as it supplies her with so many additional servants.
But in the middle classes the custom is often the cause
of bitter family dissensions. The heavy expenses of the
marriage ceremonies also occasion great domestic misery,
at least if they are celebrated according to all the established conventionalities. Debts are then incurred which
perhaps the young couple are unable at the time to dis-
charge, so that when other expenses grow, and trouble or
misfortune overtake them, they are speedily plunged in

Baptism. 259

the deepest distress and indigence. The natural consequence of this arbitrary custom is that runaway matches frequently take place. The venial act, however, is usually wisely winked at by the parents, who feign great lamentations and anger, then finally assemble their neighbours, pardon their recreant children, circulate the inevitable saki, and the marriage is considered as legitimate as if performed with all the requisite formalities.

The birth of a child is another occasion for the meeting of the whole circle of relations, and the consumption of a great many more bumpers of saki. The baptism of the young Japanese citizen takes place thirty days later, when the infant is taken to the temple of the family divinity to receive its first name. The father has previously written three different names upon three separate bits of paper, which are handed over to the officiating bonze. The latter throws them into the air, and the piece of paper which in falling first touches the ground contains the name which shall be given to the child. There are no god-parents, but several friends of the family declare themselves the infant's protectors and make it several presents, among which is a fan if it be a boy, a pot of rouge if a girl.

The Japanese child is early taught to endure hardships, and is subjected from its infancy to all the small miseries and privations of life. The mother nurses it till it is two years of age, and carries it continually about with her, attached to her back for convenience. Education is not forced too early upon the children, but nature is allowed its own way during the first years of childhood. Toys, pleasures,

260 *Sceptical Notions.*

JAPANESE NURSE.

fêtes of all kinds are liberally indulged in, for the parents find as much enjoyment in them as the children. After three years of age they attend school, where ideas are inculcated which do not fail to influence them in the smaller details of their after life. They hear on all sides and in every form that existence is but an illusion, which one day will vanish, leaving no trace behind it—a philosophy which teaches them to regard life as merely a period for enjoyment, and death as a simple accident.

A Japanese attains his majority at fifteen years of age. As soon as the time has arrived he takes a new name, and quietly discards the pleasures of infancy for the duties of a practical life. His first care, if he belongs to the middle classes, is the choice of a trade or profession. He serves an apprenticeship, for a period of more or less duration, till he is fitted to pass from the workman into the master; and then it is he provides himself with a wife.

The Japanese are as strict in the observance of etiquette at their funeral as at their marriage ceremonials. These rites take place both at the time of the actual interment, and afterwards at the festivals celebrated in honour of the gods on these occasions. There are two kinds of funerals, interment and cremation. The majority of Japanese make known during life, either to their heir or some intimate friend, their wishes respecting their mode of sepulture.

When the father or mother in a family is seized with a mortal illness, and all hope of recovery is past and the end is approaching, they take off the soiled garments worn by the dying person and change them for perfectly clean ones. This duty is performed by men to one of their own sex, and by women if the sufferer be a woman. The last wishes of the dying one are then recorded on paper. As soon as life has departed, all the relations give way to lamentations; the body is carried into another room, covered with a curtain, and surrounded by screens. In the higher classes the body is watched for two days, but in the lower it is buried the day after death.

Contrary to the customs at marriage ceremonies, the bonzes preside over all the funeral rites. It is they who watch beside the dead until the time of interment. This is usually carried out by men who make it their profession;

they first carefully wash the corpse with tepid water, and then shave the head. It is then placed in a coffin somewhat of the shape of a round tub, in a squatting position, with the head bowed, the legs bent under, and the arms crossed; the lid of the coffin is then fastened down by wooden pegs. The funeral procession forms in the following order, and proceeds to the temple :—The bonzes march first, with their assistants, some carrying flags, others different symbols, such as little white boxes full of flowers, others ringing small hand-bells; then follows the corpse, preceded by a long tablet, upon which is inscribed the new name given to the deceased; the eldest son follows, and then the family, intimate friends, and domestics; the women follow last of all in norimons. The nearest relations are dressed in white, which is the colour worn for mourning. The men wear coarse straw hats; the women do their hair up with a comb only, using no other ornament.

When the procession arrives at the temple, where the priests are in readiness, the coffin is placed before the image of the god, and then various superstitious practices commence, the length of which is regulated by the rank of the deceased. After that, all the friends and acquaintances return home, whilst the relations hasten to the spot where the body is to be laid. If the deceased has expressed the desire that his body should be burnt, the coffin is carried from the temple to a small house a short distance off. It is there placed upon a kind of stone scaffold, at the base of which a fire is maintained until the corpse is

JAPAN.—p. 262. BURNING THE DEAD.

consumed. The men employed in this work draw out the bones from the ashes by means of sticks. The first bone is drawn out by two men armed with two sticks, which has given rise to the superstition that it is an evil omen for two people to eat simultaneously of certain dishes with their chop-sticks. The remaining ashes are placed in an urn and carried to the tomb by the relations. The burials of the poor outcasts from society are very simple. The body is interred at once without entering any temple, or else it is burnt in some waste spot.

Japanese cemeteries are most carefully cherished spots, and are always bright with verdure and flowers. Each family has its own little enclosure, where several simple commemorative stones stand. Once a-year a festival for the dead is held. It is celebrated at night. The cemetery is illuminated by a thousand different-coloured fires, and the whole population resort there, and eat, drink, and enjoy themselves in honour of their dead ancestors.

Their utter incapacity for conceiving sorrow is one of the most characteristic features of the Japanese. Perhaps this psychological phenomenon is due to the influences amidst which this happy people have the privilege of living. It is an indisputable fact that where nature is always bright and beautiful, the inhabitants themselves of that particular spot, like the scenery, seem to expand under its sweet influence, and to become bright and happy. Such is the case with the Japanese, who, while yielding almost unconsciously to these influences, deepen them by their eager pursuit of all things gay and gladsome.

CHAPTER XVIII.

The Tea-houses—Picnics—The *Chiri-fouri* Dance—A Climax—A Migration to the Country—The Healing Waters—Touching Legend—Other Festivals—New Year's Day—A Time of Dissipation—An Exorcism—New Year Visits—A Return to Work—The Aïnos—Legend of the Dog—Appearance of the Aïnos—Their Dwellings—Rudeness of Manners—Decline of the Aïnos.

WHEN the fruit-gardens are blossoming, every one who can possibly afford to do so considers it his duty to spend one day at the very least in the country, where he can exchange the less wholesome pleasures of the town for some secluded tea-house, where he and his family may lie on the green sward, smoke their pipes, and listen to the chirp of the grasshopper, whilst they let their glances idly wander over the surrounding landscape. The Japanese have an innate love of nature. Upon every site and every point whence a view of any beauty is to be seen, there a tea-house will be found. And a sure sign of a genuine feeling for the beauties of nature is that they always strive to preserve its true aspect. Although the gardens they make in their own houses are conventional, yet at the same time they know how to appreciate the wonderful transformations which the successive seasons produce in the country.

Two or three families frequently join together, take a basket of provisions, and set out to spend the day in some pretty spot in the middle of a wood. On arriving there, every one sets to work at one thing or another; and soon a boundary is traced out, which they make a little enclosure of by hanging round it a kind of curtain fixed to small posts, and within which the women spread the mats, unpack the provisions, and the day speeds merrily on with song, laughter, and jest, frequently ending in music and dancing. The men rarely dance except at these rural festivities.

In Japan, dancing is especially reserved for religious festivals. The women are very fond of it, but their movements are merely a succession of postures and poisings that they make without moving from one place, rather than a dance such as we understand it. They nevertheless know the round dance, which they execute to the accompaniment of songs.

People of rank, when they go into the country, frequently engage the services of professional musicians, singers, and even dancers. The latter execute several dances very gracefully, the most original of which is the *chiri-fouri*—the classical dance, as it may be called, of Japan. The women who figure in it are usually attired in the most brilliant of costumes, painted, powdered, profusely decorated, and provided with a guitar.

"The *chiri-fouri*," says the Comte de Beauvoir, " is very

difficult to describe. It resembles in liveliness the Italian *mora*, the *parole volante*, the *pigeon vole*, &c., but slightly modified.

"The dancers divide into two sets, and while dancing and waving their hands in time, and as if in defiance of each other, one begins a rhythmical measure, which another takes up, and a third, until the whole number have successively contributed to improvise a fanciful sparkling cantata, in which the wit is as lively as the action. The cleverness of the *bon-mots* they uttered excited the greatest merriment in the bystanders.

JAPANESE FEMALE DANCERS.

"Presently the phase of the dance alters: one of the young girls has faltered in her rhyme or measure, and, as a punishment, must forfeit one of her ornaments. They all gradually become more and more animated, each striving to surpass the other, till their eyes flash fire, and loud bursts of laughter echo round the room.

"At length the right sleeve drops off, then the left one; next the scarf, the surcoat, the cartridge-box, and everything, down to their earrings; and the last muse who remains victorious upon the field of battle after having put all the others *hors de combat* is applauded, congratulated, and covered with flowers by the lookers-on. Nothing can give an idea of the vivacity of the gestures, the ringing laughter, the incessant flow of words of these dancing girls, as they move to the sound of the most inspiriting music."

These dances are frequently succeeded by lively games, of which the greatest favourite is the game of Fox. Two of the party, who are called the guardians of the Rat, hold the ends of a cord, in the middle of which a running loop is made, at a little height from the ground. Behind it is a small stool, upon which is placed a cup, a fan, or, in fact, any object which can be easily and instantly grasped by the fox, whose aim is to snatch it through the noose without being caught. When the guardians pull the cord too soon or too late, they pay a forfeit consisting of one or several cups of saki; if, on the contrary, the fox is caught, the whole company is regaled at his expense as long as they choose to hold him captive. With the help of such games, it can easily be imagined that the fun at these sylvan fêtes soon waxes fast and furious.

At the time when the whole city migrates to the country, the high-roads are lined for miles with mendicants of every description, the aged, lepers, and cripples, who have left their ordinary resorts about the precincts of the temples, and now attract the attention of passers-by by uttering piteous cries, reciting certain formularies of prayer, or by striking with a hammer a hollow vase of varnished wood placed in front of them. These people form a class of themselves, and are in some ways regarded as unclean. Filth and deformity render them often such hideous objects that they inspire more disgust than pity. Many amongst them are blind, or have their limbs fearfully enlarged by elephantiasis; others pass their lives crouching in a little cart on wheels, and are pushed along from one village to another by compassionate passers-by. Some of them, in the course of their miserable lives, have by this means traversed the whole length of Japan, never losing hope that at one or other of the many healing waters a cure may be found for their maladies.

"This touching custom," says the Comte de Beauvoir, "took its rise from an old legend. A young princess, loved by two officers, espoused the richest and rejected the youngest and bravest. After suffering two years of tyranny, her odious master died from a stroke of lightning. Still wondrously beautiful, she made a far pilgrimage to hide herself from her fellow-creatures. Each morning she drew to the nearest village the first poor cripple she came across, and the last that she brought to the holy fountain of health was he whom she had formerly known so young and handsome, but who, heartbroken at her rejection of him, had become insane, and was now dying of hunger in the high-roads. Hardly had the healing waters touched the poor sufferer than he rose from his miserable cart perfectly whole; and then only did they recognise each other. Thus did the gods recompense the charitable soul of the lady and the trueheartedness of the young warrior."

In addition to the continually-recurring public festivals, the Japanese have instituted several smaller ones, which partake more of the nature of social gatherings, and some of which are especially devoted to the amusement of the children, though the parents seem to take an equally large share in them. Two of them are perhaps worthy of mention—that of the dolls, celebrated in honour of the young girls; and the festival of the banners, held in honour of the boys.

The first is merely a merry family gathering, at which all the dolls that have ever been presented to the children of the household by their parents and friends are gaily dressed out and exhibited in a room decorated with flowers. The whole town takes part in the boys' festival, and the streets present a most brilliant sight, decked out with banners and streamers floating everywhere. Troops of boys, dressed in their best, parade the thoroughfares, some armed as soldiers, others carrying long bamboo canes from which are suspended engravings of the god of warriors and bravery. The armourers and cutlers drive a thriving trade on this day, as it is the custom for people to present the boys with helmets, breastplates, halberts, and other portions of a soldier's accoutrements.

The feast of lanterns gives to the streets a very quaint and animated appearance. Every creature—man, woman, and child—is provided with a lantern of some kind or other. The children particularly distinguish themselves, swinging their small ones about and shouting with all their might. This festival corresponds to that for the dead already mentioned.

The two other grandest festivals are those held at the commencement and at the end of the year. These, with the preceding ones, constitute the five annual fêtes instituted, so say certain authors, by the ancients for the enterment of the gods at the seasons reputed most unlucky, so that the influences of the bad spirits may be averted. But these are not all. Each month is marked in turn by several days' festivities, kept periodically according to the different phases of the moon. These monthly festivals are not, however, public holidays; those only observe them who like. But it is very rarely any of these pleasure-loving people allow opportunities of amusement to pass by without participating in them. They are instituted in honour of every kind of divinity: some celebrate the return of spring and the early fruits; others the blossoming of the orchards and the ingathering of the crops; others, again, the baptism of Buddha, the god of water, the god of the moon, the god of fish, etc. The people observe each of these by giving themselves some little additional treat;

New Year's Day.

but New Year's Day is deemed the season for universal enjoyment by high and low, rich and poor, in every grade of society.

New Year's Day in Japan corresponds to the beginning of our month of February, and the preparations for the great festival are commenced some days beforehand. The first care of every good citizen is to have his house thoroughly cleaned. Every article of furniture is carefully turned out, dusted—renewed if necessary, the mats swept, the screens repapered, and every nook and corner well scrubbed. The front of the house is then decorated by the women with garlands of rice straw, to which little strips of different-coloured paper are attached, and with ferns and branches of fir. The latter is extensively used for decoration, people adorning their own persons as well as their houses with it. As has already been mentioned, the Japanese are particularly fond of cultivating evergreens, and fir branches are always to be had, as nearly every garden is adorned with various specimens of *coniferæ*. The men, on their part, are just as busily employed collecting and discharging all their debts, for it is a universal principle in Japan that no debts incurred during the present year should be allowed to run on into the next. The people have also to lay in their year's provision of saki and rice. The former is sold by auction at the large marts in what may be called the docks of the town. The crowd of purchasers is always immense; some of them come provided with two small casks, which they carry suspended at each end of a bamboo across their shoulders; while others have ordinary buckets, tubs, or large jars. The women carry home purchases in circular baskets on their heads with almost as much ease and precision as the Dutch themselves. The saki, freshly brewed, is knocked down in large and small lots for the convenience of all classes of buyers, and every one is obliged to remove his purchase immediately, a custom which produces indescribable confusion as well as many a street row. Rice is bought in the same way, with the grain uncrushed. The flour is never sold in the market, but every household has its mortar and pestle, and pounds sufficient for its own

MARKETING.

consumption. Those able to afford it have professional pounders by the day.

The bakers, like the rice-pounders, are in great request at New Year time; for it is the fashion for every middle class household to be amply provided with rolls and cakes, which they distribute as New Year gifts. These pounders and bakers indemnify themselves thoroughly for their few days' hard labour, for when the eve of the New Year arrives, and they have received their wages, they have a regular bout of eating and drinking, and afterwards parade the streets, many of them disguised in parodied costumes of the nobles, and all singing and dancing lustily. Such masquerades are the order of the day. Servants, cooks, porters, messengers, all dress themselves up in absurd motley attire, and go from house to house demanding New Year gifts; and the money they collect in this manner enables them to take several days' holiday, which they spend in a round of dissipation.

Meanwhile crowds of people flock in from the country. Farmers come to make their purchases and to provide themselves with amulets for the protection of their fields. Players, jugglers, clowns, and pedlars help to fill the overcrowded streets as they pursue their different trades or callings. Every street is illuminated and decorated with a profusion of garlands and fir branches, and all is gaiety and confusion. But at midnight the whole scene changes, noise and laughter is succeeded by silence, and the streets become almost deserted. Not that the people are asleep, but this is the hour for certain domestic ceremonies, of which no Japanese of any respectability omits the observance.

The father of the family commences by lighting a small bundle of sticks, upon which certain religious formularies have been written, which are supposed to lend to them a particular power; he closely examines the form of the flames, and especially notes the direction of the smoke, as from these he is able to prognosticate good or evil presages for the coming year. The exorcism of evil spirits next takes place. The master of the house solemnly perambulates the whole dwelling, casting here and there roast beans as he pronounces certain cabalistic words; finally he prostrates himself before the altar of the household gods, and implores a blessing from the god of riches. These religious duties fulfilled, the family go to bed, but not for long, for the sun has hardly risen before the whole world is astir again. Everybody is dressed in his smartest; congratulations are poured forth on every side, and presents are universally exchanged. The fashion is for the husband and wife first to utter reciprocal good wishes, then the children enter and salute their parents, and finally the relations drop in to express their good wishes. All these are offered in the exaggerated form deemed necessary by the Japanese for the proper expression of courtesy, with the body bending so low that the hands almost touch the ground. The greater part of the morning is spent in the scrupulous observance of these various matters of etiquette, then breakfast is served, and about the middle of the day neighbourly visits are paid and returned.

Photography in Japan is as general as with us. The *cartes de visite* are usually of a large size, and decorated with numerous drawings. They are transmitted by messengers in envelopes, securely fastened with ribbons.

When the Japanese pay their visits, they are, as a rule, accompanied by one or several domestics laden with gifts, such as fans, etc.: these the visitor presents to his friends, who, in return, produce rice cakes and saki. A paper packet containing a small piece of dried fish is also frequently presented, signifying that frugality is the first of domestic virtues. Lobsters and oranges are also mutually exchanged, the former as the best fish of the sea, the latter as being the best fruit. The lobsters received in this way are dried, pounded, and consumed for certain diseases.

In the official world New Year visits are indispensable. The clerks employed in the various administrative departments go in a body to the house of their chief to offer their humble respects and good wishes. Visits to functionaries high in office are carried out with great formality. A traveller gives the following description of one :—" The reception-room of a functionary of the first order is approached by steps from the outer hall, from which it is separated by bamboo blinds, ornamented with wide silk bands and great bows of plaited cord of the same material. These blinds are raised like the curtain of a theatre, and disclose to sight the great man squatting upon a rich carpet in the middle of a kind of stage, his sword-rack on his left hand, and kneeling a little way behind him his aides-de-camp or secretaries. The subordinates, assembled in the other hall, prostrate themselves at the lowest step of the stairs, which are varnished black and polished like marble. While in this posture they present an address to their chief, who after a certain time requests them to partake of some refreshment, whilst their attendants bring their offerings and spread them out upon the top step."

These visits of ceremony are now only exacted by dignitaries of the state, and have more of the absurd than the imposing about them. The middle classes have long discontinued them, and employ their time far more pleasantly in a perfect round of mirth and merriment. The streets are nothing more than a vast playground overrun with school boys and girls of every age, all engaged in sports of the most childish nature—such as tops, stilts, hoops, kites, battledores, &c. The sellers of toys, confectionery, and sweets, it is needless to say, drive a lucrative trade. The absurd attire and ridiculous capers of the masqueraders are unfailing sources of amusement, and their whereabouts may be infallibly traced by the loud bursts of laughter which follow them wherever they go. The merry-makings are kept up during the whole night, the next day, and sometimes even the day following. Then things return to their usual course, and everybody, refreshed by their few days of untrammelled pleasure, betake themselves cheerfully to their work again.

So far our attention has been devoted exclusively to the

A Primitive Race. 277

Japanese proper, that is, to those people inhabiting the islands of Kiusiu, Sitkoff, and Niphon; but a few words remain to be said about a people who, while forming part of the empire of Japan, yet differ essentially from the great majority of the population. They are the Aïnos, or the original inhabitants of the Japanese archipelago, now only to be found in the island of Yezo, situated to the north of Niphon, from which it is separated by the Straits of Sangar or Matsmaï. These people are decreasing in numbers year by year, and will soon be numbered with those extinct races of whom it is only known that they have once existed.

The Aïnos, however, have had their day of glory. In olden times, several centuries before our era, they were masters of all the part north of the island of Niphon, and their power equalled that of the Japanese; but little by little their influence diminished, and, forced to abandon their possessions in Niphon, they were obliged to confine themselves to the island of Yezo. There the Japanese pursued them, and a long war ensued, which finally reduced them to complete submission about the fourteenth century. Since then, the state of servitude in which their conquerors have held them has been such as to stifle even the instinct of progress within them: thus it is that in the nineteenth century they offer the image of a people hardly past its first infancy.

Their origin is unknown; they themselves are perfectly ignorant of their own history, and they have no written document existing which could throw light upon the past. A few legends are still extant, however; one of the quaintest of which, as related by Lindau, is regarded by the inhabitants as an explanation of their origin.

"As soon as the world had emerged from the waters, a woman came and established herself in a most beautiful island, which was subsequently to be the abode of the Aïnos. She arrived in a vessel which had been driven by favourable winds and waves from the West to the East, and she brought with her arrows, bows, lances, knives, nets, and all the necessary implements for stalking the fallow deer which thronged the forests, and for despoiling the sea and rivers of the fish which overcrowded them.

"During a long succession of years this woman lived alone and happy in a garden which no longer exists, and of which no living being will ever be able to discover any trace. One day, after returning from hunting, she felt fatigued, and, to refresh herself, went to bathe in the river which separated her dominions from the rest of the world. Suddenly she perceived a dog swimming with great rapidity towards her. Terror-stricken, she hurried up out of the water and hid herself behind a tree. The animal followed her, and demanded wherefore she fled from him; she answered that she was afraid. 'Let me remain with thee,' said the dog; 'I will be thy companion and protector, and thou needst never more fear anything.' This she consented to, and from the union of these two creatures were born the Aïnos, that is to say, men."

"Other fables," adds M. Lindau, "also affirm that the Aïnos, who now inhabit the Kurile Archipelago, of which

Yezo is the most southerly, have come from the West. It is most probable they originally came from the far interior of the Asiatic Continent; at any rate, they bear not the slightest resemblance to any of their neighbours, the Guilakes, Tougouses, Manchoos, and other tribes now scattered upon the eastern coasts of the north of Asia."

The Aïnos are generally small, thick-set, and awkwardly formed; they have wide foreheads and black eyes, not sloping; their skin is fair, but sunburnt. Their distinguishing feature is their hairiness, and they never dress their heads or trim their beards. The little children have a bright, intelligent look, which, however, gradually wears away as they grow older. Before they are able to walk the parents carry them astride on their hips. For long or fatiguing journeys, they put them in a net slung across their backs and tied in front over their foreheads. The women enhance their natural ugliness by painting the outlines of their mouths blue. They usually wear one or more robes according to the season. The men have tight-fitting pantaloons and a large cloak confined at the waist by a sash. These clothes are extremely coarse in texture, some of them resembling a kind of straw matting which they make from seaweed.

The dwellings of the Aïnos are of the simplest construction, and only contain a few implements for hunting and fishing, and some cooking utensils. They are built in small groups or hamlets, but none ever contain more than a hundred individuals. They are a gentle, kindly, hospitable, even timid people, contrasting strangely with the dangerous professions they exercise. Monogamy, which seems to have been customary in the times of their independence, has disappeared since the partial introduction of Japanese customs, and now every Aïno has the right to possess as many wives as he likes.

Fishing is their chief occupation, for their coasts abound in fish, and a considerable trade is carried on with the island of Niphon. Hunting is another profitable pursuit. The fish and the wolf are the principal divinities in their rude religion. There is no sign of agriculture, nor is any breed of cattle to be found amongst these Aïnos; dogs only are utilised to drag their sledges in winter. Their organisation is quite patriarchal; they have neither king, princes, nor lords. In every hamlet the affairs of the community are invested in the hands of the oldest and most influential member. Although the intelligence of the Aïnos is very little developed, they evince great aptitude for knowledge, and eagerly seize every opportunity of acquainting themselves with Japanese laws and customs.

The Aïnos now only inhabit the centre and northern part of the island of Yezo. In the south, the population is almost entirely Japanese. There are two important towns, Matsmaï and Hakodadi, both built upon the Straits of Sangar. The latter has about six thousand inhabitants, who maintain themselves by fishing and trading. The town is built at the bottom of a harbour regarded as one of the best and finest in the world. Although the streets are wide and kept in good repair, the town has a poverty-

The Aïnos.

stricken appearance; the houses being low and thatched, and of the commonest type of architecture.

The residences of the English and other consuls are in the centre of the town, for Hakodadi is one of the ports open to foreign commerce; but business is very dull. All regular communications with the West are centred in the towns in the south of the Japanese Empire.

JAPANESE FISHERWOMEN.

CHAPTER XIX.

The Language of Japan—Four Series of Characters—Literature—Curious Mode of Measuring Time—Sam-Sin Music—Public Speaking—The Daimio's Vases—Pithy Proverbs—Fan-painting—Skill in Japanning—Sharp Shopkeeping—Bargaining Extraordinary—"*Izouchi!*"

THE Japanese tongue has for a long time been regarded merely as an offshoot of the Chinese language, or at any rate as being very nearly connected with it; study, however, and the comparison of the two languages, has rectified this error. The Japanese understand Chinese writing, because the Chinese characters form part of the numerous kinds in use in Japan. This is easily understood when it is remembered that Chinese characters represent neither letters nor meaningless sounds, which are only the constituent parts of a word, but are words themselves, or rather the ideas that these words express; consequently the same ideas can be communicated, although expressed by different words, to any one who is acquainted with the signification of the characters.

The Japanese have, like the Chinese, a great variety of terms whereby they can express personal pronouns, and at the same time indicate the respective positions of the parties speaking. Thus they are able in a certain degree to show deference towards the persons they are addressing or of whom they speak, and respect on the part of him who is speaking. This feature of the Japanese language also applies to several other words which indicate an action, a resolution, a sentiment, anything relating to the Emperor, other dignitary, or a divinity—in fact, to whatever forms the subject of discussion. So that, if a Japanese wishes to show especial respect or courtesy, the necessary deferential expressions he introduces render his sentences twice the length they would otherwise be in ordinary conversation.

The Japanese language is very soft and agreeable to the ear; but travellers declare that no one born out of the country could possibly pronounce some of the words. They have a system of forty-eight syllabic signs, which can be, so to speak, doubled by means of signs added to the consonants, which modify the sound and render it harder or softer. This system, it is said, dates from the eighth century, and can be written in four different series of characters: these are the *kata-kana*, which is considered more correct for the men only to make use of; the *kira-kana*, supposed to be only used by the women; the *manyo-kana*, composed entirely of Chinese characters, but with which the characters of the *kata-kana* and the *kira-kana* are frequently mixed; and, lastly, the *yamato-kana*, or Japanese writing, composed of Chinese characters considerably contracted. With the exception of the *kata-kana*, the different series are rarely employed alone;

the characters of two or even three of them are usually intermixed without any rule, which renders Japanese manuscript exceedingly difficult to decipher.

The art of printing in Japan, although it cannot rival the magnificence of European typography, is yet sufficiently advanced to allow an extensive propagation of the literature of the country. They are not acquainted with the moveable type, and they multiply copies of manuscripts by means of a species of imperfect stereotype, or else by engraving on wood.

Japanese literature comprises books on science, history, biography, geography, travels, philosophy, natural history and poetry, dramatic works, romances, and encyclopædias. The latter seem to be little more than picture-books with explanatory notes, arranged, like other Japanese dictionaries, sometimes alphabetically, but more often quite fancifully, and without any attempt at scientific classification. The poetical works are divided into two kinds only: the one including small poems of five verses, composed sometimes with five characters, sometimes with seven; the other, on the contrary, being poems of unlimited length. They strive to express the most comprehensive ideas in the fewest possible words, and to employ words with double meanings for the sake of typical allusions. They also delight in descriptions or similes furnished by the scenery or the rich variety of natural productions by which they are surrounded. As a rule, however, their poems are little better than ballads or songs. Of their books on science, none are of any value but those which

The Calendar.

treat of astronomy. Japanese astronomers have studied the deepest books on the subject brought over from Holland, and they have learned the use of the majority of European instruments. Several travellers have also testified to having seen very good telescopes, barometers, and thermometers that had been manufactured in the country. A proof of their progress in this science is afforded by the fact that almanacs, which were at first brought from China, have now become very general, and are composed in Japan.

The measurement and division of time in Japan is not only very singular, but exceedingly difficult to understand. The year generally reckons twelve lunar months, but it contains more than three hundred and sixty-five days, as the Mikado and his astronomers add two days to several of the months, the number and name of the months thus augmented being always announced in the calendar. The difference between the lunar year, when thus lengthened, and the sidereal year, necessitates yet another correction, which is effected by an intercalary month inserted every three years, and varying in length according to the number of days rendered necessary by the Mikado's previous short reckonings. The year, as aforesaid, commences at our month of February; and besides the monthly divisions dependent on the moon, it is divided again into twenty-four periods of about fifteen days each, which are determined by the time the sun is in the first or fifteenth degree of each sign of the zodiac. Each month is recognised by some descriptive term. The first month is named the social month, from the continued festivities of the New Year; the second is the month for the change of apparel, winter garments being then laid aside; the third is the budding month, when nature awakes from its winter sleep; the fourth is the blossoming month, when the flowers begin to open; the fifth the transplanting month, the transplantation of rice commencing; the sixth the dry month, a period when no rain falls; the seventh is the month for writing sonnets to the stars; the eighth is the leafy month, when the autumnal leaves begin to fall; the ninth is the long month, when the nights begin to lengthen; the tenth is the god-forsaken month, as it is supposed that during this month all the divinities quit their temples and take a long journey; the eleventh is the month of hoar frost; and the twelfth is the final month which terminates the season. The days are divided into twelve hours, six of which are assigned to the day and six to the night. But the calculation of these hours is wonderfully complicated. Nine being regarded as the mystic number of perfection, midday and midnight are both known as nine o'clock, while the sun always rises and sets at six o'clock both by day and night. They overcome or elude the apparently unconquerable difficulty of nine o'clock coming round twice in the twelve hours by omitting the first and the three last numbers; so that in this way they commence their computation at the number four, and end at the perfect number, nine. The intervening numbers are laboriously worked out by means of a multiplication table; the whole system being based upon the deep reverence entertained for the mystic number nine.

The Japanese have only a slight knowledge of mathematics, trigonometry, mechanics, or engineering. Their canals are principally designed for irrigation, and are crossed by a great variety of bridges. They have also learned to measure the height of mountains by means of a barometer.

History and geography are very fairly cultivated; and there is an academy at Yedo where the annals of the empire and the imperial almanac are carefully inscribed. Their geographical maps also possess a certain value.

Music is the most cultivated of the fine arts. Japanese tradition accords it a divine origin. They relate that in times of yore the sun-goddess, irritated by the violence of one of her brothers, retired into a cave, and the universe remained a prey to the horrors of darkness and anarchy. The gods in their perplexity had recourse to music to allure the goddess from her retreat, and with evident success. But if music is of their invention, certainly its present state is far from recalling it's divine origin. The Japanese have many stringed, wind, and percussion instruments—twenty-one in all; but the general favourite is the sam-sin, or guitar with three strings. There are also the lutes, several kinds of drums and tambourines, fifes, clarionets, and flageolets. The Japanese have no idea of harmony; a number of them will often perform together, but they are never in tune. They are not more advanced in melody; their airs recall neither the savage strains of the forest nor the scientific music of the West. In spite of this, their music has the power of charming them for hours together; and it is only among the utterly uneducated classes that a young girl is to be found unable to accompany herself in a song on the sam-sin. These songs are often quite *impromptu*. In the higher classes a great deal of time is devoted to music and literature.

Reading is the favourite recreation of both sexes in Japan. The women confine themselves to the perusal of romances printed in the *kira-kana* dialect, which we have already said is that chiefly used by them. Every young girl who can afford it has her subscription to a library, which for the sum of fivepence per month furnishes her with as many books, ancient and modern, as she can devour. Saving their titles, these productions seem all formed on one pattern, being all of precisely the same character as the dramatic pieces, with the same types and personages. In the choice of their characters and their subjects, the authors seem by no means desirous of breaking through the narrow limits within which prejudice and custom have confined them.

Public speaking is another favourite taste of the Japanese, as shown by the good attendances at the public conferences, which were held in Japan long before they were known in Europe. "If, on passing the door of a house," says Bousquet, "you see a collection of sandals, each docketed with a number, lying before the threshold, you should enter and take your seat amongst an audience composed principally of men, who are all squatting round

INTERIOR OF TEMPLE.

JAPAN.—p. 289.

upon mats. The subject under consideration is neither jocose nor fabulous; it is either a question of morality, science, or philosophy upon which the orator holds forth to an assembly of tradesmen and small officials. The discourse proceeds with great seriousness, and nothing interrupts the eloquence of the lecturer save a few '*He's*' of acquiescence, and the sound of the pipes being shaken out against the brazier." It is a fairly lucrative profession, and in the small villages these lay-preachers are to be met with, spreading information amongst the country population, who thirst for knowledge as eagerly as their brethren of the towns. There are also Buddhist preachers, whose sermons turn exclusively upon morality, and prove a great attraction to the women and even the children, who are permitted to attend the temples where exhortations by these priests are given. Seated with but little attempt at order upon mats, the audience commences by intoning with the priests the incomprehensible litany of their sect. Each of them sits in the easiest and most comfortable attitude for listening, with the eternal pipe in his or her hands. The preacher appears, clothed in his robes of ceremony, and discourses in a familiar manner upon morals or the catechism. His lecture sometimes takes the form of a conversation, in which the answers of the faithful are expressed by cries of "*Nammida! nammida!*" repeated with various intonations according to the exigencies of the reply. "Nothing," says the bonze, "is more impure than the human body; it is covered with fat; tears are distilled from the eyes, etc. What an error it is to regard as the perfection of beauty such a mass of corruption!" "*Nammida! nammida!*" is the contrite cry of a miserable sinner of ten years of age!

In Japan, as in every other country, popular imagination has created a number of tales, which are faithfully handed down orally from one generation to another. As we have stated in a previous chapter, the fox is almost always the hero of these legends, and enjoys with the cat, and especially the badger, the reputation of being the tormentor of men. These superstitious fables have all a great hold upon the people, so that if, for example, the wind causes the slight partitions in the rooms to shake, all the women firmly believe it is the mischievous prank of one of these animals. The badger is often supposed to assume the guise of a woman, for the purpose of ensnaring innocent young folks who do not perceive the cloven hoof, or rather the tail, protruding from beneath her skirts. A few of the many marvellous stories told about the tricks of these mischievous animals have already been given. Such tales are so universally known and believed in that, if a young Japanese was asked to relate one of the national legends, he would infallibly begin one upon either the fox or the badger, which are more celebrated than "Puss in Boots" or "Blue Beard" with us.

Besides these legends, the Japanese have fables in abundance; but it is very difficult to discover the hidden meaning which the allegory veils. Some of the anecdotes they relate are much more comprehensible, and always contain a good moral.

The Daimio's Lesson.

"A Daimio had caused twenty magnificent china vases to be made expressly for himself, and to stand and admire them became his chief pleasure in life. A servant had the misfortune to break one of them, when the rage of the Daimio knew no bounds, and he condemned the man to instant death. One of his dependants, hearing of this, presented himself before the angry lord, and offered to repair the vase by means of a receipt of which he was the fortunate possessor, so that not the slightest suspicion of a flaw would remain. He was therefore conducted into the room in which the Daimio kept these idols of his heart carefully concealed under a coverlet of silk. The man raised the drapery, and with a single push threw them all on the ground, where they lay shattered in a thousand pieces. 'These nineteen vases,' said he, 'might have cost the lives of nineteen other persons; let mine, therefore, suffice for all.' The Daimio accepted the rebuke, and granted his full and free forgiveness to all concerned."

The wisdom of these tales is enhanced by the constant intervention of pithy, shrewd proverbs and sayings which the Japanese also constantly introduce into their conversation.

"If you hate a person, let him live." (That is sufficient torment.)

"It is far better to avoid reproach than to seek for praise."

"Learn by your own sufferings the troubles that others endure."

"A flogged soldier fears the rod."

"The bottom of the candlestick is dark." (The nearer the church, the farther from God.)

These sayings and proverbs give to their conversation a piquancy and sharpness which well illustrates the nature of the people. Generally gay and laughing, often light and frivolous, the Japanese involuntarily make a jest of everything. Their great talent for caricaturing is a natural consequence of this; and they have a peculiar aptitude for combining the comic and serious sides of things. The Japanese are essentially wags; but their humour is expressed less in the attitudes than in the choice of their subjects, and the expressions of their faces. They exaggerate, but always with moderation and invariably with good taste. Their works in sculpture and painting show that the sole thought of the native artists is to portray the passions of the heart—tranquillity, ecstasy, melancholy, fear, anger, hatred, surprise, gaiety, but rarely love. The study of the human frame has no interest for them; nevertheless, however ignorant they may be of its anatomy, they succeed in producing and giving it its grandest quality—life.

The almost universal use of fans by the Japanese, and the large quantities of these and similar fancy articles now exported to the West, renders their manufacture an important branch of industry. Fan-painting is consequently much in vogue; it is a trade, but it is also an art in which all the qualities which distinguish Japanese art are combined. Indeed some of these productions are perfect little

FAN-PAINTER.

chef d'œuvres in their extreme simplicity; as, for example, a stork with a fish in its beak skimming along the surface of the waves, the horizon of the sea being invisible; or, again, a flock of small birds on the wing, a vast expanse of sky as the background. These pretty, graceful subjects are always striking from their originality, and in contrast between the slenderness of outline of the principal object and the immensity of the background and border. In Japan

FAN-MAKERS.

there are no academies or studios. Talent is considered to be hereditary, and an art is usually transmitted from father to son for generations in the same families; and thus it follows naturally that their productions have become very stereotyped, no new ideas are struck out, but the same old subjects are reproduced again and again, till at last the artists themselves are beginning to tire of them. But one quality which has never deserted them is good taste —a God-given gift rather than a thing acquired—which is principally shown in their bronzes and japanned goods, articles both largely manufactured.

The Japanese bronzes are especially distinguished for their richness of decoration. The most celebrated foundries are at Kioto, the ancient religious capital of the empire; but the articles of real artistic value are becoming more and more rare, and find no sale except amongst the rich natives. Travellers unanimously aver that the specimens which are imported into European countries give but a very imperfect idea of their proficiency in this branch of manufacture; and the same may be said of the japanned goods, of which the most inferior kinds only are sent out of the country.

The process of japanning is extremely complicated. The varnish, which is the resinous production of a shrub, has to undergo a long and careful preparation before it is ready for use. It is mixed very slowly and smoothly upon a copper palette with the colouring matter. The final operation of varnishing is also as tedious as the preliminaries. At least five or six different layers are laid on successively, with sufficient time allowed between for each to harden; it is then scraped and polished with a stone or polisher of bamboo, and it is by this patient labour alone that the varnish attains its brilliancy. The faces in mother-of-pearl are cut out in the requisite shape from the shell and coloured underneath; they are then placed upon the varnish, and the same number of coats and the same amount of rubbing and polishing given to them as to the rest; this produces the soft sheen which they always wear.

There are in every large Japanese town several shops for the sale of these japanned goods; but the intending purchaser must, on entering one, arm himself with a vast amount of patience, or else be prepared to pay at least three or four times the value of the article. The Japanese shopkeeper is fonder of a bargain even than his brethren of the West, the only difference being that he preserves a cool air of unconcern during the whole transaction, as if it were a matter of perfect indifference to him whether the bargain were a successful one or the reverse. The Comte de Beauvoir gives, in his usual amusing style, an account of the mode in which a purchase is effected.

"We enter a shop, and friendly good-morning pipes and cups of tea are immediately passed round; the shopman then shows us some articles of about the forty-fifth rate, thinking us 'young' enough to buy them. We, however, know better, and chat, offer him cigarettes, laugh, and pay compliments to the lady in the parlour. 'Ah, you French!' they say to us; 'you love laughter as much as we do; you are gone to make war in Corea; you have a beautiful frigate, La Guerrière, and officers in fine uniforms who teach us how to fight.' How many whole hours have we not thus passed with these good-natured prattlers? Presently, after rummaging about his shop in a careless and affectedly aimless sort of way, the shopman produces a pretty little japanned cabinet. *Tkoura?*' (how much?). The goodman instantly puts on a look of deep thought, rubs his thighs, hesitates, frowns, and after keeping you in suspense for some moments, says with a sigh, '*Ftaz-yack-ichi-boo!*' (three hundred and twenty francs). We have already decided the full value to be about forty francs, so we sit down again, chat on, and after a while suggest '*A la gigoto!*' which signifies, 'Show us something else.' Upon this he displays a hundred tempting things, all the while continuing to smile, laugh, and utter the drollest remarks.

"At this period of the transaction young hands would give in, offer half the price, and would then be the losers of about a hundred francs. The sharp ones, however, return to the charge another day, try to circumvent the shopkeeper by feigning to be on the point of giving a large order, and then refusing everything. Just as they are leaving the shop, the man in an indescribable voice of deep affliction cries after them, '*Mayotto! mayotto! mayotto! Ni siou boo!*' (the lowest price, twenty boos). Then follows a repetition of the whole thing—more talking, more pipes, more tea. At length they offer twelve boos, but the shopman rejects it, prostrates himself, puts everything away, and finally, at the end of about two hours, when his customers are departing for good and all, he calls them back, and despairingly hands them for twelve boos the articles for which he had demanded two hundred. They clap their hands three times, he cries '*Izouchi!*'

JAPANESE CURIOSITY SHOP.

JAPAN.—p. 296.

and the bargain is concluded. Then it seems as if all the anxiety of the last moments have vanished; the seller devotes his fullest energies to the careful packing of his customer's purchases in lovely little boxes, offers them cake, tries to tempt them afresh, and they finally part, both sides equally enchanted with their bargain."

JAPANESE WORKERS IN METALS.

CHAPTER XX.

Manufactures—Paper-making—Silk-husbandry—Lessons in the Rearing of Silkworms—A Silkworm Fête—The Legend of Toung-Young—Agriculture—Small-farming—Manuring and Irrigation—Rice-culture—Account of the Preparation of Tea—Giant and Dwarf Trees—Sailors and Seamanship—Shipbuilding—Dockyards and Railways.

THE most celebrated of the Japanese manufactures are those of porcelain, paper, and silk, and the native industry of the country in these and other articles is sufficient to supply the necessities of the inhabitants. The Japanese china, which in the sixteenth and seventeenth centuries was so justly celebrated, seems in these days to have lost much of its former superiority. This decadence has been attributed (whether rightly or wrongly we cannot say) to the increasing scarcity of the fine and peculiar clay used in making this ware; also, no doubt, the cost attending its production having considerably increased, it has been found in many instances convenient to abandon the making of the finest qualities, and to bestow more time on that which needs a less exquisite finish.

The paper used by the Japanese is usually of a creamy white, and is made of the bark of certain trees boiled in an alkaline preparation. It next goes through a most delicate process of washing, on the success of which depends the whiteness and quality of the material; and being then mixed with a viscous preparation of rice, is reduced to a smooth paste, sufficiently consistent to be formed into sheets. The moulds used for making the sheets are of straight laths of bamboo. The last process is that of drying, for which purpose the sheets are placed in piles (each one divided from the rest by a strip of bamboo) under a wooden press, and the weight is gradually increased until the water is thoroughly squeezed out. The leaves are then raised one by one by the bamboo strips and placed on a rough plank, where they are left to dry in the sun. This paper is durable enough, but after a time the surface becomes fluffy. It does not appear to have been used in Japan before the seventeenth century.

It is said that the finest silks are woven on a small barren island by criminals of high birth, who are obliged to work for their living. The art of silk-husbandry—sericiculture, as it is called—was introduced into Japan by the Chinese and the Coreans about the year 310, and has since increased to a marvellous extent. Towards the end of the sixteenth century the reigning emperor stimulated his subjects to increasing industry in this trade, and his injunctions on the subject do honour to the Japanese Government of that period. He says—"Give to your silkworms the same tender attention which parents bestow on their infants; tend them as your mother tends her new-born child. Cold, damp, and heat are alike injurious to them; watch carefully, therefore, that they may always enjoy an even temperature, and a sufficiency of pure fresh air both night and day. This precious branch of industry was given to the people by the wisdom of their princes in former ages. Nobly-born ladies, queens, and princesses have with their own hands gathered the mulberry leaves, and proved that the art of raising silkworms is an occupation worthy of their sex and rank. If, then, members of the royal family have not shrunk from this work, why

JAPANESE WEAVERS.

should not their inferiors imitate them, and interest themselves in an occupation which involves no fatigue, and can be satisfactorily carried on with an ordinary amount of zeal and care?"

The Japanese are certainly masters of the art of raising silkworms and preserving their quality and vigour; and much is to be learned from their numerous treatises on the subject if they could be got at. One of these books has in some way come within our reach, and is entitled, *Yo-Sau-Fi-Rok; or, The Secret History of the Education of Silkworms*. It is a work which no rearer of silkworms should be without, for it gives every particular on the subject, beginning with the many traditions borrowed from China. We append a specimen of its original style:—

"In the third month the eggs must be dried, at midday plunged into clear water, and afterwards carefully preserved from dust. The place destined to receive the worms after hatching must be carefully dried and warmed; and when the time has come they must be provided with young and tender leaves plucked from the side of the tree facing the rising sun. These must be distributed quietly and noiselessly before the worms compose themselves to sleep, and when they awake they must be slightly fed. Then comes the time of spinning, when the worms begin to raise themselves to turn towards the cloudy home of the Dragon (the constellation of the Lion). They lie down together, curved like a crouching tiger, and as soon as the first rays of dawn appear their instinct impels them to raise themselves heavenward."

When the silkworms are about to enclose themselves in their network, they are placed in a warm box prepared with twigs and brushwood, and shaded from the too powerful rays of the midday sun; and not until the cocoons are quite finished does the whole neighbourhood join in a fête, and libations are poured out to the tutelary gods of the silkworms. Friends pay each other visits; the old people give presents to the children; whilst the "silkworm mothers" again think of their own adornment, and attend to the arrangement of their hair and their toilet generally.

The *Yo-Sau-Fi-Rok* concludes with the most minute directions for rearing the precious nurslings, and recommends them especially to the care of the women, who are enjoined to neglect their own persons until the cocoons are safe, and to cherish especially great evenness of temper, "for it is well known that worms tended by bad-tempered people never succeed."

Early in the present century, the governor of a town in the island of Niphon made great endeavours to improve and increase the art of silkworm-rearing. He carefully studied the subject in a district of the country resembling the Cevennes or North Italy, where it is most cleverly carried on. He tested the experience there gained in another part of Japan which seemed to him favourable in climate and soil, and condensed all the knowledge which he could gather from books and from his own experience into a simple and popular treatise, which he published in 1802, and which—brought into Europe by the Dutch—has since been translated into several languages. He combats strongly the injurious superstitions prevalent in his country, in words which give a good idea of the mind of a highly-educated Japanese freed from the prejudices of Buddhism.

"Heaven favours those alone who second its efforts by their own. Those who do not understand this principle may apply in vain to the Divine Spirit—to Buddha. It is in vain that they curse the man of whom they bought the eggs of the silkworm, or covet the treasures of their next-door neighbour. For what would it avail them if Buddha or any other divinity listened to their invocations? They would still neglect the attention which alone will preserve the worms."

This book contains every precept necessary for the planting and culture of the mulberry tree; gives methodical and clear instructions in every point of the business; and closes with some noble thoughts and a pleasing legend.

"The first care of every country should be to cultivate all such things as minister to their necessities both in food and clothing, for by them great comfort is provided for the inhabitants, and the Divine Spirits have themselves taught us the art of procuring those things which are for the good of mankind. Birds, beasts, insects, fishes, plants, and trees are given for our use and comfort by the overruling spirit of the universe. Let us see that none receive these merciful gifts with thanklessness or contempt. For us they were born, and for us they live. Above all, let us beware lest in our love of gain we forget our love to man, for nothing would be more contrary to the will of the Celestial Spirit. He who should be guilty of such sin would certainly fall into trouble when he least expected it. But to him who, on the contrary, had striven to do that which is right, the Divine Spirit would assist him in the time of need, even though he did not directly pray for aid. The legend of the virtuous Toung-Young is an illustration of this fact.

"This youth was a model of filial piety. When, as a child, he followed his mother to the grave, he vowed to devote all his energies to the care of his remaining parent. As he grew older, he hired himself as a labourer in order to supply his father's wants; and when at last he died, he sold himself as his only means of raising money to defray the funeral expenses. Having accomplished this filial duty, he proceeded to the residence of his new master, and when on the road he met a most lovely maiden, who stopped him and said, 'Toung-Young, I wish to be your wife.' 'But,' replied he, 'I am poor, and my body belongs not to myself but to my master, for I have sold myself to gain the means to bury my father. How can you wish to become my wife?' 'Because Heaven wills it,' answered the beauteous maiden. 'I am clever at weaving, so let us go together to your master and he will receive us both into his service.' Toung-Young dared no longer offer further objections; he took the maiden as his wife, and together they were received into the master's service. In less than a month the clever weaver had produced more than a hundred pieces of the most exquisite silk, which she offered to her master as the ransom of her husband. Surprised and charmed, he gave them both their liberty. They had scarcely begun the journey into their own country when the wife said to Toung-Young, 'I am the celestial weaver. Heaven was touched by the sincerity of thy filial piety, and sent me to aid thee.' And with these words she disappeared into the clouds and returned to her heavenly home. True filial piety, the source of all happiness, is thus ever rewarded."

The Japanese have dedicated the art of silk-weaving to certain of the heavenly constellations, and they hold a fête in their honour on the seventh day of the seventh month of the year. The women and girls congregate at twilight as the stars begin to appear, and amidst a brilliant assemblage they solemnly spread out silk threads of various colours, offering at the same time fruits and flowers, and imploring the divinities to grant them the dexterity necessary for making the most perfect tissues. If, during the night, a spider, the emblem of spinners, rests upon the offerings, it is hailed as the best possible omen, and as a sign that their prayers will be granted.

Agriculture is followed in Japan as assiduously as the manufacture of which we have been speaking. With the exception of the roads and the forests necessary for providing the country with fuel, there is not an acre of uncultivated ground; where it is impossible to work the plough, the ground is prepared by the hand. Wherever the coast is not too precipitous and rocky, the eye of the traveller is delighted by the richness of the cultivation to be seen on approaching the country. The law commands that no portion of land shall remain unproductive, and every variety of vegetable may be seen covering the ground in successive intervals.

There are some rich landed proprietors, but as a rule

the land is divided and rented out in small portions, from half-an-acre up to two or three acres at the most. There is consequently no great bustle at harvest-time, but each farmer arms himself with a blade fastened to a wooden handle about a foot long—for they do not use scythes or sickles—and with this instrument he can complete his own ingathering. These small plots of ground are manured, watered, and drained with the most minute care, and are sown alternately with wheat, rye, and barley; several different kinds of these cereals succeed equally well, and they cultivate both common and bearded wheat, and long and short-

MANURING THE TEA PLANT.

eared barley. The manure employed is nearly always in a liquid state. The people are thoroughly alive to the importance of such manure in agriculture, store it up with the greatest care, and carry it to the fields in barrels, out of which it is ladled with large pails. The nose of the traveller is consequently assailed during the spring season with stenches which seem to harmonise but ill with the blossoming hedge-rows and the pure air of the country. Threshing is a very simple process, for they merely strike the sheaves against a beam to separate the grain from the straw. Winnowing is often witnessed by the sailors as their vessels pass within sight of the shore. The women stand in long lines and shake the grain in baskets held above their heads, while the sharp sea breeze carries away the chaff. They sometimes use hand pestles and mortars to grind the corn, but the ordinary method is to bruise it in a mill turned by several people.

The Japanese think much of the importance of irrigation, and always water their land well before sowing it. Their plough is a heavy piece of wood fastened obliquely to a beam, and hollowed out so as to receive a piece of iron which serves as a ploughshare. A bullock or a horse is fastened to the beam and led by one man, while another guides the plough. This instrument acts well enough in the light moist soils, but does not make very deep furrows. For strong clayey lands they use hoes made of hard wood, the edges and sides of which are strengthened with iron. Having worked the ground over with this instrument, they water it till it is well saturated, and then harrow it backwards and forwards. The high grounds are especially devoted to the cultivation of strong coarse reeds, of which they make light and at the same time solid roofs to the houses; and they use a disagreeable weed which is common on the heights as manure. Along the coast, especially in the isle of Yezo, is found a kind of seaweed which the lower classes gather and use for food. Broad and kidney beans, lentils, and potatoes abound in the islands; and there are a few plantations of maize. Vines grow in abundance in many places, and bear very fine-tasted fruit, but the wine made from them is inferior to that obtained from European grapes. Almost every kind of fruit common to Europe is grown, such as plums, apricots, peaches, pears, apples, figs, oranges, raspberries, cherries, etc.; and to these numerous products may be added the cam-

JAPANESE WOMEN GATHERING SEAWEED.

Rice-culture. 309

phor and vegetable wax tree, from the latter of which is extracted, by means of incisions cut in the trunk, the precious sap of which the Japanese varnish is made.

Rice is the principal object of culture in Japan. In the early spring the rice plantations are thoroughly inundated by water from the canals, and when in this state the soil is ploughed and broken up till it becomes a kind of liquid paste. The grain is then cast by hand into the ground, which is

TRANSPLANTING THE RICE PLANTS.

turned over afresh by a species of harrow. When the young rice is beginning to shoot, the Japanese dig it up and transplant it in clusters to another piece of ground, where it finishes its growth. The month of October is the time when the rice reaches maturity. To keep the birds from attacking it, the Japanese hang strings of plaited straw round and about the plantations, and attach to them various floating appendages, which a child is employed to keep constantly in motion.

Next in importance to rice is the cultivation of the tea-plant, which was introduced into Japan about the

PICKING THE TEA LEAVES.

beginning of the ninth century. The tea-plant is a branching shrub, which grows to the height of five or six feet; the leaves are hard, oval, elongated or elliptical, of a shiny green colour, smooth at the base, but the rest of the margin serrated. The head of the plant is lopped off to render it more bushy, and consequently more productive, and it is carefully tended for several years before its leaves are gathered. The best tea is cultivated in the neighbourhood of Odsi, a small town on the coast not far from Kioto. People are placed in charge to watch that the leaves are kept as free as possible from dust and insects.

PREPARATION OF TEA—SIFTING.

312 *Gathering Tea Leaves.*

The persons chosen to gather the leaves usually pluck them with gloved hands and with the most particular care and attention. This tea is generally reserved for the use of the imperial family. Ordinary tea is harvested by workmen, who show the most astonishing skill in the speed and delicacy with which they handle the leaves. They pluck from ten to fifteen pounds a-day, and this not by handfuls, but separately, one by one. After being gathered, the leaves are carefully sifted and selected, according to size and quality.

The leaves thus selected are carried to buildings provided

PREPARATION OF TEA—RUBBING THE LEAF.

Drying the Tea.

with the furnaces used for the preparation of the tea. Each furnace is covered with a sort of wide, flat metal slab. When this is hot, a certain quantity of fresh leaves are placed upon it, the workmen stirring them continually with their hands till the heat becomes unbearable. After this semi-baking, a greyish juice, acid to the taste, exudes, and they are then taken out, thrown upon mats or paper, rubbed by workmen between the palms of the hands to make them roll better, then thoroughly shaken in baskets, or cooled with a fan on paper, to chill them the quicker, and the better to preserve their curliness. They are next

PREPARATION OF TEA—FANNING AND COOLING.

put back upon the metal slab, this time only half heated, and rubbed again, an operation which is repeated a third and even a fourth time, until they are perfectly free from moisture. Finally, to complete the process, after the tea has been warehoused for some months, it is taken from the vases in which it has been packed, and for the last time placed over a gentle fire to dry any moisture which might have gathered since the first preparation. The leaves thus prepared are rolled and coloured more or less according to their kind and quality.

Horticulture is another art in which the Japanese excel. They have camphor trees whose trunks are forty feet in circumference, and cedars of even larger growth. Certain of the temples have in their gardens cedars shaped like circular columns of extraordinary height and perfect symmetry. The traveller Meylan mentions a palm tree covered with blossoms, each one equal in size to four fine roses. Siebold also speaks of a garden lettuce which produces leaves a yard long. By a singular contrast, these people, who have succeeded in producing such gigantic specimens of trees and shrubs, are equally celebrated for their skill in dwarfing plants without destroying their productive qualities. There may be seen in a box five inches long by two in width, a fir, a bamboo, and a cherry tree, all apparently in the healthiest state of vigorous vegetation.

The paucity of animals existing in Japan is rather singular; it, however, may arise from the great extension of cultivated lands to the exclusion of pastures. There are very few draught horses and no sheep. The Japanese were astonished on learning that the woollen garments worn by Europeans were fabricated from the clothing of the sheep. There is an equal scarcity of pigs; not that pork is repudiated by the Japanese, for they eat with great relish any and every kind of meat placed before them on board foreign vessels. Their main food consists, as already said, of rice, vegetables, poultry, and especially fish. This absence of ordinary animal food in Japan is severely felt by Europeans on their first residence in the country, until their constitutions become gradually habituated to the lighter aliment on which the natives have learned to subsist.

It is impossible that navigation and nautical science could have made much progress in a country where the coasting trade forms almost their only maritime commerce, and where the laws regarding the building of vessels have been such as virtually to prohibit the undertaking of any long voyages. Nevertheless, the Japanese sailors and bargemen are remarkable for their agility, their knowledge of seamanship, and the hardihood with which they brave the worst weather in their frail barks; and a coast trade is actually carried on, thanks to the facilities afforded by numberless sheltered bays, ports, and good canals. They never make use of the roads unless no passage by water exists. The natural tendencies of an insular population has caused the development of a considerable mercantile marine in addition to the imperial navy of Japan; and it is an ascertained fact that, so early as the end of the second century, they had a sufficient fleet wherewith to effect a descent on Corea, and to conquer the greater part of that peninsula.

It is probable, according to Siebold, that the ancient Japanese vessels were made after the model of those of the Coreans, who have been common frequenters of the coasts of Japan ever since the year sixty-three of our era. The build of the Japanese vessels of the second century, which are represented in the pictures placed in the temples by the piety of the faithful, justify this opinion. But those constructed by them in the present day neither bear any resemblance to the Chinese vessels nor to ours, although the Japanese have for several centuries had the opportunity of acquainting themselves with both. The precise period of the present style of shipbuilding, and the political motives which led to its adoption, is a point which has not yet been sufficiently elucidated. However this may be, there is no doubt that the construction of Japanese vessels renders them utterly incapable of coping with the dangers and perils of a long voyage, in accordance with the existing laws which forbid expatriation. The timber used in shipbuilding is cedar, fir, and camphor; pine and elm are also sometimes employed. They have hardly any keel, an open stern, and bows terminating in a figure-head. Those built expressly for navigating rivers have a flush deck fore and aft; they are heavier and less elegant than the seagoing ships, and, with the exception of those used as pleasure boats, are by no means remarkable for cleanliness. All, or nearly all, have only a single mast, composed of several pieces, and carrying one large sail. The bolts and fastenings are of copper, the rigging of hemp, and the sails of calico, those for the small boats being of plaited straw. Their anchors are iron and four-fluked; for boats, wooden grapnels are used instead of anchors, which they sink to the bottom with a stone. The merchant vessels are from fifty to one hundred feet in length, by twenty or more in breadth, and a large one can carry about one hundred and fifty tons of cargo. Since the opening of Japan, its navy has undergone important changes, and it now possesses several steamships, most of which have been purchased in England or America. In many of the Japanese towns, however, dockyards for shipbuilding have been established.

Thanks to the facilities presented by the numerous ports on the Japanese coasts, and to the variety of the country's productions, internal commerce is pursued with immense activity. Merchandise is conveyed on land by horses and oxen. The frequent accidents which occur in this mountainous country, when they often have to climb to the tops of mountains and descend by paths which are merely steps cut in the rock or shaped on the ground, render it impossible for wheeled vehicles to be extensively used. Lines of railway are, however, gradually making their way throughout the country. One already runs from the port of Yokohama to the capital town of Yedo.

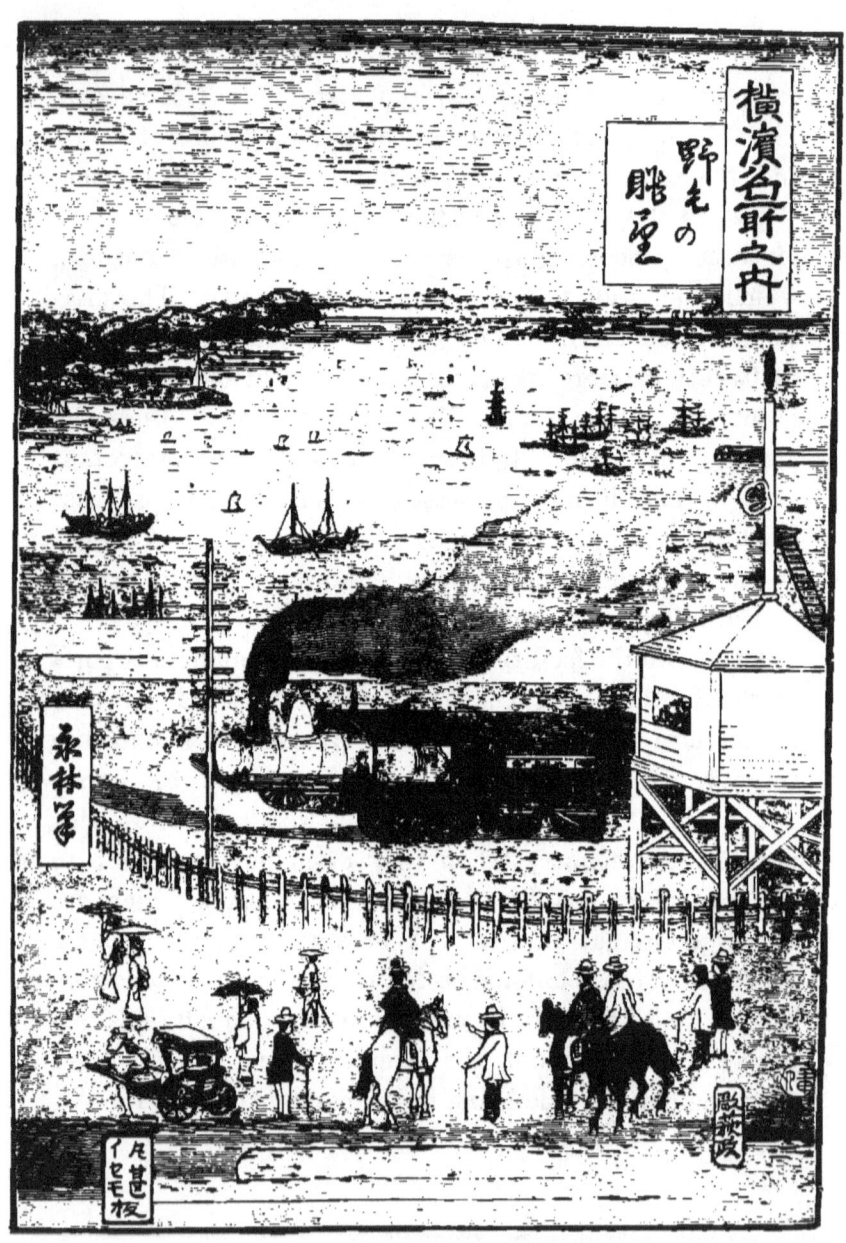

JAPANESE RAILWAY—FAC-SIMILE OF NATIVE WATER-COLOUR DRAWING.

CHAPTER XXI.

Foreign Relations of Japan—The Rise and Decline of Nagasaki—Yokohama—Hakodadi—Hiogo—Osaka—Niegata—Commercial Intercourse with Great Britain and America—Probable Future of Japanese Commerce.

A FEW words remain to be said upon the commercial relations Japan at present holds with the nations of the West, and especially with Great Britain. On the 20th of August, 1858, a treaty was concluded, as related in the early pages of this book, at Yedo, between Japan and Great Britain, guaranteeing to the latter country the highest privileges that one nation could concede to another. Permission was granted her to nominate a diplomatic agent to the town of Yedo, with liberty to travel anywhere throughout the empire, and consuls were sent to all the open ports. British subjects were also allowed to hire or buy houses, build warehouses, and even churches; but fortifications of any kind are strictly forbidden. The British are entirely under the jurisdiction of their own representatives. Free trade is allowed, with the proviso that certain dues are paid by those engaged in it. The Government do not object to any native entering the service of an Englishman settled in the country. All foreign monies are accepted in Japan, and valued according to their corresponding weight in Japanese coins. Japanese moneys of all kinds, excepting copper, can be exported, as well as gold and silver bullion. Such is a summary of the principal clauses contained in the treaty of 1858. The French treaty is precisely similar. Foreigners have the liberty of residing and trading in any of the maritime towns of Nagasaki, Yokohama, Hakodadi, Hiogo, Niegata, Kanagawa, and in the inland towns of Yedo and Osaka.

Nagasaki, or Nangasaki, is situated on the south-west coast of the island of Kiusiu, and is built in the form of an amphitheatre. The European quarter, in the east, stands upon land reclaimed from the sea at considerable labour and expense; on the highest point is seen the church, flanked by a gigantic acacia, and the residence of the British consul. Desima, the ancient Dutch factory, lies at the foot, and behind it is the native part of the town; the whole is sheltered by high wooded mountains.

The town of Nagasaki was almost the first which attracted the attention of foreigners—partly from its being already known by name from the Dutch colony established there; partly because it was the nearest point to China, and a port of great beauty; and also because, before the political revolution which overthrew the power of the Tycoonate, the Daimios of the south were there enabled, owing to its distance from Yedo, to transact their foreign affairs unmolested. This comparative importance did not last long, for affairs soon began to be concentrated in Yokohama, and the opening of the ports of Hiogo and Osaka further reduced it to a secondary rank amongst commercial

Its Decline. 321

towns. It still, however, drives a very fair trade, exporting annually from three to four million pounds of tea, besides a certain quantity of camphor and vegetable wax. It also supplies the island of Kiusiu with foreign products; and a great portion of the navigation of the Japanese seas passes by its beautiful port. But it is not a town of the

BRITISH CONSULATE AT NAGASAKI.

future, and will lose much of its prosperity in proportion as Japan ceases to require large instalments of firearms and steamers, which for many years have been its staple stock-in-trade.

Yokohama, situated on the Gulf of Yedo, owes its rise and importance to the English merchants who came to seek their fortunes in the Empire of the Rising Sun immediately after the signature of the treaty which threw open the heretofore impenetrable coasts of Japan to adventurous foreigners. It is in the form of a parallelogram, traversed from east to west by three great arteries, crossed by streets of little importance. Facing the sea, and parallel with the principal highways, is a row of fine houses with small gardens in front and behind. To the east is the native quarter, which extends itself towards the north; to the west, slight eminences, having no connection with the surrounding hills, covered with houses, range towards the sea. A railway unites Yokohama with the not far distant town of Yedo. Business is carried on in the lower part of the town, where are the banks, the counting-houses of the principal firms, the offices of three steamboat companies, stores and warehouses, and a great number of grog-shops. This quarter bears very little resemblance to the industrial commercial centres of Europe and America. Houses and people all wear a quiet, respectable, even countrified look. Yokohama has become the great mercantile centre of European trade.

Hakodadi, already mentioned, is situated in the south of the island of Yezo. It is a town of only mediocre importance, and its principal trade is with China in alimentary plants.

Hiogo, or rather Kobi, as it has been called since the concession, adjoins Osaka, both towns being situated in the island of Niphon. They were thrown open to foreign trade, January 1st, 1863. The former has already many fine houses and spacious warehouses, and is built on the western side of a gulf of great extent. On the east, the large town of Osaka extends up the two banks of a river, which, running from north to south, flows into the gulf a little way below the town. The distance from Kobi to Osaka by sea is very short, and several small steamers, belonging to native companies but manned by Englishmen, ply continually between the two towns.

Osaka, which reckons about half-a-million of inhabitants, is the trading capital of Japan. All foreign merchandise imported into the empire passes through it. In spite of the shallowness of this part of the gulf and the awkwardness of the bar, the amount of shipping to be seen here is very great. The quarter for foreigners is situated in the southern extremity of the town, and is bordered on every side by rivers and canals. It contains two or three European houses, the British consulate, and a few native huts adapted for the use of foreigners.

Niegata is to the north-east of Yedo; the entrance to the port is dangerous for ships of even moderate draught, and it is only after a considerable expenditure that a proper roadstead has been formed. Nevertheless, this town is an important market for Japanese silks, as it is situated in a province which produces them in great quantities. At the town of Yedo, a steady and profitable trade is carried on in fancy articles.

Relations between the Western nations and Japan are extending year by year; but the country by no means offers the great openings for trade that might reasonably be expected after an isolation of nearly three centuries, for home manufactures in a great measure suffice for the needs of the inhabitants. The flags of the different countries take rank according to tonnage, as follows—English, American, German, French, Dutch, Norwegian, and Swedish. The *Statesman's Year-Book*, for 1875, says:— "The commercial intercourse of Japan is carried on mainly with two countries, namely, Great Britain and the United States of America, the former absorbing more than two-thirds of the whole. The extent of trade with the United Kingdom is shown in the subjoined table, which gives the value of the total exports from Japan to Great Britain and Ireland, and of the total imports of British and Irish produce and manufactures into Japan in each of the five years, 1869 to 1873.

Years.	Exports from Japan to Great Britain.	Imports of British Home Produce into Japan.
1869	£167,308	£1,442,104
1870	96,173	1,609,367
1871	109,224	1,584,517
1872	184,342	1,961,327
1873	561,390	1,680,017

The principal articles of export from Japan to Great Britain, in the year 1873, were tobacco, unmanufactured, of the declared value of £121,614; rice, of the value of £71,621; and wax, of the value of £65,356. The staple article of British imports into Japan consists of cotton goods, the value of which was £792,235 in 1873. Besides cotton manufactures, the British imports consisted chiefly of iron, wrought and unwrought, of the value of £137,837, and of woollen fabrics, of the value of £347,237, in the year 1873." All mercantile transactions, especially the silk trade, are regulated by the state of the Liverpool and London markets; and there is a greater demand for British goods than for any other. The Americans import from Oregon and California sawn timber and flour; in exchange, they export large quantities of tea, which is consumed in immense quantities in the United States.

To sum up: the study of the natural resources of Japan and its manufacturing powers leave no doubt as to the future reserved for its trade. The efforts which up to the present time have been made to establish civilisation and preponderating European influences have only partially succeeded; but they are still persevered in from a strong feeling of self-interest, for the population of the Old World requires a new area for its enlarged spheres of activity. It is no longer the spirit of conquest which leads us towards new countries, we now search only for a fresh market for our goods. Our neighbours may perhaps sneer, but there is no other enterprise so useful and legitimate; and it is much to be desired that no complications will

326   *The Future.*

arise to distract Europe from this pacific intercourse with the countries of the far East.

What Japan stands in need of at present is a solid central Government, with complete security for property. It would be unreasonable to expect that, after the political revolutions which the country has lately undergone, either of these boons should exist to the same extent as with us. But there is a manifest tendency towards improvement, and we shall be surprised if, within a single generation, Japan does not rise to a degree of prosperity unequalled among the kingdoms of the East.

JAPANESE LANDSCAPE—FUSI-YAMA (AN EXTINCT VOLCANO) IN THE DISTANCE.

INDEX.

Actors, Japanese, 215, 217.
Agriculture, 52, 305.
Ainos, the, 277, 279.
Americans, the, in Japan, 43, 52.
Amusements, 184.
Ancestors, worship of, 73, 92.
BAPTISM, 259.
Barber's shop, 151.
Bargaining in shops, 296.
Bath-houses, 169.
Bonzes, 110, 261.
Bootmaker's shop, (*cut*) 153.
British Consulate at Nagasaki, (*cut*) 321.
Bronzes, Japanese, 294.
Buddhism, 78, 94
Buddhist priest, (*cvt*) 30 ; temple, (*cut*) 81.
Builder, Japanese. (*cut*) 151.
Burning the dead, (*cut*) 262.
Butterfly, the magic, 199.
CARICATURES, 104.
Cat, the demon, story of, 228.
Cemeteries, 263.
Characteristics of Japanese, 23, 66, 254, 263.
Children, training of, 259.
"Chiri-fouri" dance, 265.
Christianity introduced, 28.
Christians persecuted, 32, 89.
Classes in Japan, (*cut*) 122, 123.
Comedy, Japanese, 210.
Commerce, increase of, 317, 324.
Commercial relations, 319.
Confucius, 132.
Coolie, (*cut*) 156.
Cooper, Japanese, (*cut*) 120.
Corea, lion of, 190.
Costumes, Japanese, (*cut*) 122, 127, (*cut*) 241, (*cuts*) 243, 244.
Courtesans, 115.
Courtesies, (*cut*) 149, 274.
Creation, Japanese account of, 74.
Cremation. (*cut*) 262.
Cuisine, Japanese, 187.
Curiosity shop, (*cut*) 296.
DAIMIOS, the, 56, (*cut*) 57, 63, 123, 145 ; anecdote of one, 291.
Dancing, 180, 265, (*cut*) 266.
Desima, 32, (*cut*) 37.
Dining, a Japanese family, (*cut*) 252.
Discussions in bath-houses, &c., 170, 222.
Doctors, 244.
Dolls, festival of, 269.
Dutch, the, in Japan, 35, 41.
Dwellings, Japanese, 249, 252.
EARLY history of Japan, 25.
Earthquakes, frequency of, 14, 246.

Embassy, Japanese, to Europe, 54.
English, the, in Japan, 37.
Execution by the sword, (*cut*) 85.
Exorcism, 274.
Exports and imports. 324.
FABLES, Japanese, 200.
Fair at Yomasta, 187.
Fairy lore, 134.
Family at table, (*cuts*) 185, 252.
Fan-making, 292, (*cut*) 293.
Fan-painting, (*cut*) 292.
Fan, the, tricks with, 197.
Fatal star, the, 133.
Fertility of Japan, 65, 129.
Festivals, 184, 269 ; religious, (*cut*) 111.
Fêtes, 110, 305.
Fide-Yosi, 82.
Fireproof storehouses, 249.
Fires, frequency of, 15, 224.
Fisherwomen, Japanese, (*cut*) 231.
Fishing, 280 ; fish markets, 155.
Foreigners unpopular, 59.
Fox, the, stories about, 234 ; game of, 267.
French, the, in Japan, 39, 54.
Fruit trees, 308.
Funeral ceremonies 261.
Fusi-Yama, (*cut*) 326.
GARDENS, 249.
Ghekos, the, 179.
Gods, Japanese, 74, (*cut*) 75, 98.
Grades of society, (*cvt*) 122, 123.
Gymnasts, 191, (*cut*) 192.
HAKODADI, 52, 280, 322.
Hamlet, Japanese, (*cut*) 131.
Hara Kiru, the, 20.
Healing waters, 268.
Hermit of Kioto, (*cut*) 84.
Hero worship, 131.
Hiogo, 320, 323.
Hondjo, 145, 150.
Horticulture, 66, 250, 314.
Houses, Japanese, 246 ; interior, (*cut*) 248.
IDOLS, Japanese, 26, 74, (*cut*) 75, 109.
Imports and exports, 324.
Irrigation, 307.
JAPANESE empire, 65 ; origin of name, 8.
Japanning, 294.
Jesuits, the, in Japan, 28, 86.
Jinrikisha, the, 160.
Joros, the, 178, 181.
Jugglers, 190, 193 ; juggling girls, (*cut*) 195.
KAGOSIMA, 60.
Kami, worship of, 73, 92, 106, (*cut*) 107.
Kango, the, 160.
Kioto, 83, 119, 294 ; hermit of, (*cut*) 84.

Kiusiu, 86, 89, 321.
Kobi, 323.
Kurile Archipelago, 278.
LADIES, Japanese, (*cut*) 67.
Language of Japan, 282.
Legends, 268, 278, 290, 303.
Libraries, 288.
Life, disregard of, 127.
Literature, 131, 284; specimens of, 133, 134, 136, 139, 158, 228, 232.
Lonins, 123, 157; story of, 158.
MANURING the land, (*cut*) 306, 308.
Manufactures, 51, 298.
Marco Polo, 25.
Marionettes, 196.
Marketing, (*cut*) 272.
Marriage customs, 256.
Matsmaï, town of, 280.
Mats, much used, 252.
Matsouris, 110, (*cut*) 111.
Masquerading, 273, 276.
Meals, (*cut*) 185, (*cut*) 252, 254.
Mendez Pinto, 27.
Mendicants, 123, 268.
Metals, Japanese workers in, (*cut*) 297.
Mikado, the, 10, 117, 123; court of, (*cut*) 11.
Modesty, Japanese, 168, 180.
Music, 287.
NAGASAKI, (*cut*) 32, 320, (*cut*) 321.
New Year's Day, 271.
Niegata, 323.
Night-houses, 175.
Nipon, 25; Niphon-Bas, 151.
Norimon, the, 160, (*cut*) 161.
Nurse, Japanese, (*cut*) 260.
OFFICIAL costumes, (*cut*) 244.
Ogava, river, 150.
Opening of Japanese ports, 53.
Origin of Japanese, 66, 71.
Osaka, 18, 184, 320, 323.
PAINTER, Japanese, (*cut*) 254, 255.
Palace of the Sovereign, 247; of the Tycoons, 248.
Paper-making, 298.
Physical appearance of Japanese, 239.
Picnics, 265.
Playthings, passion for, 255.
Ploughing, 307.
Porcelain, manufacture of, 298.
Portuguese, the, in Japan, 28.
Postman, Japanese, (*cut*) 163.
Printing, 284.
Processions, 114, 164.
Proverbs, 291.
RAILWAYS introduced, 317, (*cut*) 318.
Religions, 73, 78, 92, 97.
Revolution in Japan, 119.
Rice, cultivation of, (*cut*) 309.
Rivers, crossing, 165.

Russians, the, in Japan, 38.
SAILORS, (*cut*) 122, 315.
Salutations, Japanese, (*cut*) 149.
Samurais, the, 145; child, (*cut*) 213.
"Sannoo," festival of, 113.
Scenery, picturesque, 130.
Scientific knowledge, 287.
Sculptor, Japanese, (*cut*) 141.
Seaweed, women gathering, (*cut*) 308.
Shipbuilding, 316.
Shops, 151; shopping, 295.
Sibaïa, the, 184, 210, 223.
Sikono, story of, 69.
Silk manufacture, 299.
Silkworms, rearing, 299.
Simoda, town and bay of, (*cut*) 7.
Simonasaki, 60.
Society, Japanese, 123.
Soldier, Japanese, (*cut*) 64.
Spaniards, the, in Japan, 35.
Speaking, public, 288.
Spinning, (*cut*) 238.
Stealing, punishment for, (*cut*) 55.
Superstitions, popular, 227.
Surgery, Japanese, 245.
TABLE, Japanese family at, (*cut*) 185.
Tea, cultivation of, (*cuts*) 310, 311, 312, 313.
Tea-houses, 170, (*cuts*) 172, 187, 264.
Tea-kettle, (*cut*) 253.
Temple, interior of, (*cut*) 289; at Yokohama, (*cut*) 82; Buddhist, (*cut*) 81.
Temple, Kami, (*cut*) 107.
Theatre, the Japanese, 16, 209.
Time, division of, 285.
Tocado, the, 160, 164.
Toilet, Japanese, 211, 240.
Tops, performance with, 197.
Treaties with Japan, 52-54, 319.
Trees, 314.
Tycoon, the, 13, 118, 248.
Types of Japanese, (*cuts*) 128, 240.
Tzanaghi, legend of, 75.
VINE, cultivation of the, 308.
Visits, paying, 275.
WARRIORS, ancient Japanese, (*cuts*) 48, 125.
War vessel, Japanese, (*cut*) 46.
Watchmen, 224, (*cut*) 225.
Weavers, Japanese, (*cut*) 300.
Winter dress, (*cut*) 242.
Wives, plurality of, 258.
Women, Japanese, (*cuts*) 72, 103, 240, 242.
Wrestling matches, 200, (*cut*) 203.
YAKONINS, 123, 145, (*cuts*) 146, 147.
Year, mode of dividing the, 285.
Yedo, 14, 142, 156; street in, (*cut*) 143
Yezo, island of, 277.
Yokohama, 59, (*cut*) 61, 317, 322; temple at, (*cut*) 83.
Yomasta, 184; fair at, 187.

Marcus Ward & Co. Royal Ulster Works, Belfast.

FEBRUARY, 1878.

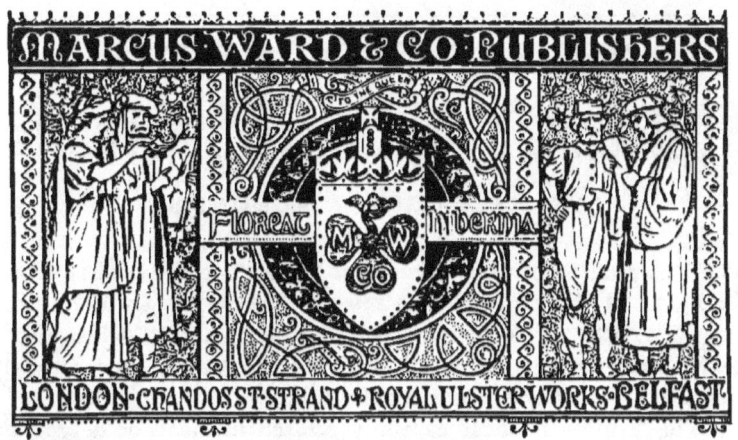

 llustrated &  ducational Works.

	PAGE		PAGE
Illustrated Waverley Novels	2	Annual Publications	17
Poetry	3	Concise Diaries	18
Important Illustrated Volumes	4	Atlases	19
Art Embroidery	5	Mythology of Greece and Rome	21
Historical and Topographical Volumes	5	Works on Drawing and Design	22
Birthday Registers	6	Fret-Cutting and Wood-Carving	22
Books of Travel	6	Aunt Charlotte's Histories for Young Children	22
Books for Boys	8		
Book on Fishing for Boys	8	A New System of Shorthand	24
New Editions of Standard Works	9	Handbook for Agricultural Students	24
Novels and Novelettes	10	Sunday School and Reward Cards	24
Books of Fairy Stories	11	Card Packets, by F. R. Havergal	27
Books for Young People	12	Temperance Cards	28
Books at 5/- for Children	12	Wall Greetings and Texts	28
Books at 2/6 for Children	13	Vere Foster's Writing Copy-Books	29
Books at 2/- for Children	15	Vere Foster's Water-Colour Drawing Books	30
Books at 1/6 for Children	16		
Children's Coloured Picture Books	17	Vere Foster's Drawing Copy-Books	31

MARCUS WARD AND CO.,
67, 68, Chandos Street, Strand,
LONDON;
ROYAL ULSTER WORKS, BELFAST.

MARCUS WARD'S
Illustrated Waverley Novels.
IN HALF-CROWN VOLUMES.

THE expiration of Copyright in Sir Walter Scott's Novels enables MARCUS WARD & CO. to offer to the Public an ENTIRELY NEW EDITION, at a popular price, with numerous Illustrations (drawn and engraved expressly by first-class Artists), and strongly bound in a New Style, ready for the Library.

The Edition is most carefully printed in clear, bold type, on fine paper, and the text is identical with the Original Edition, containing all the Author's Notes, etc.

As each Volume contains one or more Complete Tales, this Edition compares favourably in cost with other Illustrated Editions, in which one tale generally occupies two half-crown volumes.

NOW PUBLISHED.

WAVERLEY,	with 35	Illustrations	(10 full-page).
IVANHOE,	,, 36	,,	(10 full-page).
KENILWORTH,	,, 35	,,	(10 full-page).
GUY MANNERING,	,, 35	,,	(10 full-page).
HEART OF MID-LOTHIAN,	,, 32	,,	(8 full-page).
QUENTIN DURWARD,	,, 36	,,	(10 full-page).

Others will follow Monthly.

Crown Octavo, price 2/6 per Volume.

OPINIONS OF THE PRESS ON THE ILLUSTRATED WAVERLEY NOVELS.

"Decidedly the best produced at a moderate charge."—*Liverpool Courier.*
"The best one-volume edition we have yet seen."—*Sunday Times.*
"Convenient and handsomely brought out."—*Irish Times.*
"An excellent new edition."—*Daily News.*
"Will prove a general favourite."—*Academy.*
"A cheaper and handsomer form than we have hitherto been able to obtain."—*Bath Herald.*
"Ought to become popular, more especially as the drawings, besides being remarkably spirited, show a good deal of unusual knowledge of 'the periods' that are severally illustrated."—*Illustrated Sporting and Dramatic News.*
"Nothing more handsome or more perfect could be desired at the price."—*Belfast Northern Whig.*

LIST OF ILLUSTRATED BOOKS.   3

ELEGANT GIFT-BOOKS.

Poetry.

English Echoes of German Song. Translated by Dr. R. E. WALLIS, Dr. J. D. MORELL, and F. D'ANVERS. Edited by N. D'ANVERS. With Twelve beautiful Steel Engravings. Small quarto, cloth elegant, gilt edges. Price 10/6.
"Gracefully rendered into English. . . . Engravings remarkable for delicacy. . . . . very pretty and wholly unconventional."—*Daily News.*
"Successfully and faithfully rendered into musical English. . . . . The illustrations on steel are very worthy of the poetry."—*Standard.*

Floral Poetry and the Language of Flowers. A collection of choice poems on Flowers, with most complete Indexes to the Language of Flowers, and eight exquisite Illustrations in colours. Small quarto, cloth elegant, gilt edges. Price 10/6.
"A tasteful and well-chosen collection of flowery lyrics."—*Graphic.*
"Contains some of the choicest pieces of English verse about flowers."—*Bath Chronicle.*
"Poems of real merit, culled by a skilful and discriminating hand from the whole garden of English Poetry."—*The Nation.*
"Marvels of pictorial excellence."—*Standard.*
"Illustrations carefully coloured after nature."—*Daily News.*

The Quiver of Love: a collection of Valentines, Ancient and Modern. With Eight exquisite Full-page Illustrations in Gold and Colours, by WALTER CRANE and KATE GREENAWAY. Full gilt cover, gilt edges. Price 7/6.
"Look at it as we may, the book is a marvel, and its cheapness is not its least noticeable feature."—*Morning Advertiser.*

The Latin Year: a Collection of Latin Hymns, Ancient and Modern. Edited by the Rev. W. J. LOFTIE, B.A., F.S.A. With numerous Illustrations by R. BATEMAN, after the manner of the best period of early Wood Engraving. Rough edges, quaint binding. 15/-.
N.B.—A few copies with special binding may be had. Price 40/-.

Logroño: a Metric Drama in Two Acts. By FREDERICK CERNY. Twenty-nine Illustrations by T. WALTER WILSON. Royal octavo, cloth extra, gilt edges. Price 10/6.
"Historical in plot, the incident is realistic, and the language well chosen."—*Irish Times.*
"This composition is of a high order of merit; the poetry is bright and musical, the movement of the piece is rapid, and the various scenes are very effectively presented."—*Nation.*
"The story of this drama is pretty, and the author's treatment of it displays much power. The book is splendidly produced, and the engravings—which are in fac-simile —show that the artist has much originality of conception and execution."—*Irishman.*
"Has considerable merits, the pastoral stanzas possessing an exceptionable sweetness and beauty."—*Court Journal.*
"The style of the drama, though florid and declamatory, often rises to eloquence, the lyrics are generally musical and simple, there are several effective situations, and the author displays considerable power in the delineation of fiery southern passion."—*Scotsman.*

ELEGANT GIFT-BOOKS—*Continued.*

Language and Poetry of Flowers. A New Edition, carefully Revised and Amplified. With Six Illuminated Pages in Gold and Colours. Cloth, black and gold, 2/6; Gilt Edges, 3/-.

LANGUAGE AND POETRY OF FLOWERS. Pocket Edition, Illustrated in Gold and Colours. Cloth extra, 1/-; gilt edges, 1/3.

"An exceedingly nice little volume, well brought out and well illuminated."—*Ulster Examiner.*

"In addition to the ordinary dictionary of flower language . . . . beautifully coloured illustrations are given of such plants as the Azalea, Cyclamen, Arum, Pansy, &c."—*Cork Examiner.*

IMPORTANT ILLUSTRATED VOLUMES.

Shores of the Polar Sea: a Narrative of the Arctic Expedition of 1875-76. By Dr. EDWARD L. MOSS, H.M.S. "Alert." With Sixteen large Chromo-Lithographs, and numerous Engravings, from Drawings made on the spot by the Author. Imperial Folio. Price Five Guineas. [*In preparation.*

New Zealand Scenery. Fifteen Chromo-Lithographs after Original Water-colour Drawings by JOHN GULLY, with descriptive letter-press by Dr. JULIUS VON HAAST. Imperial Folio, in portfolio or bound, full cloth extra, gilt edges. Price Five Guineas.

"The drawings are fifteen in number, and are devoted almost entirely to lake, mountain, and river scenery, the peculiar characteristics of which are suggested with striking effect."—*Daily News.*

"May go far to encourage emigration among the enterprising, and pleasure-travel among the lovers of nature who have means and time for the enjoyment of their healthful taste."—*Daily Telegraph.*

"Cannot fail deeply to interest the British public, not only because of its great merit as an art-work, but as introducing us to the glorious picturesque of a new world, with which we have become of late years very intimately associated."—*Art Journal.*

Thalassa: an Essay on the Depth, Temperature, and Currents of the Ocean. By JOHN JAMES WILD, Member of the Civilian Scientific Staff of H.M.S. "Challenger." With Charts and Diagrams by the Author. Price 12/-.

"Well worthy of the attention of all students of Physical Geography."—*Academy.*

"The essay compresses within narrow bounds an extraordinary amount of useful and interesting information."—*Daily Express.*

"The diagrams and maps are capitally executed, and illustrate effectively the lucid letterpress."—*World.*

At Anchor: Sketches from many Shores visited by H.M.S. "*Challenger,*" *with a Narrative of Experiences on Sea and on Land.* By JOHN JAMES WILD, Artist and Secretary to the Expedition.

[*In active preparation.*

Bards and Blossoms; or, the Poetry, History, and Associations of Flowers. With Eight Floral Plates, Illuminated in Gold and Colours. By F. E. HULME, F.L.S., F.S.A., Marlborough College. Price 10/6.

"It is written in an easy, agreeable style, with short dissertations on the beauty, teaching, utility, and symbolical value of flowers."—*Irish Times.*

"Very charmingly written."—*Irishman.*

"A magnificent gift-book, which, at the same time, contains much valuable information not easily attainable."—*Glasgow News.*

IMPORTANT ILLUSTRATED VOLUMES—*Continued.*

Mrs. Mundi at Home. R.S.V.P. Lines and Outlines by WALTER CRANE. Twenty-four Plates. New Edition, cloth, Decorated by the Artist, gilt extra, gilt edges, large oblong quarto. Price 15/-.
"A quaint and clever book of drawings."—*Times.*
"Every picture in the twenty-four is a study in itself."—*Standard.*
"The humour is so intense, and at the same time so delicate, that the most fastidious hypochondriac must be forced to laughter."—*Morning Post.*

Topo: a Tale about English Children in Italy. By G. E. BRUNEFILLE. With numerous Illustrations by KATE GREENAWAY. Square octavo, cloth extra, gilt edges. Price 4/6.
"This is a delightfully naïve and natural little story."—*Nonconformist.*
"We are much mistaken if 'Topo' fail to secure the joyousest of welcomes."—*Illustrated Sporting and Dramatic News.*
"The illustrations are the most life-like representations of children we have come across this year, and would stand favourable comparison with the best sketches of Richard Doyle and George du Maurier."—*Globe.*

Art Embroidery: a Treatise on the Revived Practice of *Decorative Needlework.* By M. S. LOCKWOOD and E. GLAISTER. With Nineteen Plates, printed in Colours, from Designs by THOMAS CRANE. Royal quarto. Price One Guinea.

Christopher Columbus and the Discovery of the New World. From the French of M. LE MARQUIS DE BELLOY. With Fifty-one Drawings on Wood and Six Etchings, by LEOPOLD FLAMENG. Demy quarto. Price Two Guineas.

The Black Crusoe. From the French of ALFRED SEGUIN. With Seventy Illustrations engraved on Wood by M. MEAULLE, from Designs by MM. H. SCOTT, MEYER, FERDINANDUS, &c.
[*In preparation.*

Bible Biographies; or, Stories from the Old Testament. By Rev. W. E. LITTLEWOOD, M.A., Vicar of St. James's, Bath. With numerous Illustrations and Coloured Frontispiece. [*In preparation.*

Companion to Killarney. By S. C. HALL. A Complete Guide to this interesting and much-visited spot. With numerous Illustrations and good-sized Map (scale, 1 inch to mile), and all necessary Tourists' arrangements. Small octavo, cloth limp. Price 2/6.
[*In preparation.*

HISTORICAL AND TOPOGRAPHICAL VOLUMES.

Historical Records of the 2nd Royal Surrey Militia. With Introductory Chapters, giving a Sketch of the History of the English Militia, and of events in the Military History of Surrey. By JOHN DAVIS, Captain in the Regiment. Frontispiece and numerous Full-page Illustrations specially prepared for this work. Large 8vo. 21/-.
"A mass of information which will be found sufficiently interesting, not only by the members of the Second Royal Surrey, but by the general reader as well."—*Globe.*
"The local antiquary—whether a man of peace or war—will find much to interest him in Captain Davis's pages."—*Graphic.*
"Both amusing and instructive."—*Morning Post.*

HISTORICAL AND TOPOGRAPHICAL VOLUMES—*Continued.*

A History of Belfast, from the Earliest Times to the Close of the Eighteenth Century. By GEORGE BENN. Maps and Illustrations. Large octavo, 770 pp., cloth gilt. Price 28/-.

"The book is full of quaint and curious details, as well as of more solid information bearing on the subject with which it deals; and the Maps and Illustrations with which it is enriched add greatly to its value."—*North British Daily Mail.*
"A contribution to the library much wanted and of great value."—*Art Journal.*
"Worthy of being regarded as a standard work of reference to the locality of which it treats."—*Belfast News-Letter.*
"In all respects this work is very complete."—*Northern Whig.*
"We are inspired with confidence in the author's ability as a historian."—*The Irish Builder.*

Birthday Registers.

The Poets' Year: a Birthday Register. With Selections from Chaucer to Longfellow, chronologically arranged, printed on Writing Paper. With Illuminated Title-page. Cloth extra, 2/-; gilt edges, 2/6; and in Limp French Morocco, Morocco and Russia, from 3/6 to 10/6.

A superb edition of the above, with Illuminated Pages, and Vignette Portraits of the Poets, handsomely bound in cloth, gilt edges.
[*In preparation.*

Links of Memory: a Birthday Register and Daily Text Book. Compiled by FRANCES A. SHAW, with a Preface by FRANCES R. HAVERGAL. With Illuminated Frontispiece. 32mo. Price 1/-.
[*In preparation.*

BOOKS OF TRAVEL.

South by East: Notes of Travel in Southern Europe. By G. F. RODWELL, Science Master in Marlborough College. 102 Full-page Original and other Illustrations. 4to, cloth extra. Price 21/-.

"He is able to give freshness to his chapters by faithfully recording the ideas and impressions of a cultivated observer.... Descriptive passages that are admirable in their way."—*Daily News.*
"Interesting and instructive volume, abounding with evidences of intelligent study, profound appreciation, refined taste, and general cultivation."—*Illustrated London News.*
"His descriptions of scenery, life, and manners are excellent."—*Spectator.*
"A very welcome addition to this season's best hand-books of travel."—*Standard.*

Heroes of North African Discovery. By N. D'ANVERS. Map and numerous Illustrations. Crown octavo, cloth extra. Price 5/-.

"The narrative is swift, full of information and of interest."—*Irish Times.*
"A very readable book."—*Nation.*
"The book is as interesting as any average sensational novel, and far more profitable in perusal."—*Irishman.*
"A complete and vividly written record of exploration and explorers."—*World.*
"A mass of carefully-digested information, drawn from over forty different works. ... The work is well and carefully printed, contains numerous illustrations, and what is especially essential, a good map of Africa, corrected down to the present date, and giving in red the routes of travellers."—*The Colonies and India.*

BOOKS OF TRAVEL—Continued.

Heroes of South African Discovery. By N. D'ANVERS. Author of "Dobbie and Dobbie's Master." Map and numerous Illustrations. A companion volume to "Heroes of North African Discovery." Crown octavo, cloth extra. Price 5/-.

China, Historical and Descriptive. By C. H. EDEN. With an Appendix on COREA. Numerous Illustrations, Map, and Coloured Frontispiece by a Native Artist. Crown octavo, cloth extra. Price 5/-.

"Eagerly perused at the present time by giving useful and pleasant details of a country and a people of which our knowledge hitherto has been anything but extensive or precise."—*Irish Times.*
"A most entertaining account of an interesting country and a wonderful people."—*Nation.*
"The book is extremely readable."—*Irishman.*
"A concise and interesting account of China, and of the manners and customs of the inhabitants of that vast country."—*Academy.*
"Carefully compiled from recognised authorities, and here presented in a convenient shape."—*World.*
"The four chapters on Corea, which are chiefly based on the valuable introductory matter prefixed to Dallet's 'Histoire de l'Eglise de Corée,' bear signs of being carefully written, and will be read with the greater interest, as the subject is quite new to English readers."—*The Overland Mail.*
"The book will be found useful by all those who wish to obtain a good general view of a very wide and important subject."—*Standard.*
"He has admirably succeeded in his task of collecting all the latest and most reliable information within reach, and placing it in a form likely to be interesting and attractive to the general reader."—*Mayfair.*
"In a thick small octavo, Mr. Eden tells the story of China in an attractive manner."—*Scotsman.*

Japan, Historical and Descriptive. A comprehensive account of Japanese History, Life, Character, and Manners. By C. H. EDEN, Author of "India, Historical and Descriptive," &c. Seventy-five Illustrations, Map, and Coloured Frontispiece. Crown octavo, cloth extra. Price 3/6.

"A very clear and comprehensive view of Japanese life, character, and manners."—*Morning Advertiser.*
"There have been few books at once so valuable and so accessible. . . . . . Another right good work to the many rare issues of the Belfast Press."—*Art Journal.*
"A clever, cheerful book."—*Morning Post.*
"A complete history of the growth of Japan. . . . A good, valuable, and profoundly interesting book."—*Times.*
"Written in good, easy style, and very well illustrated."—*Scotsman.*

India, Historical and Descriptive. With an Account of the Sepoy Mutiny of 1857-58, by C. H. EDEN, Author of "Ralph Somerville," &c. Sixty-six Illustrations, Map, and Coloured Frontispiece. Crown octavo, cloth extra. Price 3/6.

"The illustrations are well executed."—*Standard.*
"A clever little book, containing an excellent and most readable account of our greatest dependency."—*Daily Telegraph.*
"An interesting volume."—*Graphic.*

Notes of Travel in Egypt and Nubia. By J. L. STEPHENS. Revised and enlarged, with an account of the Suez Canal. Seventy-one Illustrations, Map, and Coloured Frontispiece. Crown octavo, cloth extra. Price 3/6.

"A very entertaining, well-written little volume."—*Graphic.*
"The little volume is unexceptionable."—*Daily Telegraph.*

Books for Boys.—Tales, Travel, and Adventure.

Stirring Tales of the Sea, by S. Whitchurch Sadler, R.N.

The Flag-Lieutenant : a Story of the Slave Squadron. With Coloured Frontispiece and Illuminated Title-page, and numerous Original Illustrations. Post octavo, cloth extra. Price 5/-.

"A stirring and evidently faithful story of adventure, this handsome book forms an excellent present for a boy, who would revel in its exciting incidents, and gloat over its striking illustrations."—*Glasgow News.*
"Well arranged and vigorously written."—*World.*
"Will probably be a favourite with boys."—*Academy.*
"Captain Sadler constructs his story neatly, and knows how to throw in his incidents, never obtruding the lessons he would teach in such a way as boys would not like."—*Nonconformist.*
"A rattling naval romance which will delight any schoolboy who has a taste for salt water."—*Bath Herald.*
"Is clearly the work of an old sailor, who knows, from long experience, what life at sea is like, and has found out the shape in which boys like to have the yarn spun for their express edification."—*Standard.*
"A good rattling sea story."—*Scotsman.*
"A capital book for boys, full of excitement and gallant deeds."—*Vanity Fair.*

Last Cruise of the Ariadne. With Coloured Frontispiece and Illuminated Title-page, and numerous Original Illustrations. Post octavo, cloth extra. Price 5/-.

"A stirring story of the sea."—*Academy.*
"A narrative of adventure that will delight any reader."—*Lloyd's Weekly News.*
"A pleasant and spirited tale."—*Spectator.*

Perilous Seas, and how Oriana sailed them. With Coloured Frontispiece and Illuminated Title-page, and numerous Original Illustrations. Post octavo, cloth extra. Price 5/-.

"All through 'Perilous Seas' there is enough stirring incident to arouse, and enough good writing to sustain, the interest of its youthful readers."—*Hour.*

The Ship of Ice : a Strange Story of the Polar Seas. With Coloured Frontispiece and Illuminated Title-page, and numerous Original Illustrations. Post octavo, cloth extra. Price 3/6.

"Not only a 'Strange Story,' but one full of exciting interest. The author writes in a vigorous, manly style, and the book is one which most English boys, with their love of daring and adventure, are likely heartily to relish."—*Pall Mall Gazette.*
"A capital book of adventure."—*Manchester Guardian.*

BOOK ON FISHING.

The Boy's Walton. By ULICK J. BURKE, B.A., Author of "The Great Captain : an Eventful Chapter in Spanish History." Numerous Illustrations. Small octavo, cloth extra. Price 2/6.

By C. H. Eden.

Coralie; or, the Wreck of the Sybille. With Coloured Frontispiece and Illuminated Title-page, and numerous Original Illustrations. Post octavo, cloth extra. Price 5/-.

"The details of savage life and adventure localising the story are carefully and accurately given."—*Morning Post.*

"An ingenious little romance."—*Times.*

"The whole tone and drift of the book, too, are good, and young people will find in it much that is curious to interest and instruct them in the doings of brave men."—*Standard.*

Ralph Somerville; or, a Midshipman's Adventures in the Pacific Ocean. With Coloured Frontispiece and Illuminated Title-page, and numerous Original Illustrations. Post 8vo, cloth extra. Price 5/-.

"There is always an air of reality about Mr. Eden's descriptive passages which makes one feel that they are the result of actual experience."—*Morning Post.*

Three Years at Wolverton: a Public School Story. By a Wolvertonian. With Coloured Frontispiece and Illuminated Title-page, and numerous Original Illustrations. Post octavo, cloth extra. Price 5/-.

"The best purely boy's book we have seen since 'Tom Brown.'"—*Saturday Review.*

"Well conceived and worked out."—*Athenæum.*

"Written throughout with a high tone and manly spirit."—*Academy.*

"The book is manly, and has but little of the unreal sentiment which is so apt to disfigure public school stories. Bertram is a well-conceived and natural character; and schoolboys can get nothing but good from reading of his failures and successes. . . . We can recommend the book."—*Guardian.*

"A capital book for boys, which is likely to instil right principles to guide them in their school life."—*Blackheathen School Magazine.*

"A decidedly interesting book."—*Magdalen College School Journal.*

"Lively and well sustained, and the tone good and healthy throughout."—*Uppingham School Magazine.*

"A book which we would recommend as a useful picture of school life."—*Epsomian School Magazine.*

"Superior to the generality of schoolboy books."—*The Meteor—Rugby School Magazine.*

"Really good."—*Cheltenham College School Magazine.*

New Editions of Standard Works.

Robinson Crusoe. By DANIEL DEFOE. Crown octavo, cloth extra. With Coloured Frontispiece and Title-page, and numerous Illustrations. Price 3/6.

"Remarkable as possessing the very best illustrations with which any popular edition has been issued."—*Sunday Times.*

Swiss Family Robinson. A New Translation from the German, with numerous Illustrations and Coloured Frontispiece. Crown octavo, cloth extra. Price 3/6.

"A new edition, bountifully enriched with excellent pictures."—*Daily Telegraph.*

"A goodly volume, adorned with some clever and picturesque woodcuts."—*Standard.*

"Could not be found in a better form than this."—*Scotsman.*

"Beautiful edition, with coloured prints and fine wood engravings."—*Nonconformist.*

"Well printed, well bound."—*World.*

NEW EDITIONS OF STANDARD WORKS—*Continued*.

The Vicar of Wakefield. By OLIVER GOLDSMITH. Crown octavo, cloth extra. With Coloured Frontispiece and Title-page and numerous Illustrations. Price 3/6.

"A charming edition."—*Morning Post.*
"A really pretty and cheap edition."—*The Nonconformist.*

Novels and Novelettes.

Em; or, Spells and Counter-Spells. By M. BRAMSTON, Author of "The Panelled House." *Second edition*, with a Frontispiece by PERCY MACQUOID. Crown octavo. Price 6/-.

"It is long since we read a story more satisfactory from every point of view."—*John Bull.*
"Containing in one volume a good deal more than the ordinary value of three. . . . Miss Bramston has given to us one of the freshest and healthiest tales of the year."—*Nonconformist.*
"It is the merit of the author that, without much resort to incidental subjects of interest, she manages to make all her characters distinct, if not ambitious in their proportions. The best of them is Em, a by no means faultless though very winning heroine, who learns much in the period of suspicion and humbled pride which separates her for a time from happiness."—*Athenæum.*
"Agreeably told, and Em herself is a pleasant sketch."—*Daily News.*
"The character of the heroine is cleverly conceived, and very consistently worked out."—*Academy.*
"Pleasantly written."—*Standard.*
"Em is a good story, told with much spirit and humour."—*Spectator.*
"The author's characters are carefully drawn and well sustained. . . . 'Em' is the produce of culture, good taste, and generous sympathies."—*Pall Mall Gazette.*
"One of the pleasantest of stories."—*Court Journal.*
"We hope that the book will make its way to all our readers who care for a well-told tale, with high feeling and delicate portraiture."—*Guardian.*
"A pretty and well-written love story."—*Morning Post.*

Country Maidens: a Story of the Present Day. By M. BRAMSTON, Author of "The Panelled House," &c. With Full-page Original Illustrations, Coloured Frontispiece, and Illuminated Title-page. Post octavo, cloth, gold and black. Price 3/6.

"A charming fresh little story, which must give pleasure to both old and young . . . deserves to be heartily commended."—*Morning Post.*
"As charming a tale of home life as we have often met."—*Standard.*

A Very Young Couple. By the Author of "Mrs. Jerningham's Journal." With Original Full-page Illustrations. Post octavo, cloth extra. Price 3/6.

"Affords some excellent sketches of private life in pursuit of comfort under difficulties."—*Morning Post.*
"A simple story of true love, told with much grace and naiveté."—*Sunday Times.*
"A very lively and pleasant little tale."—*Spectator.*
"The young wife relates her own distress so touchingly that she quite wins our sympathy."—*Athenæum.*
"We must thank the author for having given us an hour or two of genuine pleasure, and cordially recommend the book to all readers."—*Graphic.*

Miss Hitchcock's Wedding Dress. By the Author of "Mrs. Jerningham's Journal," &c. Post octavo, cloth extra. Price 5/-.

"One of those pleasant stories, in an attractive dress, which are becoming almost a specialty of Marcus Ward & Co."—*Morning Advertiser.*

LIST OF ILLUSTRATED BOOKS. 11

NOVELS AND NOVELETTES.—*Continued.*

Myrtle and Cypress: a Tale of Chequered Life. By ANNETTE CALTHROP. With Original Full-page Illustrations. Post octavo, cloth extra. Price 5/-.
"The tale is altogether above the average, healthy in tone, and worked out with no little ability."—*John Bull.*

Mildred's Mistake. A Still-Life Study. By F. LEVIEN, Author of "Maggie's Pictures," &c. With Coloured Frontispiece, Illuminated Title, and Full-page Original Illustrations. Small octavo, cloth extra. Price 2/6.
"A book that young maidens will delight in."—*Academy.*

Eldergowan; or, Twelve Months of my Life, and Other Tales. By ROSA MULHOLLAND, Author of "l'uck and Blossom," "The Little Flower-Seekers," &c. Full-page Original Illustrations, Coloured Frontispiece, and Illuminated Title-page. Small octavo, cloth, gold and black. Price 2/6.
"One of the pleasantest little books we have met for some time; charmingly illustrated."—*Illustrated Review.*

Where the Rail Runs Now: a Story of the Coaching Days. By F. FRANKFORT MOORE. With Illustrations. Small octavo, cloth extra. Price 2/6.
"There is no lack of sensational incidents, but the story is told in very simple language, and will serve to create no other than a healthy excitement."—*The Times.*
"Capitally written, and full of spirit. The interest never once flags."—*Irish Times.*
"A clever little novel."—*Saturday Review.*
"We can strongly recommend this little book."—*Spectator.*
"The author's descriptions of English scenery are picturesque and unaffected."—*Daily News.*
"A capital book for a railway journey, or to amuse an idle hour."—*Pall Mall Gazette.*

Told by the Sea: Tales of the Coast. By F. FRANKFORT MOORE. With Illustrations. Small octavo, cloth extra. Price 2/6.
"Few readers having once begun, will care to lay down the book till they have finished."—*Belfast Northern Whig.*
"'Told by the Sea' is a collection of stories very different in character, and only alike in merit. The earliest in order, which is entitled 'The Last Yarn of Our Cruise,' is a powerful, if rather sensational, narrative. That which follows, entitled 'Mr. Plassington's Journal,' is one of the cleverest comic sketches we have ever read. It absolutely overflows with drollery—genuine, irresistible drollery—and in the description of an old sailor whom it introduces shows a power of observation worthy of Dickens. If Mr. Frankfort Moore can write many stories like this, he will maintain a permanent place in literature."—*Sunday Times.*

Books of Fairy Stories.

Fairyland Tales of Dwarfs, Fairies, Water-Sprites, &c. From the German of Villamaria. Twenty-five Illustrations and Coloured Frontispiece. Crown octavo, cloth extra. Price 3/6.
"A genuine book of fairy tales."—*Spectator.*
"The translator's style is pure and graceful."—*Daily News.*
"Very quaint and graceful, and very well translated."—*Times.*
"A nicely executed and pleasantly illustrated translation."—*Saturday Review.*
"A capital little volume."—*Athenæum.*
"Will prove a welcome offering."—*Academy.*

BOOKS OF FAIRY STORIES—*Continued.*

***Fairy Circles: Tales and Legends of Dwarfs, Fairies, and**
Water-Sprites. From the German of Villamaria. A Sequel to
"Fairyland Tales." Numerous Illustrations and Coloured Frontispiece. Crown octavo, cloth extra. Price 3/6.
"An attractive book of Fairy Stories."—*Pall Mall Gazette.*
"All are smoothly translated."—*Academy.*
"Capital reading, while its illustrations are excellent."—*Scotsman.*
"Very pretty they are, and read as though they were well translated."—*Times.*
"Have all the charm which the Teutonic fairy tales always possess."—*Bath Herald.*

Books for Young People.
By Sarah Tytler.

Childhood a Hundred Years Ago. By the Author of "Papers for Thoughtful Girls." With Six Chromographs, after Paintings by SIR JOSHUA REYNOLDS. Small quarto, cloth elegant, gilt edges, 10/6.
"A very fascinating account of juvenile doings a century back."—*Graphic.*

Landseer's Dogs and their Stories. By the Author of "Citoyenne Jacquelline," &c. With Six Chromographs, after Paintings by Sir Edwin Landseer. Small quarto, cloth elegant, gilt edges, 10/6.
"Charming stories."—*Spectator.*
"Thoughtful and sensible essays."—*Saturday Review.*

The Good Old Days; or, Christmas under Queen Elizabeth.
By ESME STUART. With Five Coloured Illustrations, from Drawings by H. STACY MARKS, A.R.A. Foolscap quarto, cloth extra, bevelled boards. Price 5/-.
"Not only will interest be derived from the story, but instruction as to the manners and habits of the people in the days of good Queen Bess."—*City Press.*

Melcomb Manor: a Family Chronicle. By F. SCARLETT POTTER. Six Illustrations, in Gold and Colours. Foolscap quarto, cloth extra, bevelled boards. Price 5/-.
"Altogether a very pretty book, whether as regards the pictures or the story."—*Saturday Review.*

Chronicles of Cosy Nook: a Book of Stories for Boys and Girls. By Mrs. S. C. HALL. With Full-page Original Illustrations, Coloured Frontispiece, and Illuminated Title-page. Post octavo, cloth, gold and black. Price 3/6.
"Mrs. Hall never in her best days wrote a better story for youngsters."—*Morning Advertiser.*

BOOKS AT FIVE SHILLINGS FOR CHILDREN.
Chromograph Series.

Puck and Blossom: a Fairy Tale. By ROSA MULHOLLAND, Author of "The Little Flower-Seekers," "Eldergowan," &c. Six Illustrations, in Gold and Colours. Foolscap quarto, cloth extra, bevelled boards. [*New Edition.*
"Pretty stories, beautifully illustrated in gold and colours."—*Daily News.*

LIST OF ILLUSTRATED BOOKS. 13

BOOKS AT FIVE SHILLINGS FOR CHILDREN.—*Continued.*

The Little Flower-Seekers ; or, the Adventures of Trot and
Daisy in a Wonderful Garden by Moonlight. By ROSA MULHOLLAND, Author of "Puck and Blossom," "Eldergowan," &c. With Twelve Chromographs of Flowers, by various Artists. Foolscap quarto, cloth extra, bevelled boards.

"A charming volume."—*Daily News.*
"Contains some of the finest coloured plates of flowers ever published, and the story is in itself telling and fresh."—*Standard.*
"A prettier book for young children we have not seen for a long while."—*Pall Mall Gazette.*

A Cruise in the Acorn. By ALICE JERROLD. Six Illustrations, in Gold and Colours. Foolscap quarto, cloth extra, bevelled boards.
[*New Edition.*

"A simple little story, very prettily told, with illustrations in colours and gold."—*Graphic.*
"Told in a charming style, by aid of beautiful print, and illustrated in gold and colours."—*Liverpool Albion.*

Katty Lester : a book for Girls. By Mrs. GEORGE CUPPLES, Author of "The Children's Voyage," &c. With Twelve Chromographs of Animals, after Harrison Weir. Foolscap quarto, cloth extra, bevelled boards. [*New Edition.*

"A capital book for girls."—*Globe.*
"Is deserving of high commendation for its artistic beauty."—*Figaro.*
"A delightful collection of stories for little girls, adorned with a dozen capital chromographs, after Harrison Weir."—*Times.*

The Children's Voyage ; or, a Trip in the Water Fairy.
By Mrs. GEORGE CUPPLES, Author of "Katty Lester," &c. With Twelve Chromographs of Ships, Boats, and Sea Views, after Edward Duncan. Foolscap quarto, cloth extra, bevelled boards.

"Well adapted to the comprehension of children."—*Standard.*
"Mrs. Cupples deserves to be congratulated on a success, and so assuredly does the artist."—*Pall Mall Gazette.*

BOOKS AT TWO-AND-SIXPENCE FOR CHILDREN.

Esther: a Story for Children. By GERALDINE BUTT. Author of "Christmas Roses," "Lads and Lasses." Numerous Woodcut and Chromograph Illustrations. [*In preparation.*

Kaspar and the Seven Wonderful Pigeons of Würzburg.
By JULIA GODDARD. With Coloured Frontispiece, Illuminated Title, and Full-page Original Illustrations. Small octavo, cloth extra.

"Thank you, good Pigeons, for the very pleasant hours you have given us."—*Academy.*

Dobbie and Dobbie's Master : a Peep into the Life of a
Very Little Man. By N. D'ANVERS, Author of "Little Minnie's Troubles," &c. With Illustrations. Small octavo, cloth extra.

"A genuine child's story."—*Spectator.*
"A fascinating story."—*Academy.*
"We can recommend this book with all confidence to all fathers and mothers who have a nursery of small children."—*Standard.*

BOOKS AT TWO-AND-SIXPENCE FOR CHILDREN.—*Continued.*

Tom: the History of a very Little Boy. By H. RUTHERFURD RUSSELL. Full-page Original Illustrations, Coloured Frontispiece and Illuminated Title-page. Small octavo, cloth, gold and black.
"Almost as good, in its way, as Mr. Carroll's 'Alice in Wonderland.' Parents and lovers of childhood will like it much, as the childish reader is sure to do."—*Illustrated London News.*

Tom Seven Years Old: a Sequel to "Tom." By H. RUTHERFURD RUSSELL. Full-page Original Illustrations, Coloured Frontispiece and Illuminated Title-page. Small octavo, cloth, gold and black.
"The truest and purest exhibition of a natural little boy's mind that we have seen in any story of child life."—*Illustrated London News.*

Minna's Holiday, and other Tales. By M. BETHAM-EDWARDS. Full-page Original Illustrations, Coloured Frontispiece and Illuminated Title-page. Small octavo, cloth, gold and black.
"Simple, pleasantly written stories."—*Daily News.*

Doda's Birthday: the Record of all that befell a Little Girl on a Long, Eventful Day. By EDWIN J. ELLIS. Full-page Original Illustrations, Coloured Frontispiece and Illuminated Title-page. Small octavo, cloth, gold and black.
"A charming book."—*Daily News.*

The Markhams of Ollerton: a Tale of the Civil War, 1642–1647. By E. GLAISTER. Full-page Original Illustrations, Coloured Frontispiece and Illuminated Title-page. Small octavo, cloth, gold and black.
"Abounds with thrilling incidents of that eventful period."—*Morning Post.*

Nanny's Treasure. From the French of Madame DE STOLZ. Nineteen Full-page Illustrations and Coloured Frontispiece. Small octavo, cloth extra.
"A very delightful story for children."—*Academy.*

The Little Head of the Family. From the French of Mdlle. FLEURIOT. Fourteen Full-page Illustrations and Coloured Frontispiece. Small octavo, cloth extra.
"Natural and pleasant."—*Times.*

Christmas at Annesley; or, how the Grahams spent their Holidays. By M. E. SHIPLEY. Small octavo, cloth, gold and black.
[*New Edition.*

Turnaside Cottage. By MARY SENIOR CLARK, Author of "Lost Legends of the Nursery Rhymes." Small octavo, cloth, gold and black. [*New Edition.*

The Fairy Spinner. By MIRANDA HILL. Small octavo, cloth, gold and black. [*New Edition.*

Pollie and Jack: a Small Story for Small People. By ALICE HEPBURN, Author of "Two Little Cousins." Small octavo, cloth, gold and black. [*New Edition.*

BOOKS AT TWO-AND-SIXPENCE FOR CHILDREN—*Continued*.

All in a Garden Green, and Talk of a Sheet of Paper.
By ELIZABETH C. TRAICE, Author of "A Forlorn Hope," "Gerard Marston's Wife," &c. With Illustrations by T. M. LINDSAY. Small octavo, cloth extra.
"An attractive book for children, agreeably illustrated."—*Sunday Times*.
"Two delightful stories, and extremely well told. The manner in which the accessory incidents are clearly and sharply indicated, with just enough and not too much detail, shows much aptitude, and that natural sense of the right proportion of things which makes all the difference between a well-told story and one awkwardly developed."—*Athenæum*.
"An interesting and instructive book of stories for small children."—*Pall Mall Gazette*.

BOOKS AT TWO SHILLINGS FOR CHILDREN.

Two Little Cousins. By ALICE HEPBURN, Author of "Pollie and Jack." Five Coloured Illustrations, Cloth, Illuminated.
"Adorned with bright chromographs, and printed in large, clear type to suit beginners."—*Standard*.

Percy's First Friends. By M. D. Five Coloured Illustrations, Cloth, Illuminated.
"An agreeable account of the early adventures of a motherless boy."—*Lloyd's Weekly London News*.

Five Little Farmers. By ROSA MULHOLLAND, Author of "Puck and Blossom," "The Little Flower-Seekers," "Eldergowan," &c. Five Coloured Illustrations, Cloth, Illuminated.
"Contains a number of cunningly worked-out chromo-lithographs, in which children and their domestic pets are grouped in a most artistic and effective manner."—*Figaro*.

Maggie's Pictures; or, the Great Life told to a Child. By FANNY LEVIEN, Author of "Mildred's Mistake," "Little Ada's Jewels." Five Coloured Illustrations, and Illuminated Title-page. Cloth, Illuminated.
"Will be welcome for the simplicity of its early lessons."—*Lloyd's Weekly London News*.

The Brothers; or, Tales of Long Ago. By FANNY LEVIEN. Five Coloured Illustrations, and Illuminated Title-page. Cloth, Illuminated.

The Twin Brothers of Elfvedale: a Story of Norwegian Peasant Life. By CHARLES H. EDEN, Author of "Ralph Somerville," "India, Historical and Descriptive," &c. Coloured Illustrations, Cloth, Illuminated.
"Full of adventure. . . Schoolboys will welcome the book."—*Guardian*.

Our Games: a Story for Children. By MARY HAMILTON. Five Coloured Illustrations, Cloth, Illuminated.
"A pleasant little book. . . . Attractive illustrations."—*Standard*.
"Adventures of children, drawn in a charmingly natural manner."—*Guardian*.

Ella's Locket, and what it brought her. By G. E. DARTNELL. Five Coloured Illustrations, Cloth, Illuminated.
"Pleasantly conceived, and prettily told."—*Hour*.

BOOKS AT EIGHTEEN PENCE FOR CHILDREN.

Nellie's Playmates. By HOPE MYDDLETON. Numerous Illustrations and Coloured Frontispiece. Small octavo, cloth extra.
"A pretty story for children."—*Irishman.*
"Written in a style to please and attract juvenile readers."—*Belfast Morning News.*

The Magic Rose : a Story for Children. By BLANCHE MARY PEYTON. Numerous Illustrations and Coloured Frontispiece. Small octavo, cloth extra.

My Dolly. By H. RUTHERFURD RUSSELL, Author of "Tom Seven Years Old." Numerous Illustrations and Coloured Frontispiece. Small octavo, cloth extra.

Children of the Farm : A Tale of Country Life. With Illustrations and Coloured Frontispiece. Small octavo, cloth extra.

Wildflower Win : the Journal of a Little Girl. By KATHLEEN KNOX. Numerous Illustrations and Coloured Frontispiece. Small 8vo, cloth extra.
"The very name is tempting enough to make one buy the book, which, besides a great number of woodcuts, contains a nicely painted picture of the little heroine."—*Irish Times.*

The Little Bog-Trotters. By CLARA MULHOLLAND. Numerous Illustrations and Coloured Frontispiece. Small octavo, cloth extra.
[*In preparation.*

Master Trim's Charge. By ESME STUART, Author of "The Good Old Days; or, Christmas under Queen Elizabeth." Numerous Illustrations and Coloured Frontispiece. Small octavo, cloth extra.
[*In preparation.*

Lily of the Valley : a Story for Little Boys and Girls. By KATHLEEN KNOX. Coloured Illustrations, Cloth, Illuminated.
"A pretty little gift-book, the value of which will be appreciated by the very youngest of readers."—*Leeds Mercury.*

Meadowleigh : a Holiday History. By KATHLEEN KNOX. Coloured Illustrations, Cloth, Illuminated.
"Another of those irresistible little books for children in which Messrs. Marcus Ward & Co. so cunningly combine frolicsome narrative with some of the best executed and most satisfactory coloured illustrations that have ever come under our notice."—*Figaro.*

Elsie's Victory. By ELEANOR P. GEARY. Coloured Illustrations, Cloth, Illuminated.
"Sure to delight children."—*Guardian.*

Katie Summers : a Little Tale for Little Readers. By Mrs. C. HALL. Coloured Illustrations, Cloth, Illuminated.
"We hardly know whether most to praise binding, printing, or literary merit."—*Morning Advertiser.*
"Another tempting story of and for little people."—*Lloyd's Weekly London News.*

Roses With and Without Thorns. By ESTHER FAITHFULL FLEET. Coloured Illustrations, Cloth, Illuminated.
"Daintily decorated with delicate coloured illustrations."—*Scotsman.*

Little Ada's Jewels. By FANNY LEVIEN, Author of "Maggie's Pictures," "Mildred's Mistake." Coloured Illustrations, Cloth, Illuminated.
"Nicely written, and beautifully illustrated."—*Morning Advertiser.*

CHILDREN'S COLOURED PICTURE VOLUMES.

The House that Jack Built: a New Building on the Old Foundation. Set forth in twelve Full-page Drawings, in Colours, in the Antient Style, by J. R. HARRIS. Large 4to, cloth extra, 5/-.

"An illustrated children's book, got up in a style which surpasses anything of the kind we have seen."—*Standard.*

Struwwelpeter. Funny Picture Stories in the Struwwelpeter Manner, "In merry mood for children good; with moral sad for children bad." Twenty-four pages in Colours, enamelled covers. Price 1/-.

"Much genuine humour, along with healthy, moral lessons."—*Leeds Mercury.*

ANNUAL PUBLICATIONS.

The Shaksperean Calendar. Highly-decorated Daily Date Calendar, for the Library and Boudoir. Illustrated with a scene from one of the Plays. Beautifully printed in Colours. A leaf to be torn each day from the block-tablet. The information comprises Sunrise and Sunset, Moon's Changes, Festivals, Holidays, Days past and Days to come, &c., with an appropriate Quotation from Shakspere. Price 1/-.

"Time Flieth, Time Trieth." A Calendar for the Year in Chromo-Lithography, with Poetry and General Information. Price 1/-.

Season's Calendar. Size, 4 × 2¾ inches, containing four highly-finished pictures, representing "Spring," "Summer," "Autumn," "Winter," and four pages consisting of Calendar and other Useful Information. Price 6d.

Pocket-Book Calendar. A Bijou Almanac, size, 1¾ × 1¼ inches, with gilt edges, suitable for purse, pocket-book, or waistcoat pocket. Price 1d.

CHRISTMAS, NEW YEAR, AND EASTER CARDS.

An annual issue of an extensive series of new and beautiful designs in the highest style of Art, specially prepared for these seasons by the first Artists. With special poems and appropriate wishes by well-known writers.

BIRTHDAY CARDS.

A similar issue of special designs, with appropriate verses and wishes, suitable for all classes.

MARCUS WARD'S CONCISE DIARIES.

For the Pocket—Published Annually—Lightest, Cheapest, Handiest, Best.

THE CONCISE DIARIES meet the universal objection to all other Pocket Diaries—their cumbrousness and unnecessary weight in the pocket. They are beautifully printed in Blue and Gold, on a light, hard, Metallic paper, and combine the following advantages:—

1. Maximum of Writing Space.
2. Minimum of Weight.
3. Useless Matter Omitted.
4. Equal Space for Sundays.
5. Daily Engagement Record.
6. The Writing is Indelible.

THE CONCISE DIARIES are made both in "Upright" and "Oblong" form, and in Three sizes of each form.

Only one part (Three Months) need be carried in the pocket at once.

All so-called "Useful Information," which few ever read, is excluded.

OPINIONS OF THE PRESS.

"By a capital arrangement, the maximum amount of writing space is secured in these handy little books, with the minimum amount of weight, by the simple expedient of changing the Diary every quarter, instead of only once a year."—*Daily Telegraph.*

"The *Concise Diaries* are singularly good in the four-part arrangement, and the finish of the leather-work leaves nothing to be desired, whilst a new patent bolt lock, which cannot readily be put out of order, stamps the present issue as the most complete series yet published."—*Standard.*

"The Diary pages are furnished *separately* in quarterly parts, ... and are much smaller and handier than they would otherwise be. It is a very good plan."—*Pall Mall Gazette.*

"Elegant and tasteful little pocket-books, with movable diaries, divided into quarterly parts so as to save room. We have never seen anything better—if so good—of the kind."—*Fun.*

"The *Concise Diaries* are as convenient in form as they are beautiful in appearance."—*Globe.*

"Like everything published by this firm, the *Concise Diary* is handsome and handy. The Diary itself being divided into four parts, the well got-up Russia leather case, in which it is enclosed, makes the book much more eligible for the pocket than the majority of so-called pocket diaries."—*Sportsman.*

"The diary is in arrangement perfect for keeping a cash account, memoranda, and engagements, besides containing a deal of useful information. It is bound in a strong Russia pocket-book, making altogether as good a present as one would wish to give or receive on New-Year's Day."—*Hour.*

"Conspicuous for the taste displayed in their manufacture."—*Morning Post.*

"The idea is so simple, that the wonder is that nobody thought of it before."—*Daily News.*

Educational Works.

ATLASES.

Adopted by the Board of National Education in Ireland.

EDITED BY J. HARRIS STONE, B.A.

MARCUS WARD'S SIXPENNY ATLAS.

LIST OF MAPS—Fully Coloured.

Eastern Hemisphere	North America	France
Western Hemisphere	South America	German Empire
Europe	England and Wales	Austrian Empire and
Asia	Scotland	Hungary
Africa and Arabia	Ireland	India or Hindustan
United States & Canada	Australia & Tasmania	New Zealand
Canaan or Palestine		

The largest Sixpenny Atlas ever offered.

MARCUS WARD'S SHILLING ATLAS.

Twenty-four Maps, printed in Colours, in the best style.

WITH GEOGRAPHICAL DEFINITIONS, DIAGRAMS OF THE GLOBES, &c.

This Atlas contains extra Maps and information, suitable for more advanced pupils, is printed on strong paper, and bound in durable cloth cover.

LIST OF MAPS.

Eastern Hemisphere	Kingdom of Italy	India or Hindustan
Western Hemisphere	Sweden, Norway, and	Africa and Arabia
Europe	Denmark	North America
England and Wales	Switzerland	South America
Scotland	Spain and Portugal	United States of America
Ireland	Netherlands and Belgium	Dominion of Canada
France	Russia in Europe	Australia and Tasmania
German Empire [Hungary	Turkey in Europe & Greece	New Zealand
Austrian Empire and	Asia	Canaan or Palestine

The largest Shilling Atlas ever offered to the Public.

OPINIONS OF THE PRESS.

"The Sixpenny and Shilling Atlases are *marvels of cheapness*, and the Home and Portable Atlases, each containing thirty maps, with indexes to upwards of 4000 places, are *very complete for ordinary use*."—*Guardian, March 15th, 1876.*

"The series of Atlases issued by the Messrs. Marcus Ward & Co., of London and Belfast, merit attention. The maps are beautifully printed and neatly coloured; the coast-lines, rivers, and mountains are clearly shown, and the names are not too crowded."—*Public Opinion, April 1st, 1876.*

MARCUS WARD'S HOME ATLAS.
Thirty Maps, printed in Colours,

From New Plates, specially engraved, with all the latest information from the best authorities, and Index to upwards of 8000 places. Crown Quarto, Paper Boards, 2/-; Cloth, Extra, 2/6.

LIST OF MAPS.

Explanatory Map	Ireland	Spain and Portugal
Eastern Hemisphere	France	Turkey in Asia, Syria,
Western Hemisphere	German Empire	Persia, Afghanistan, &c.
Europe	Austrian Empire and King-	India or Hindustan
Asia	dom of Hungary	The Dominion of Canada
Africa	Kingdom of Italy	United States of America
North America	The Netherlands & Belgium	Australia and Tasmania
South America	Sweden, Norway, and	Central America and West
Oceania	Denmark	Indies
The British Islands	Turkey in Europe & Greece	New Zealand
England and Wales	Russia in Europe	Canaan or Palestine
Scotland	Switzerland	Bible Maps

MARCUS WARD'S PORTABLE ATLAS.
Thirty Maps, printed in Colours, on one side only of Superfine Drawing Paper, with full Index.

Demy Octavo, handsomely bound in Cloth—India Rubber binding, to open perfectly flat. 3/6.

Advantages of this Atlas over others at similar or higher prices:—
1. Pictorial Illustrations of Geographical Terms.
2. Diagrams to illustrate the use of the Globes.
3. In the Maps of England, Scotland, and Ireland, the Sizes of the Towns by their Populations are distinguished by varied letterings.
4. The Countries where French is spoken are shown on one Map.
5. The Countries where German or kindred languages are spoken are shown on one Map.
6. The whole of the Russian Empire depicted on one Plate.
7. The whole of the Turkish Empire depicted on one Plate.
8. Map of Overland Route—Mediterranean to the Indus—Asiatic Russia—Khiva—Kokand—Syria—Euphrates Valley—Persia—Afghanistan—Biluchistan, &c. Illustrating the advance of the Russian Empire towards India.
9. The British Isles in one Map.
10. Several enlarged Maps of British Colonies.
11. Special Biblical Maps, for Sunday Lessons.

MARCUS WARD'S SCHOOL ATLAS.
This Atlas contains Thirty Maps, printed in Colours.

The lettering of the places is plain and readable, the Index is specially adapted for quick reference, and it will be found a most useful Atlas for Schools and Colleges. Imperial Octavo, Maps folded, Decorated Cloth Cover, Elastic Binding, to open perfectly flat, with complete Index. 5/-.

MARCUS WARD'S EVERY-DAY ATLAS.
Thirty Maps, printed in Colours.

With Geographical Illustrations, Coloured Illuminated Title-page, and a complete Index. Imperial 4to, Strong Boards, Cloth Back, Printed Design on Side. Price 3/6.

Atlases of Blank Projections & Outlines.

MARCUS WARD'S SIXPENNY OUTLINE ATLAS.
Sixteen Maps, Quarto, Stout Drawing Paper, Stiff Paper Wrapper.

CONTENTS.

Eastern Hemisphere	North America	France
Western Hemisphere	South America	German Empire
Europe	England and Wales	Austrian Empire and
Asia	Scotland	Hungary
Africa and Arabia	Ireland	India or Hindustan
United States & Canada	Australia and Tasmania	New Zealand
Canaan or Palestine		

MARCUS WARD'S SIXPENNY ATLAS OF BLANK PROJECTIONS.
Consisting of Sixteen Maps, Quarto, printed on Fine Paper, Stiff Wrapper.

SINGLE MAPS can be had from the Outline and Projection Atlases on specially prepared Superfine Drawing Paper. 1d. each.

CLASS-BOOK FOR CLASSICAL AND ART SCHOOLS.

The Mythology of Greece and Rome, with special reference to its use in Art. From the German of O. Seemann. Edited by G. H. BIANCHI, B.A., late Scholar of S. Peter's College, Cambridge. 64 Illustrations, Crown Octavo, Cloth, 3/6.

"To those who, like the Germans, are beginning to feel that the art of the ancients is no unimportant branch of classical study, a handbook like this commends itself."—*Graphic.*

"Will be received as a real boon by a large portion of the public."—*Standard.*

"To schools and to private students this book may be strongly recommended. It is likely soon to replace most cheap works on the subject."—*Sunday Times.*

"Complete account of ancient mythology."—*Daily News.*

"Agreeably written . . . the illustrations are remarkably good, being fine in execution, and faithful to the originals."—*Glasgow News.*

"The art student has here a considerable treasure, such as will place him in possession of a knowledge of art forms which will live for ever, and will serve as a fitting preliminary before practically dealing with these forms in the round."—*Industrial Art.*

☞ *Placed on the Prize-List of H.M. Department of Science and Art.*

Works on Drawing and Design.

By F. E. HULME, F.L.S., F.S.A., of Marlborough College.

Plants: their Natural Growth and Ornamental
Treatment. Containing 44 plates, printed in Colours from Drawings made by the Author, accompanied by a careful Treatise on the subject. Large imperial 4to, cloth extra, bevelled boards. Price 21/-.

Hulme's Freehand Ornament.
Sixty Examples, for the use of Drawing Classes. Imperial 8vo. Price 5/-, or mounted millboard, cloth-bound edges, 10/-.

☞ *Both these Works have been adopted by H. M. Department of Science and Art, for Copies and Prizes.*

Examples for Fret-Cutting and Wood-Carving.
Containing Twenty-four Large Plates of Original Designs. Large Imperial 4to. Price 7/6.

Illuminating: a Practical Treatise on the Art.
By MARCUS WARD, Illuminator to the Queen. With 26 examples of the styles prevailing at different periods, from the sixth century to the present time; Chromographed in facsimile and in outline. Foolscap 4to, cloth extra, bevelled boards, gilt edges, 5/-, or, in Morocco extra, 10/6.

"A very creditable and remarkably cheap little book."—*Architect.*

"Of all the volumes that we have seen, none equals this as a compact and cheap book of instructions."—*Standard.*

Aunt Charlotte's Histories for Young Children.

Profusely Illustrated, Square Octavo, Cloth Extra, Bevelled Boards, Gilt Edges. Price 6/- each.

Stories of English History for the Little Ones.
By CHARLOTTE M. YONGE, Author of "The Heir of Redclyffe," &c. In Fifty easy Chapters, with a Frontispiece in Colours by H. S. Marks, A.R.A.; 50 Illustrations, and an Illuminated Title-page. New Edition, with Questions.

"So simple that a child of the tenderest years will be perfectly able to comprehend all that the writer wishes to convey . . . adorned with numerous illustrations . . . the title-page is a lovely piece of art in illuminated printing."—*Edinburgh Courant.*

☞ *A Cheap Edition of MISS YONGE'S HISTORY OF ENGLAND, for Schools, is now ready; with 41 Engravings, and Questions, neatly bound in cloth. Price 1/6.*

LIST OF EDUCATIONAL WORKS. 23

AUNT CHARLOTTE'S HISTORIES—*Continued.*

Stories of Bible History for the Little Ones.
By CHARLOTTE M. YONGE. Three Readings and One Picture for each Sunday in the Year, with an Illuminated Title-page and Frontispiece in Colours.

"Illustrations numerous and well executed."—*Daily Telegraph.*
"Embraces the whole story from the creation to the ascension; told as Miss Yonge knows so well how to tell it."—*Guardian.*
"Nicely illustrated; got up in an attractive style."—*Birmingham Gazette.*

☞ *A Cheap Edition of STORIES OF BIBLE HISTORY, price 2/-, just published.*

Stories of French History for the Little Ones.
By CHARLOTTE M. YONGE. In Forty-eight easy Chapters, with a Frontispiece in Colours by H. STACY MARKS, A.R.A. Twelve Full-page Illustrations, and an Illuminated Title-page. New Edition, with Questions.

"The stories are well and clearly written."—*Saturday Review.*
"Charmingly bound, printed, and illustrated."—*Manchester Guardian.*

Stories of Greek History for the Little Ones.
BY CHARLOTTE·M. YONGE. In Forty-five easy Chapters, with Frontispiece in Colours by WALTER CRANE, Illuminated Title-page, and numerous Illustrations.

"An extremely handsome and attractive volume. . . . marked by a simplicity and clearness of language which should bring the book within the comprehension of those to whom it is addressed."—*Scotsman.*

Stories of Roman History for the Little Ones.
By CHARLOTTE M. YONGE. In Forty-six easy Chapters, with Frontispiece in Colours, Illuminated Title-page, and numerous Illustrations.

"Clear and interesting style. . . . . well illustrated."—*Saturday Review.*
"Admirably suited to convey to juvenile minds correct impressions concerning the manners and life of the people depicted."—*Sunday Times.*

Stories of German History for the Little Ones.
By CHARLOTTE M. YONGE. In Fifty easy chapters, with Frontispiece in Colours, Illuminated Title-page, and numerous Illustrations.

"Quite as entertaining and gracefully written as Scott's 'Tales of a Grandfather,' and teaches history with the same simplicity and charm, while having the further advantage of multitudes of beautiful pictures to illustrate the pleasing narrative."—*Irish Times.*
"Miss Yonge tells the story with her usual charm of manner, and it is evident that she has made an effort to study the subject."—*Spectator.*

A NEW SYSTEM OF SHORTHAND.

Shorthand for General Use. By J. D. EVERETT, Professor of Natural Philosophy in the Queen's College, Belfast. Foolscap octavo. Price 2/6.

A system which furnishes the means of noting down the leading sounds of spoken discourse, both vowels and consonants, with a rapidity comparable with that obtained in other systems by writing the consonants only. In a competition of the Belfast Phonetic Shorthand Writers' Society, held the 18th May, 1876, the speed attained by this system was one hundred and sixty words per minute, which exceeded by ten words per minute the fastest performance of every rival.

" Professor Everett's book does great credit to the enterprising publishing house that has brought it out."—*The Phonetic Journal.*

"Judging from an outsider's point of view, we should be inclined to recommend this little work to all would-be phonographers."—*Chemical News.*

"An excellent manual."—*Athenæum.*

"As regards speed and legibility, it stands pre-eminent as the soundest work on Phonetic Shorthand that has yet appeared. The whole principle of it can be acquired by a few hours' study."—*Ballyshannon Herald.*

"We have seen enough of it to feel assured that it is quite eligible—and perhaps better than any other system—for general use."—*Stockton Times.*

HANDBOOK FOR AGRICULTURAL STUDENTS AND FARMERS.

Animals of the Farm: their Structure and Physiology. By JOHN F. HODGES, M.D., F.C.S., &c. Second Edition, revised by the Author. Numerous Illustrations. Small Octavo, Cloth, 2/6.

" This work discusses succinctly, and without too many technicalities, the physiology of the greater number of domestic animals. It is written in a somewhat popular style, but at the same time preserves great accuracy of diction and detail, and it is well illustrated."—*Academy.*

POPULAR SERIES OF 6d. AND 1/- PACKETS, SUNDAY-SCHOOL CARDS, REWARD TICKETS, &c.
IN HANDSOME WRAPPERS.

A PACKET OF POESY. Twelve Floral Cards, printed in Colour on Black Grounds. Price 1/-. (25)

BIBLE PICTURES. Twelve scenes from Old Testament History, printed in Colours, with appropriate selections from Scripture. Price 1/-. (15)

BEES FROM THE BIBLE. Twelve Monitory Texts on Cards, with Floral Borders and various Coloured Grounds. Price 6d. (32)

BLESSINGS OF OUR LORD. Twelve Floral Cards, on Black Grounds, with verses from Holy Scripture. Price 6d. (52)

CHRIST THE FIRST FRUITS. A set of Twelve Floral Cards, with Gold Grounds, Texts, and appropriate sacred poetry. Price 1/-. (23)

REWARD TICKETS, PACKETS, &c.—*Continued.*

COMFORTING WORDS FROM HOLY SCRIPTURE. Twelve Floral Cards. Texts from Scripture. Price 1/-. (96)
FLORAL REWARD CARDS.—Two packets, each containing Twenty-four Cards, with Floral Borders in Gold and Colours. Price 6d. each. Packet A.—Sacred Verses. (21) | Packet B.—Texts of Scripture. (22)
FLOWERS OF THE MONTHS. A set of Twelve Cards, printed in Gold and Colours, with appropriate Poetry and Descriptive Notes. In Wrapper. Price 1/-. (67)
GRACE AND GLORY. Twelve Texts from the Bible, Illuminated on Floral Cards. Price 1/-. (70)
GOLDEN PRECEPTS. A Series of Nine Floral Illuminated Texts. Size, $6\frac{1}{4}\times 8$ inches. In Three Packets, price 1/- each; or in Mounts, Gilt Bevelled Edges, 2/6 each Packet.
GOLDEN THOUGHTS FROM KEBLE'S CHRISTIAN YEAR. A set of Twelve Floral Cards. Price 1/-. (36)
HYMNS FOR THE LAMBS OF CHRIST'S FLOCK. Twelve Cards of Birds and Flowers for Children. In handsome Wrapper. Price 1/-. (38)
LEAVES FROM THE BOOK OF LIFE. Transcribed and Illuminated after the manner of Religious MSS. of the Fifteenth Century. Price 6d. (33)
LIGHTS FOR THE HEAVENWARD PATH. Twelve Floral Illuminated Text Cards. Price 1/-. (68)
MEMORABLE WORDS FROM SCRIPTURE. Twelve Mediæval Illuminated Cards. Price 6d. (41)
MONTHLY MUSINGS. Twelve Illuminated Cards, with descriptive and entertaining notes concerning Birds and Flowers. Price 1/-. (39)
MOTTOES FOR THE MEMORY. Twelve Mottoes for the memory from Holy Writ, Illuminated on Floral Cards. Price 6d. (44)
PROVERBS POETICALLY APPLIED. A set of Twelve Cards, with Floral Designs on Gold Grounds. Price 1/-. (37)
PROMISE, PRECEPT, & PRACTICE CONCERNING PRAISE. Twelve Designs, with Illuminated Texts in Panels. Price 1/-. (45)
PROMISE, PRECEPT, & PRACTICE CONCERNING PRAYER. Twelve Designs, with Illuminated Texts, in Plain Roman Letters. Price 1/-. (53)
SACRED SELECTIONS. Twelve Richly Illuminated Cards. Floral Borders on Gold Grounds, with Sacred Texts and Poetry. Price 6d. (35)
SACRED TEXTS FROM THE OLD TESTAMENT. On Twelve Floral Cards. Price 6d. (79)
SACRED TEXTS FROM THE NEW TESTAMENT. On Twelve Floral Cards. Price 6d. (80)
SACRED THOUGHTS, in Verse. Twelve Floral Cards, with Black Backgrounds. Price 1/-. (24)
SAYINGS OF OUR LORD. Twelve Floral Cards, on Black grounds, with Verses from Holy Scripture. Price 6d. (51)
SPIRITUAL SONGS FOR LITTLE SINGERS. Twelve Hymns, on Cards, with Highly-decorated Borders on Gold Grounds. Price 1/-. (54)

REWARD TICKETS, PACKETS, &c.—*Continued.*

THE HISTORY OF OUR LORD. Twelve Scenes from the Life of Our Lord, printed in Gold and Colours, with appropriate Selections from Scripture. Price 1/-. (14)

THE GOOD SHEPHERD AND HIS SHEEP. Twelve Scripture Texts, on Floral Cards, with Gold Repp Backgrounds. Price 1/-. (46)

THE APOSTLES' CREED. A Packet of Twelve Highly-decorated Cards. Price 6d. (28)

THE TEN COMMANDMENTS. Six Double Cards Illuminated. Price 6d. (30)

THE LORD'S PRAYER. A Packet of Twelve Highly-decorated Cards. Price 6d. (29)

HOLY COMMUNION CARDS. Twelve Cards in a Packet, beautifully Illuminated Borders on Gold grounds, containing suitable Texts and Verses. Price 6d. (48)

WORDS OF COUNSEL from the Sacred Scriptures, Illuminated on Twelve Floral Cards. Price 1/-. (34)

WATCHWORDS FROM SCRIPTURE FOR CHRISTIAN WAY-FARERS. Eighteen Floral Text Cards, on Dark Coloured Grounds. Price 6d. (47)

WORDS OF CHRIST. Twelve Sayings of OUR LORD inscribed in plain readable characters, with Illuminated Borders and Initials. Size, $6\frac{1}{4} \times 4\frac{3}{4}$ ins. Price 1/-. (40)

SUNDAY SCHOOL PACKETS AT 9d.—6d.—4d.
IN HANDSOME WRAPPERS.

SUNDAY SCHOOL REWARD CARDS. Twenty-four Floral Decorated Texts. Price 9d. (31)

SUNDAY SCHOOL CARDS. Eighteen Double Floral Cards in a Packet, on Black Ground, Two Designs on each, Twelve Texts repeated three times. Price 6d. (26)

SUNDAY SCHOOL CARDS. Twelve Cards in a Packet, Four small Floral Designs on each. Forty-eight Texts. Price 6d. (27)

SUNDAY SCHOOL CARDS. Eight Cards in a Packet, Four simple Floral Designs on each. Thirty-two Texts. Price 6d. (55)

SUNDAY SCHOOL CARDS. Twelve Cards in a Packet, Ten Floral Designs with Black Grounds on each, One Hundred and Twenty Texts. Size of Card, $5\frac{1}{4} \times 3\frac{3}{4}$. Price 6d. (56)

SUNDAY SCHOOL CARDS. Eight Cards in a Packet, Four Designs on each, Thirty-two Scripture Texts in Elizabethan Panels. Size of Card, $5\frac{1}{4} \times 3\frac{3}{4}$. Price 4d. (57)

SUNDAY SCHOOL CARDS. Eight Cards in a Packet, Eight Designs on each, Sixty-four Scripture Texts in Elizabethan Panels. Size of Card, $5\frac{1}{4} \times 3\frac{3}{4}$. Price 4d. (58)

SUNDAY SCHOOL CARDS. Eight Cards in a Packet, Ten Designs on each, Eighty Scripture Texts in Elizabethan Panels. Size of Card, $5\frac{1}{4} \times 3\frac{3}{4}$. Price 4d. (59)

SUNDAY SCHOOL PACKETS —*Continued.*

SUNDAY SCHOOL CARDS. Eight Cards in a Packet, Eighteen Designs on each, One Hundred and Forty-four Scripture Texts in Elizabethan Panels. Size of Card, 5¼ × 3¾. Price 4d. (60)

SUNDAY SCHOOL CARDS. Eight Cards in a Packet, Eight Floral Designs on each, Sixty-four Scripture Texts. Size of Card, 5¼ × 3¾. Price 6d. (61)

SUNDAY SCHOOL CARDS. Ten Cards in a Packet, Twelve Floral Designs on each, One Hundred and Twenty Scripture Texts. Size of Card, 5¼ × 3¾. Price 6d. (62)

PACKETS OF CARDS FOR BIRTHDAYS, CONFIRMATIONS, MISSION SERVICES, ETC.

By FRANCES RIDLEY HAVERGAL.

LILIES FROM THE WATERS OF QUIETNESS. Twelve Mediæval Illuminated Cards, with Texts selected by F. R. H. Price 6d. (63)

GIFTS FROM THE KING'S TREASURE. Twelve Mediæval Illuminated Cards, with Texts selected by F. R. H. Price 6d. (64)

CONSECRATION CARDS. "THINE FOR EVER." For Confirmations, &c. Twelve richly Illuminated Cards, with Texts and Original Verses. By F. R. H. Two Packets. Price 6d. each. (65), (66)

SONGS IN THE NIGHT; OR, VISIBLE MUSIC FOR SILENT HOURS. Texts, and Original Verses by F. R. H. Designs of Alpine Flowers by Baronesse Helga Von Cramm. (74)

BIRTHDAY CARDS. Texts, and Original Verses by F. R. H. Designs of Alpine Flowers by Baronesse Helga Von Cramm. (76)

GOLDEN COMMANDMENTS WITH GREAT REWARDS. Twelve Jacobean Floral Cards. The first reference on each card is to the "Commandment," the second to the "Great Reward." Price 1/. (69)

ROYAL ACTS; OR, WHAT GOD IS DOING FOR US. Twelve Floral Cards, with Texts selected by F. R. H. Price 6d. (71)

ROYAL PRECEPTS; OR, LAWS FOR THE KING'S HOUSEHOLD. Twelve Texts selected by F. R. H., Illuminated in Floral Wreaths. Price 1/-. (73)

ROYAL GRACE; OR, PRESENT POSSESSIONS OF THE KING'S CHILDREN. Twelve Floral Cards. Texts selected by F. R. H. Price 1/-. (72)

ROYAL PATHWAYS FOR THE KING'S PILGRIMS. Twelve Jacobean Floral Cards. Texts selected by F. R. H. Price 1/-. (75)

ASCENSION CARDS. Six Floral Cards, with Texts, and Original Verses by F. R. H. Price 6d. (77)

SONGS OF MY PILGRIMAGE. Twelve Coloured Cards of Wild Fruits, with Texts from Scripture selected by F. R. H. Size, 7¼ × 5¼ inches. Price 2/-. (78)

POPULAR PACKETS OF TEMPERANCE CARDS.

THE WATER PACKET. A set of Twelve Cards, with Borders of Water Plants, &c., and Original Verses by S. C. Hall, F.S.A. Price 1/-.
(43)

THE TEXT PACKET. Twelve Selections from Scripture, chosen for their bearing on Temperance. Beautifully Illuminated in Gold and Colours. Price 6d. (42)

WALL GREETINGS AND TEXTS,

Suitable for the Decoration of Schoolrooms and Homes, or for Framing.

GOLDEN WORDS ABOUT JESUS. Six Floral Illuminated Texts. Size, $6\frac{1}{4} \times 8$ inches. In Two Packets. Price 1/ each; or in mounts, gilt bevelled edges, 2/6 each.

GOLDEN WORDS ABOUT THE GOOD SHEPHERD. Three Floral Illuminated Texts. Size, $6\frac{1}{4} \times 8$ inches. In one packet. Price 1/ each; or in mounts, gilt bevelled edges, 2/6 each.

LIGHTS FOR LIFE'S JOURNEY. Four large Floral Wall Texts in a Packet. Oblong. Size, 19×6 inches. Price 2/-.

WORDS OF CHRIST. Twelve Cards in a Packet, with Illuminated Texts. $6\frac{1}{4} \times 4\frac{3}{4}$ inches. Price 1/-.

A Set of Placards, "**A Merry Christmas**," "**A Happy New Year**," "**Welcome.**" Size, $24\frac{3}{4} \times 9\frac{1}{2}$ inches. Price 3/- per set.

A Pair of Placards, Garland of Flowers with the words, "**A Happy New Year to Everyone;**" Garland of Fruit with the words, "**A Merry Christmas to You All.**" Size, $34\frac{3}{4} \times 13\frac{1}{4}$ inches. Price 4/ per pair.

A Pair of Placards, Festoon of Flowers with the words, "**Welcome to our Hearth,**" the companion with "**Welcome to our Board.**" Size, $34\frac{3}{4} \times 13\frac{1}{4}$ inches. Price 4/ per pair.

Long Wall Text, "**Glory to God in the Highest.**" Size, $68\frac{3}{4} \times 13\frac{1}{4}$ inches. Price 4/- each. (D)

Long Wall Text, "**On Earth Peace, Good-will towards Men.**" Size, $68\frac{3}{4} \times 13\frac{1}{4}$ inches. Price 4/- each. (E)

Long Wall Text, "**Unto us is Born a Saviour.**" Size, $68\frac{3}{4} \times 13\frac{1}{4}$ inches. Price 4/- each. (F)

Long Wall Text, "**Behold I Bring you Good Tidings.**" Size, $68\frac{3}{4} \times 13\frac{1}{4}$ inches. Price 4/- each. (G)

LIST OF VERE FOSTER'S WRITING COPY-BOOKS.

1. STROKES, EASY LETTERS, SHORT WORDS.—Traced Lines under each Copy, to be written over by the Pupil. ROUND HAND.

1½. LONG LETTERS, SHORT WORDS, FIGURES.—Sanctioned by the Committee of Council as satisfying the requirements of the Second Standard, Revised Code, 1875. HALF TEXT.

2. LONG LETTERS, SHORT WORDS, FIGURES.—Guide Lines to regulate the length of Tailed Letters. SMALL ROUND HAND.

2½. WORDS OF FOUR, FIVE, OR SIX LETTERS, for Practice in forming different difficult combinations. SMALL ROUND HAND.

3. CAPITALS, SHORT WORDS, FIGURES.—Analysis of Capitals. Showing how the stiff Printed Capitals become transformed into Running Hand. MEDIUM HAND.

3½. SENTENCES OF SHORT WORDS, spaced by Perpendicular Lines. This is the first book in which Sentences are introduced. SMALL ROUND HAND.

4. SENTENCES, mostly composed of Short Words. The Perpendicular Spacing Lines are omitted in this and all succeeding numbers. MEDIUM HAND.

4½. SELECT QUOTATIONS FROM SHAKSPERE.—Principally Long Sentences. Suitable for preparing Pupils to write from Dictation. MEDIUM HAND.

5, 6. SENTENCES.—Maxims, Morals, and Precepts, in progressively Small Writing; each Line a complete Sentence. SMALL HAND.

5½. SENTENCES, in Writing of Three Sizes, continuation of preceding Books Nos. 3½, 4½, and 5. SMALL ROUND, MEDIUM, AND SMALL HANDS.

½. SENTENCES, in Writing of Two Sizes, in continuation of Books Nos. 6 and 7. SMALL HAND.

7. SENTENCES AND CHRISTIAN NAMES.—A collection of over 200 of the Christian Names in most common use, affording scope for a great variety of Elegant Capitals. SMALL HAND.

8. SENTENCES.—One Line on each Page. This Book is prepared for those who prefer at this stage to have only one line on each page. SMALL HAND.

9. SENTENCES.—Two Lines on each Page. Smaller Writing than in any of the preceding books. Some prefer this as a Finishing Hand to Nos. 7 and 8. SMALL HAND.

10. PLAIN AND ORNAMENTAL LETTERING.—Single Letters, Words, and Sentences. Alphabets in Thirty-three different Styles. The most perfect Collection yet published.

11. EXERCISE BOOK.—Wide Ruling, with Margin, for Parsing, Dictation, Composition, or other Exercises.

12. EXERCISE BOOK.—Narrow Ruling in Squares, for Arithmetic, Book-keeping, Geometry, and proportionate enlargements or reductions.

13. EXERCISE BOOK.—Ruled for Book-keeping.

HOME EXERCISE BOOK.—Same Ruling as No. 12 (but Octavo Size). Price One Penny.

COPY-BOOK PROTECTOR AND BLOTTER.—Price One Penny. Keeping the Books fresh, neat, and clean.

Adopted by the Science & Art Department, South Kensington.

VERE FOSTER'S WATER-COLOUR DRAWING BOOKS.
With Full Instructions in Painting.
ELEMENTARY BOOKS, 3d.   ADVANCED BOOKS, 6d.

THE object of this Publication is to place a knowledge of the higher branches of Drawing, hitherto the accomplishment only of the few, within the reach of all. It comprises a series of Simple and Practical Examples, in the various departments of Painting, by eminent Artists, together with useful and practical hints for Sketching from Nature.

The prices place them within the reach of everyone, and they are adapted either for Self-instruction or for study with the aid of a Master.

SEPIA.—By JOHN CALLOW, Member of the Society of Painters in Water-Colours. A series of lessons in one colour, to accustom the pupil to handle the brush and lay on washes, before beginning the use of colours. Six Numbers, 3d. each, with Instructions.

LANDSCAPE.—Painting in Water-Colours, by JOHN CALLOW. A series of elementary lessons in colours, in the various stages of simple landscape, calculated to impart a clear and effective style of handling; specially adapted to sketching from Nature. Two pictures in each book. Six Numbers, 3d each, with Instructions.

MARINE.—Advanced lessons in Water-Colour Painting, by E. DUNCAN. A series of highly-finished chromographed drawings of Marine Views and Coast Scenery, illustrating the treatment of the various effects of the ever-changing aspect of the sea. Three pictures in each book. Advanced Lessons, Four Numbers, 6d. each, with Instructions.

ANIMALS.—In Water-Colour, by HARRISON WEIR. Twelve chromographed studies of Animals. An invaluable series of characteristic drawings pictorially treated, useful alike to the student and the artist, as models or as a work of reference. Three pictures in each book. Advanced Lessons, Four Numbers, 6d. each, with Instructions.

FLOWERS—1st SERIES.—By various Artists. Twelve chromographed drawings of Garden and Wild Flowers, affording excellent practice in beginning the delightful study of Flower-painting. Two pictures in each book. Six Numbers, 3d. each, with Instructions.

FLOWERS—2nd SERIES.—By HULME, FRENCH, FITCH, &c. Twelve highly-finished chromographed studies of the most attractive Wild and Garden Flowers, singly and in groups. A set of interesting and beautiful Examples, fitting the pupil to begin Flower-painting from Nature. Three pictures in each book. Four Numbers, 6d. each, with Instructions.

ILLUMINATING.—By MARCUS WARD, Illuminator to the Queen. A series of 24 plates, from illuminated MSS. of the Middle Ages, illustrating the principal varieties of style practised from the sixth to the sixteenth century, with plain practical directions as to materials and modes of working. Two coloured and four outline plates in each book. Four Numbers, 6d. each, with Instructions.

VERE FOSTER'S WATER-COLOUR BLOCKS.

Specially prepared for Vere Foster's Water-Colour Drawing Books, and for Sketching from Nature. Composed of a number of sheets of best Drawing Paper, ready strained for the Pupil to begin painting.

No. 1 (6½ × 4½), THREEPENCE. | No. 2 (9 × 6½), SIXPENCE.

VERE FOSTER'S LARGER SERIES OF DRAWING COPIES.

ANIMALS—By HARRISON WEIR. Six Parts of Four Plates each. Imperial 4to. 2/6 each Part.

LANDSCAPE AND TREES—By J. NEEDHAM. Six Parts, Four Plates each. Imperial 4to. 2/6 each Part.

THE VERE FOSTER DRAWING PENCILS.

Specially prepared for Vere Foster's Drawing Books. Warranted to work well and rub out readily.

Price ONE PENNY each.—In Four Degrees—Superior Quality—HB, B, BB, and H, adapted for the Vere Foster Penny Drawing Books. The best Pencil it is possible to procure at the price.

Price TWOPENCE each.—In Five Degrees—Best Quality—HB, for General Work; B, for Shading, &c.; BB, for Deep Shading; F, for Light Sketching and Outlining; H, for Sharp Outlining and Mechanical.

Adopted by the Science & Art Department, South Kensington.

VERE FOSTER'S DRAWING COPY-BOOKS.
WITH INSTRUCTIONS AND PAPER TO DRAW ON.
POPULAR EDITION, 1d. SUPERIOR EDITION, 3d.

IN a country where Mechanical, Architectural, and Decorative Skill is in so much demand, a knowledge of Drawing is essential alike to the Artizan, the Employer, and the Connoisseur. The success of Mr. VERE FOSTER'S *Writing* Copy-Books suggested that a knowledge of Drawing might be spread among all classes by a series of *Drawing* Copy-Books by the best masters. It is believed that these books have already called forth much latent talent, and the advantage of a development of Taste and practical Artistic Knowledge cannot be overrated.

A—ELEMENTARY.—First Book for beginners, specially suited to practise the hand in drawing simple Geometric forms, and to accustom the eye to measure distances accurately, by an easily understood method.

B—SIMPLE OBJECTS.—Mostly in straight lines, subjects calculated to interest the pupil, and fix in the mind the first principles of correctly depicting the outlines or shape of Common Objects.

DRAWING COPY-BOOKS.—*Continued.*

C—FAMILIAR OBJECTS—Two Books.—No. 1, Objects of beauty and utility affording excellent practice in accurate drawing; No. 2, A series of Familiar Objects, interesting to youthful artists, familiarising the hand to the work.

D—SIMPLE FLOWERS—Two Books.—No. 1 begins with the simplest forms of Leaves, symmetrically arranged, with Guiding Lines, showing how a regular or irregular forms may be accurately drawn. No. 2 is more advanced.

E, G—FLOWERS—Three Books.—Native Flowering Plants, artistically drawn and botanically correct. Admirable training for Designers, Vegetable Forms being the basis of nearly all Ornamental Art.

I—ORNAMENT—Four Books.—By F. E. HULME, F.L.S., F.S.A., and other eminent Artists. A graduated series of examples, from elementary design to the more complex forms of the Classic and Renaissance.

J—TREES—Three Books.—By J. NEEDHAM. 1, Oak and Fir; 2, Beech and Elm; 3, Ash and Chestnut. For crayon or pencil drawing, showing the peculiar character and touch necessary to the proper rendering of each.

K—LANDSCAPE—Four Books.—By J. NEEDHAM and E. WIMPERIS. No. 1 Simple elementary outline; Nos. 2, 3, 4, suited for teaching the charming art of sketching from Nature in pencil or crayon.

M—MARINE—Four Books.—By CALLOW, WHITAKER, &c. A wide range of Marine subjects are represented in this series, beginning with the simplest. No. 4 contains lessons on drawing Waves, &c., by E. DUNCAN.

O—ANIMALS—Ten Books.—By HARRISON WEIR. No. 1, Domestic Animals 2, Families of Animals; 3, British Song Birds; 4, British Wild Animals 5, 6, The Horse; 7, Dogs; 8, Cattle; 9, Australian Animals; 10, Various An invaluable series of characteristic drawings.

Q—HUMAN FIGURE—Four Books.—By T. SCOTT, and other eminent Artists No. 1, Details of the Face; No. 2, Heads; No. 3, Rustic Figures; No. 4, Outlines from the Antique.

R—GEOMETRY—Three Books.—By J. MANGNALL. A thoroughly practical and useful manual, showing the application of geometrical principles to the uses of nearly every Trade and Profession.

T—MECHANICAL—Six Books.—By J. MANGNALL. A series of examples, to scale and measurement. Specially adapted for young Mechanics or Engineers.

Z—BLANK BOOK.—Plain drawing paper, for making enlarged copies, for sketching from Nature, or for working drawings.

LONDON : 67 & 68, CHANDOS STREET, STRAND.

BELFAST: ROYAL ULSTER WORKS.

www.ingramcontent.com/pod-product-compliance
Lightning Source LLC
Chambersburg PA
CBHW030348230426
43664CB00007BB/570